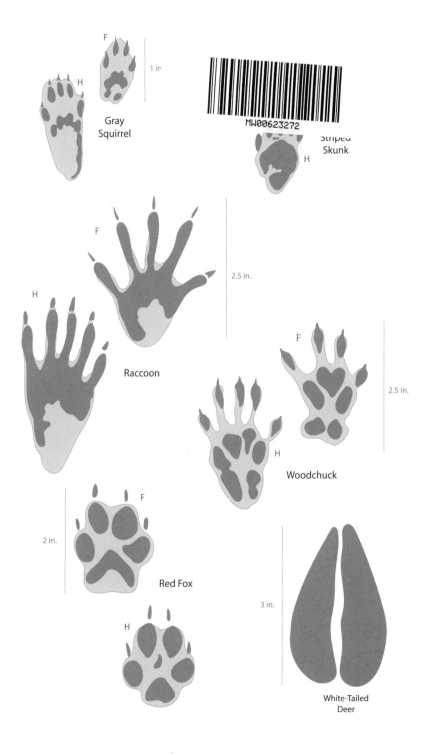

F

H

Gray
Squirrel

1 in

MW00623272

Striped
Skunk

H

F

2.5 in.

H

Raccoon

F

2.5 in.

H

Woodchuck

F

2 in.

Red Fox

H

3 in.

White-Tailed
Deer

A Field Guide to the
CONNECTICUT RIVER

The first 15 feet of the Connecticut River, flowing from the Fourth Connecticut Lake, on New Hampshire's border with Quebec, Canada.

A Field Guide to the

CONNECTICUT RIVER

From New Hampshire to Long Island Sound

PATRICK J. LYNCH

*All illustrations, maps, & photography by
the author unless otherwise noted*

Yale
UNIVERSITY
PRESS

To the late Carl Jaffe, MD, FACC, my longtime mentor and friend.

Carl had nothing to do with the making of this book but much to do with forming the person who wrote it.

To Susan, my best friend.

coastfieldguides.com

Yale University Press books may be purchased in quantity for educational, business, or promotional use. For information, please e-mail sales.press@yale.edu (US office) or sales@yaleup.co.uk (UK office).

Designed by Patrick J. Lynch.

Printed in China.

ISBN 978-0-300-26420-3

Library of Congress Control Number: 2023945276

This paper meets the requirements of ANSI/NISO Z39.48-1992 (Permanence of Paper).

10 9 8 7 6 5 4 3 2 1

CONTENTS

The young Connecticut River exits its origin in the Fourth Connecticut Lake and plunges 480 feet in less than a mile, emerging to fill the Third Connecticut Lake.

For the past 40 years I have benefited from the good company and deep birding and natural history expertise of Frank Gallo. Thanks, Frank, for all the great times, for the expert advice on many topics, and for dragging me to those wonderful out-of-the-way birding spots, many of which enrich this book.

I thank John Atherton for an angler's eye on streams and rivers, Rick Beebe for the flight over the Connecticut River, Jim Carr for his reference photographs of Bobcats, Wendolyn Hill for the excellent tips on Lyme locations, Lynn Jones for her advice on River Otters, Matthew Male for his gorgeous river photographs, Robin Ladouceur for her photographs of tidal marshes and streams, David Skelly for his general advice on the freshwater world, and Sue Sweeney for her photographs and advice on stream wildlife.

I would particularly like to thank Twan Leenders for lending me his magnificent frog, salamander, and turtle photographs. These photo treasures add immeasurably to the book.

I thank Ralph Lewis, professor of geology at the University of Connecticut Avery Point campus and former State Geologist of Connecticut. Ralph went above and beyond in sharing his expertise on the East Coast's complex geologic history, particularly on the Wisconsinan Glaciation. I offer particular thanks to Jean Thomson Black, senior executive editor for life sciences at Yale University Press, for her faith in my work over the years and for being my constant advocate at the Press. I also thank the manuscript editor on this project, Laura Jones Dooley, for her wisdom, expertise, and guidance on every page here.

I also thank my teacher, mentor, and friend, the late Noble Proctor, for his 43 years of wise counsel, for countless days of great birding and whale watching, and for introducing me to advanced birding and natural history. I know that I and Noble's hundreds of friends throughout the world miss his good humor, sharp eyes, and awesome breadth of knowledge about the natural world. This book would not exist without Noble's decades of wisdom and support.

Most of all I thank my wife, Susan Grajek, my mentor, muse, wise woman, and best friend. I literally could not have done this book without you.

Pat Lynch
North Haven, Connecticut

coastfieldguides.com
https://www.facebook.com/patrick.lynch1
patrlynch1@gmail.com

This book is a general introduction to the natural history of freshwater environments near the Connecticut River, from its origin at the Fourth Connecticut Lake in New Hampshire to where it meets Long Island Sound in Old Saybrook, Connecticut. I have organized this book around environments, not particular locations. Although I focus on this region's plants, animals, and physical foundations, you cannot write about the natural world these days without constantly referencing the effects of environmental history and anthropogenic climate change. We live in the Anthropocene Epoch: human activity and climate change have become the dominant forces that shape our geophysical and biological environments.

This region's geologic and human history also reminds us that we live on shifting ground. Sea level rise and the rapidly changing climate are now part of our daily news cycle. The accelerating pace of climate change has altered all freshwater environments along the 406 miles of the Connecticut River. In the coming decades, sea level rise will profoundly affect the river valley, from its mouth in Old Saybrook to at least central Massachusetts and beyond. Here my emphasis is on the growing physical effects of climate change on natural environments. Once you know the subtle but pervasive signs of warming, you see the changes everywhere.

My primary focus is on the southern stretches of the Connecticut River, for several reasons. The Massachusetts and Connecticut sections of the river are by far the most populous and rich with both natural and human history. ***Public access to natural environments is a key issue for me:*** the lower Connecticut River offers the visitor many public parks and other accessible places to visit the Connecticut River. Although the northern region of the Connecticut River can be breathtakingly beautiful, the states of Vermont and New Hampshire seem oddly indifferent to one of America's greatest rivers and offer just a few public parks with general access to Connecticut River environments.

This guide cannot be an exhaustive catalog of everything that lives in or near the freshwater environments of this region—such a book would be neither practical as a field guide nor very useful to the typical hiker, birder, kayaker, angler, or boater. I have emphasized the most dominant and common plants and animals. I intend to show you the major plants and animals that populate our freshwater environments so you can walk into a wet meadow or along a stream and identify much of what you see. This is the first step in developing a deeper, more ecological understanding of the New England landscape's unique and beautiful aspects. This guide to the what of plants and animals also attempts to show why and how the human and natural aspects of the landscape coevolved into what we see today.

For recommended field guides to plants, wildflowers, geology, birding, insects, and other natural history topics, please see the works listed in "Further Reading."

CONNECTICUT RIVER REGION
Major tributaries, dams, and
watershed of the Connecticut River

QUEBEC, CANADA

3rd *Connecticut Lakes*
2nd
Pittsburg
1st
Francis
Canaan
Mohawk
Bloomfield
Colebrook
Nulhegan
Northumberland

MAINE

Passumpsic
Upper Ammonoosuc
St. Johnsbury
Lancaster
Moore
Gillman
Littleton
Comerford
Macindoes
White Mountains
Montpelier
Ryegate
Ammonoosuc
Woodsville

VERMONT

Lake Winnipesaukee

Portland

Lake George

White
Hanover
White River Junction
Wilder
Mascoma
Cornish

Green Mountains
Weathersfield
Sugar
NEW HAMPSHIRE

Saratoga Springs

Bellows Falls

West
Townshend
Keene
Merrimack River
Brattleboro
Vernon
Ashuelot
Portsmouth

Taconic Mountains

Albany

Hudson River

Turners Falls
Northfield Mountain Pump Storage
Deerfield
Cabot *Millers*
MASSACHUSETTS
Cape Ann

Berkshire Mountains
Quabbin Reservoir
Boston
Massachusetts Bay

Northampton
Worcester

Holyoke
Chicopee
Charles River
Westfield
Springfield
Westfield
Enfield Dam
historic, breached
Rainbow
Taunton River
Cape Cod

Farmington
CONNECTICUT
Providence
Cape Cod Bay

Poughkeepsie
Hartford
RHODE ISLAND

Waterbury
Salmon
Leesville
Eightmile
Thames River
Newport
Buzzards Bay
Nantucket Sound

New Haven
New London
Old Saybrook

Hudson River Estuary
Housatonic River
Block Island Sound
Block Island
Martha's Vineyard
Nantucket

Stamford
Long Island Sound

New York City

Long Island

ATLANTIC OCEAN

Dams and hydroelectric facilities
Connecticut River and major tributaries
Connecticut River watershed
Other regional rivers

North

0   25   50   75
MILES

INTRODUCTION

The marina at Essex, Connecticut, on the tidal estuary section of the Connecticut River.

Quinatucquet, Quinnehtugut, Quenticutt, Connecticut. No one is quite sure how the Mohegan transliterations of "the long tidal river" became settled on "Connecticut" in English. New England's longest river arises as a trickle of water from a tiny mountain pond, the Fourth Connecticut Lake, in northern New Hampshire. The young Connecticut River drops more than 1,000 feet in altitude within its first 10 miles. Four hundred and six miles downstream, the now-vast Connecticut River flows at 18,400 cubic feet per second and supplies 70 percent of the freshwater that enters Long Island Sound.

This river landscape is ancient. The Central Valley of New England formed early in the Age of Dinosaurs, during the birth of the Atlantic Ocean and the breakup of the supercontinent Pangaea. The new valley was steep, surrounded by jagged peaks, and inhabited by dinosaurs who famously left their tracks in the red tropical mud of wetland streams and ponds. Two hundred million years later, something like the modern Connecticut River began to flow in more or less its current track.

An odd thing about a river is how difficult it can be to see. Stand on the bank of the Connecticut River at almost any point, and you can see barely a mile or two up and down the river, and often much less. About 2.4

million people live within a few miles of the river, yet most rarely glimpse the water except when crossing bridges. You will see no mighty vistas as at the Grand Canyon or Yosemite, yet the quiet Connecticut River has had far more influence and importance to US history than all of the national parks combined. For 10,000 years before Europeans landed, the river was the life-giving backbone of the Algonquin peoples of central New England. In American colonial times, the river was crucial to commerce, and its rich riverine meadows were the birthplace and breadbasket of New England's prosperity.

Oddly and often tragically, the history of the Connecticut River could be told through its dams. Before steam power and electricity became widely available, the power of running water fueled New England's early industries. That river hydropower was the basis for the industrial and mercantile prosperity of nineteenth-century New England. Most of the 65 major dams on the Connecticut River and its tributaries have long since become obsolete. Yet the old dams remain a fatal obstacle to the great migratory fish runs that once enriched the whole river and the people who lived by it. The fish ladders at our major river dams have failed at restoring or even maintaining anadromous fish runs. The once-abundant Connecticut River run of Atlantic Salmon is now just a trickle of fish. Although American Shad do pass the Holyoke Dam in numbers (192,074 in 2022), even shad numbers have plunged from previous decades. For most anadromous fish species, the vaunted "fishways" at the large dams amount to little but greenwashing by the hydroelectric power companies and state and federal agencies.

Not all river obstructions are as obvious as dams. The Connecticut River watershed has about 44,000 river and stream road bridges. Many of the concrete supports for those crossings are undersized for the rivers that flow beneath them. These poorly designed bridges squeeze the flowing water into high-speed channels that are dangerous to wildlife and the people who depend on the bridges. The high flow rates in these concrete channels can be fatal to many kinds of aquatic life and almost as bad as dams for migratory fish species.

Yet today's Connecticut River is both a local and national treasure. In 2012 the Connecticut River was named a National Blueway by the Obama administration, and international ecological groups have recognized the various river environments as world treasures. The mighty Connecticut has more than endured. Despite all the challenges of the past 400 years of relentless development activity, it has thrived.

This stream may, with more propriety than any other in the world, be named THE BEAUTIFUL RIVER.

Travels in New England and New York, *vol. 2 (1822)*

—*Rev. Timothy Dwight IV, President of Yale College, 1795–1817*

Is the Connecticut worth saving? I need not offer an opinion. I need only mention that I have seen rather more of the world's surface than most men ever do, and I have chosen the valley of this river for my home.

—*Roger Tory Peterson, quoted in* The Connecticut River, *by Evan Hill (1972)*

The Connecticut River just north of Middletown, Connecticut, looking south.

The Connecticut River

① Map location, p. 10

The Fourth Connecticut Lake in Pittsburg, New Hampshire, on the Canadian border with Quebec.

This 2.5-acre boggy alpine pond surrounded by dense spruce-fir forest is the origin of the Connecticut River. The lake is no deeper than five feet and is mostly much shallower. Biologists classify the lake as a mountain tarn with highly acidic water. Given the acidic conditions, much of the vegetation fringing the lake has a bog-like character, mixed with emergent grasses and such acid-loving shrubs as Highbush Blueberry, Leatherleaf, and Labrador Tea and scattered pitcher plants. The lake hosts a small population of Rainbow and Brook Trout.

Larger animals in and around the lake include North American River Otters and North American Beavers. Beavers sometimes modify the exit stream of the pond with their dams, slightly shifting the exact origin of the river by a few yards. Here the exit stream runs through the small marsh at the far left of the picture.

The well-marked trail around the lake offers interesting birding for boreal specialties including Canada Jays and Spruce Grouse, as well as Black-Throated Blue and Black-Throated Green Warblers. Waterfowl such as Common Mergansers, Buffleheads, and the occasional Common Loon sometimes drop in during migration.

The Connecticut River

② Map location: p. 10

The first few feet of the Connecticut River exit a small marsh and enter the lush subalpine forest south of the lake. The young river then makes a steep 480-foot drop in just half a mile to enter the Third Connecticut Lake. Biologists call the forest in this far northern location an Acadian spruce-fir forest. The forest around the lake has a distinctly different alpine character than even nearby forests around the more southerly Connecticut Lakes. The surrounding forest is fascinating, with a thick, slow-decaying carpet of pine needles covered with a dense layer of mosses. Most trees are Red Spruce, Mountain Ash, Balsam Fir, and Paper Birch. In wetter locations near

the lake, Black Spruce enters the mix. Northern shrubs and herbs such as Bunchberry and Creeping Snowberry dominate the understory. In spring the southern end of the lake can be rich in such northern wildflowers as Pink Lady's Slipper, Goldthread, Canada Mayflower, Wild Sarsaparilla, and Wakerobin. Cinnamon Ferns are common. The hike to the lake from the Border Station is rugged. The steep trail up the hillside, though beautiful, is often rocky and muddy, with very slippery surfaces. Moose and Black Bears are regularly seen, so clap your hands or

The Connecticut River

③ Map location,
p. 10

The Second Connecticut Lake, Pittsburg, New Hampshire.
This gorgeous natural lake was later enlarged by construction of the first major dam on the Connecticut River. The lake and dam are used as a reservoir for flow control to downstream hydroelectric projects and for local water sports and recreation. The shoreline is almost entirely undeveloped. The Connecticut Lakes region is a designated National Audubon Society Important Bird Area and contains some of New England's best unspoiled spruce-fir and northern hardwood forests.

Birders consider the Second Connecticut Lake an excellent area to see boreal forest specialists including Black-Backed Woodpeckers and Spruce Grouse. Northern songbirds such as Bay-Breasted Warblers and Boreal Chickadees nest in the forests.

The Second Lake is also a great fly-fishing location for Brook Trout, Lake Trout, and landlocked Atlantic Salmon.

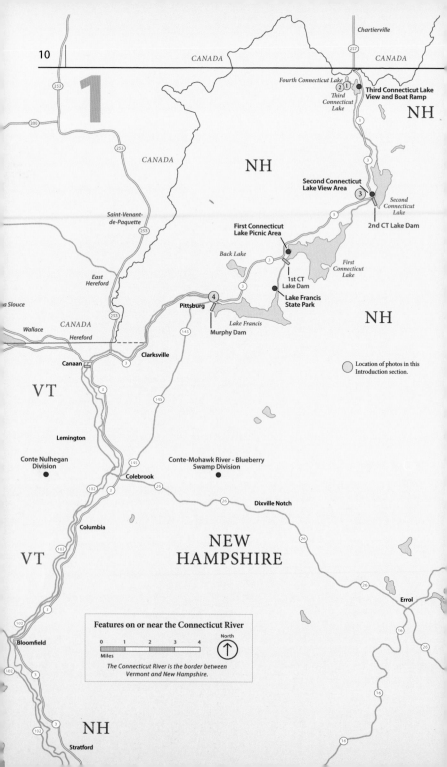

CANADA

CANADA

Chartierville

257

Fourth Connecticut Lake

253

200

253

CANADA

NH

Saint-Venant-de-Paquette

253

East Hereford

a Slouce

CANADA

Wallace

Hereford

253

Canaan

5

Clarksville

VT

3

145

Lemington

145

Conte Nulhegan Division

102

3

Colebrook

26

Columbia

VT

102

3

102

Bloomfield

102

3

NH

Stratford

Third Connecticut Lake

2 1

Third Connecticut Lake

● **Third Connecticut Lake View and Boat Ramp**

3

NH

3

Second Connecticut Lake View Area

3

Second Connecticut Lake

3

2nd CT Lake Dam

First Connecticut Lake Picnic Area

Back Lake

3

●

3

First Connecticut Lake

1st CT Lake Dam

● **Lake Francis State Park**

NH

4

Pittsburg

145

Murphy Dam

Lake Francis

Location of photos in this Introduction section.

Conte-Mohawk River - Blueberry Swamp Division

●

26

Dixville Notch

26

NEW HAMPSHIRE

26

26

Errol

16

26

16

16

Features on or near the Connecticut River

0   1   2   3   4

Miles

North

↑

The Connecticut River is the border between Vermont and New Hampshire.

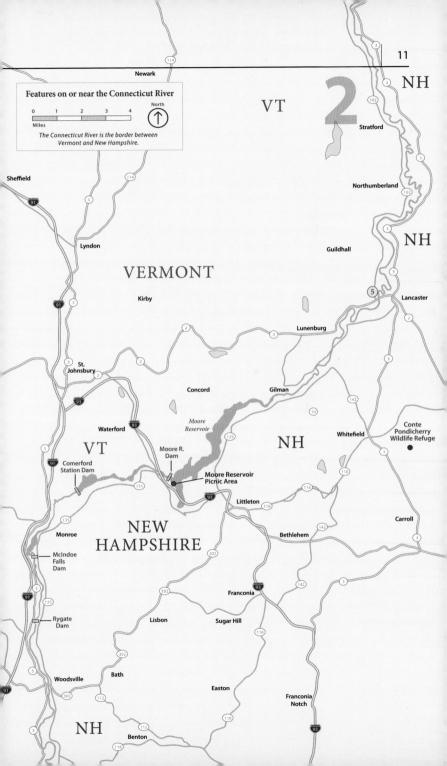

The Connecticut River

④ Map location,
p. 10

Connecticut River from the Mill Road Bridge (NH-145), Pittsburg, New Hampshire.
A glimpse of what the wild Connecticut River must have looked like before the Connecticut Lakes were dammed. Small wonder that the river at Pittsburg is wild, fast-flowing, and unnavigable: in the first 16 linear miles from the Fourth Connecticut Lake to Pittsburg, the river drops 1,348 feet in elevation. Although attempting to kayak this stretch of the river might be suicidal, the trout fishing is world-class.

The icy river water is home to Brook, Brown, Rainbow, and Lake Trout and landlocked Atlantic Salmon. Water released just upstream at the Murphy Dam on Lake Francis is typically 50–55 degrees Fahrenheit, so the water is cold even in the August heat. If you wish to fly-fish in this river area, hire a local guide. There are periodic water releases from the Connecticut lake dams, and you must know the schedule to wade safely.

The Connecticut River south of Pittsburg transitions from the shallow, rocky stretch shown here to a deeper but still swift-flowing character, punctuated by stretches of rapids where the river can drop 20 feet or more.

The Connecticut River

5 Map location, p. 11

EH Wilson

Looking south from Guildhall, Vermont, with the Connecticut River on the left and New Hampshire's Weeks State Park hills on the southern horizon. See pp. 84–85 for a view west across the Connecticut River Valley from the observation tower at Weeks State Park.

The broad, flat farm fields lie on the glacial lake deposits of ancient Glacial Lake Hitchcock (see pp. 75–79). The higher ground on either side of the river are terraces formed by a combination of varying glacial lake levels, later shaped by the action of the Connecticut River. These rich, stone-free ancient lake sediments are ideal for farming.

This part of the Connecticut River is a study in contrasts. Just a few miles north of Guildhall, the Connecticut looks like a younger, wilder river, running over a series of white-water rapids as it descends from Pittsburg, New Hampshire, south to Colebrook, New Hampshire. Then at Bloomfield, Vermont, the river enters the flat plains and gentle gradient of the old glacial lake bed. North and south of Guildhall, there are many meanders in the Connecticut River, something usually seen only in ancient rivers running across flat plains.

The Connecticut River

(6) Map location,
p. 20

The Connecticut River at Fairlee, Vermont.

Aside from the classically beautiful river countryside, this view east from the Palisades above the town of Fairlee is geologically interesting. Here the river runs in the Ammonoosuc Fault (p. 54), and the west (closer) side of the fault has been uplifted to form the Palisades hills. Interstate 91, the town of Orford, New Hampshire, on the far (eastern) side of the river, and the farm fields on either side of the river all sit on old lake-bed terraces formed by Glacial Lake Hitchcock about 13,000 years ago (see pp. 75–79 for more on Lake Hitchcock).

Bram Reusen

As the Ice Age glaciers melted, they formed a vast glacial lake, whose level gradually lowered in several stages, leaving steplike terraces showing each water level. On the farther New Hampshire side of the river, there are higher, if less defined, terraces stepping up to the hills of the valley's eastern edge. All of the lowlands near the river and most of the lower hills to the east were under the surface of Glacial Lake Hitchcock until about 15,500 years ago, when the lake drained away. The nutrient-rich, mostly stone-free lake-bed sediments attracted early settlers to Vermont and New Hampshire, and the area is actively farmed today.

The Connecticut River

Map location, p. 20

For 40 miles north of the Dartmouth College rowing docks (visible at right), the Connecticut River is essentially a placid lake, sheltered from wind by the riverbanks. The lakelike conditions are created by the impounded water behind the Wilder Dam downstream in West Lebanon, New Hampshire. This quiet, relatively straight stretch of river has made Dartmouth's rowing facilities world-famous as a site for practicing long-distance rowing.

The lakelike waters might also be ideal for many kinds of river recreation besides boating, but access to the river is limited to a few boat launch sites in this and many other areas of the Connecticut River.

The multiple dams on today's Connecticut River were created mostly in the early to mid-twentieth century for two purposes: to control the river in flood conditions and to generate hydroelectric power. The dams also create recreational opportunities. Each river dam impounds miles-long stretches of river water, and the lakelike conditions are ideal for boating, fishing, and swimming. But there are consequences in turning a wild natural river into a long lake. Aside from bringing about the almost total loss of migratory fish species, the placid water behind

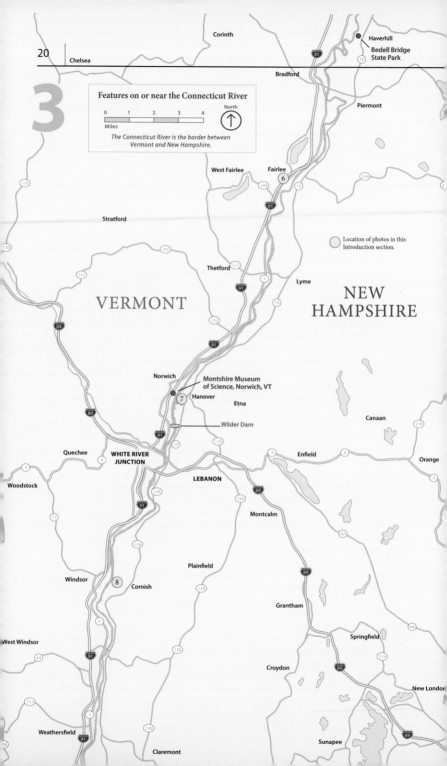

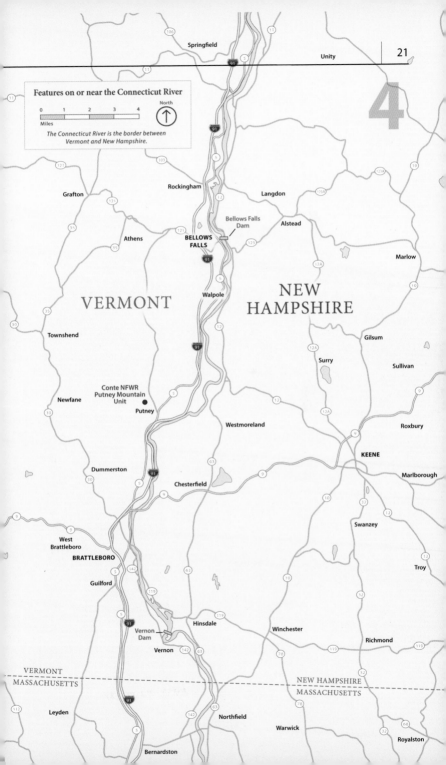

Features on or near the Connecticut River

0   1   2   3   4
Miles

North
↑

The Connecticut River is the border between Vermont and New Hampshire.

Springfield

Unity

Rockingham

Langdon

Grafton

Bellows Falls Dam

Alstead

Athens

BELLOWS FALLS

Marlow

Walpole

NEW HAMPSHIRE

VERMONT

Townshend

Gilsum

Sullivan

Surry

Conte NFWR Putney Mountain Unit

Newfane

Putney

Westmoreland

Roxbury

KEENE

Dummerston

Chesterfield

Marlborough

Swanzey

West Brattleboro

Troy

BRATTLEBORO

Guilford

Hinsdale

Winchester

Richmond

Vernon Dam

Vernon

VERMONT
MASSACHUSETTS

NEW HAMPSHIRE
MASSACHUSETTS

Leyden

Northfield

Warwick

Royalston

Bernardston

The Connecticut River

(8) Map location, pg. 20

At 449 feet in length, the Cornish–Windsor Covered Bridge is one of the longest such structures in North America. Many New England bridges were covered to protect the wooden structures from rotting in the moist and often icy environment. Uncovered wooden bridges typically have a lifespan of only 20 years because of the effects of weather, but a covered bridge may last over 100 years before it needs reconstruction. The current Cornish–Windsor Covered Bridge was built in 1866, but this is the third bridge here since colonial times.

Craig Zerbe

Vermont's Mount Ascutney rises to 3,144 feet elevation on the horizon. The mountain is an isolated peak or monadnock, part of the same igneous magma plutons that created the White Mountains much farther north. From mid-May to mid-October, the Mount Ascutney State Park road leads to the summit of the mount, with magnificent views across the Connecticut River region.

The Connecticut River

9 Map location, p. 36

The French King Bridge and the confluence with the Millers River in Massachusetts.

In the early 1700s, a French raiding party coming down the Connecticut River from Quebec encountered a massive rock in the middle of the river and claimed it as French territory in the name of King Louis XV. The name French King Rock stuck even after the English defeated the French in the French and Indian Wars, and the bridge was named after the nearby rock. Today the rock is barely above the river level because of the water impounded by the Turners Falls Dam, but French King Rock once rose 16 feet above the water.

An earlier wooden version of the French King Bridge was replaced by a modern three-arch steel span that opened to traffic in 1932. The current bridge was refurbished and repaired in 1992 and today attracts thousands of admirers every year for its graceful span and dramatic views over the river gorge.

The confluence of the Connecticut and Millers Rivers is just south of the French King Bridge span (middle right edge of the photo). The Millers has a strong flow for its size and can generate unpredictable currents as it enters the Connecticut.

The Connecticut River

⑩ Map location,
p. 36

The Turners Falls Dam spillway, Turners Falls, Town of Montague, Massachusetts.

The present Turners Falls Dam shown here was rebuilt and raised to its current height in 1970. The dam spillway is at the bottom, with the exposed riverbed in the upper left. The original wooden dam at Turners Falls of 1794 was built as part of a transportation canal system to bypass a treacherous series of rapids and waterfalls—the original "Turner's Falls." However, the transportation canal and dam were made irrelevant within 20 years by the rise of regional railroads. The mid-1800s were when hydropowered factories were the height of modernity and new

technology, and in 1868 a consortium of business people redesigned the old transportation canal to support hydropowered factories along the canal and renovated the dam to ensure a constant supply of water.

You can still see the stony stretch of the rapids in the original riverbed, but the river in this area is chronically starved of water by the dam and bypass canal, so there is little river life here in the mostly dry bed of the old "falls."

The Connecticut River

⑪ Map location,
   p. 36

The northernmost region of the Pioneer Valley, at Sunderland, Massachusetts.
This view east over the Connecticut River from Mount Sugarloaf State Reservation shows 1,269-foot Mount Toby
on the horizon. The farms on the river's eastern bank sit on lake-bed terraces of the ancient Glacial Lake Hitch-
cock. Geologically, Mount Toby is a layer cake of elements that make up the Pioneer Valley and its neighborhood.
The middle cliff layer most visible in this view is the same basalt that forms the series of traprock ridges at Mount
Holyoke Range State Park, 13 miles to the south in Amherst, Massachusetts.

The Mount Toby region is famous for its exceptional biodiversity. It is home to 42 of Massachusetts's 45 possible native fern species, as well as such rare wildflowers as the Showy Lady Slipper and the Ram's Head Lady Slipper. One possible reason for the unusual mix of species is that the rugged topography of the Mount Toby region was never logged as extensively as the more accessible lowland forests, so more of the biological richness of the primeval New England forests survived here.

The Connecticut River

⑫ Map location, p. 36

The view from the summit of Mount Holyoke, Massachusetts, looking west over the Pioneer Valley and the Oxbow. Northampton's famous Oxbow Lake has been chopped up a bit since the painter Thomas Cole's time (center right in the photo; see pp. 120–21), but the circular lake is still one of the landmarks of a region rich with historical and natural landmarks. Most of what you can see from the foot of the mountain and west to the Berkshires on the horizon was the lake bed of Glacial Lake Hitchcock. These lake sediments were the foundation of pioneer European agriculture in the mid-1600s and still support extensive farms today.

The Connecticut River is relatively placid most of the time in this region. Still, during the historic floods of the 1930s, the river flooded virtually all the lowlands you can see here. In 1936, after multiple warm rainstorms caused the sudden melting of the northern New England snowpack, the river rose to over 30 feet above flood stage and caused 150–200 deaths. Multiple dams built since then have helped tame the worst of the river floods. However, with climate change, storms are getting warmer and wetter, so floods remain a concern on the Connecticut River.

The Connecticut River

13 Map location,
p. 36

The Oxbow Lake, Massachusetts, with the Mount Holyoke Range in the distance.

The Oxbow is now primarily a resource for pleasure boating and fishing. A large portion of the center of the loop has been excavated to form one of the Connecticut River's largest marinas. Interstate 91 and Route 5 also cross the Oxbow center. But much of the area's natural environment has been preserved and protected by Mass Audubon's Arcadia Wildlife Sanctuary. Portions of the lake are also within the Silvio O. Conte National Fish and Wildlife Refuge.

This original Massachusetts "Oxbow Lake" gave its name to the general geologic phenomenon of oxbow lakes, seen in older, slow-flowing rivers throughout the world.

The Arcadia Sanctuary offers a beautiful range of riverine freshwater habitats: wet meadows, vernal pools, marshes, wooded swamps, the Mill River (see pp. 274–75), and Hulberts Pond—really a calm extension of the Mill River where it meets the Oxbow. As well as offering excellent birding, the area is popular with anglers and kayakers. An observation tower on the Fern Trail offers fine views over Hulberts Pond and its marshes.

The Connecticut River

(14) Map location,
p. 36

A view to the northwest along the Connecticut River at Holyoke, Massachusetts, with the Holyoke Dam along the bottom of the frame. The entrance to the First Level Canal is just visible on the lower left.

The current Holyoke Dam, sometimes also referred to as the Hadley Falls Dam, dates from 1900. Two previous and unsuccessful dams were created in 1847 and 1848. The first failed catastrophically. The second, though structurally unsound, was successfully reinforced and supported the construction of the industrial canal system that defined Holyoke as a manufacturing city in the late nineteenth and early twentieth centuries.

AerialMA

The current Holyoke Dam now operates primarily as a hydroelectric facility, producing 33 megawatts of power. There is a fishway on the south side of the dam (left in the photo), but the fishway has been unsuccessful at limiting the sharp decline of migratory river fish. The mountain with the communications towers on the distant center horizon is Mount Tom, with the peaks of the Mount Tom State Reservation running to the right.

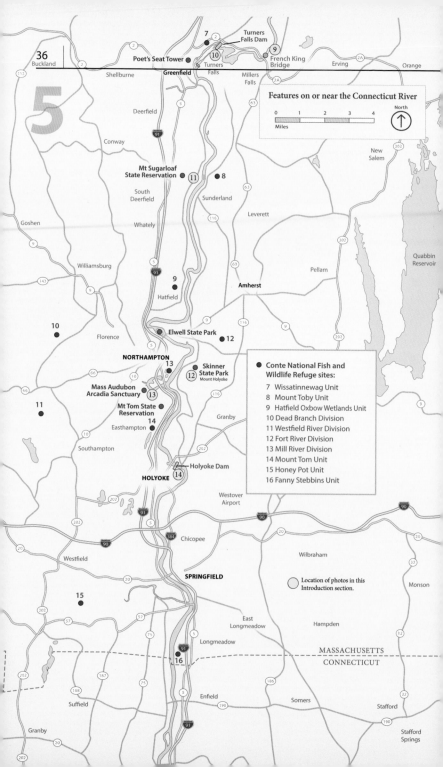

5

Buckland

7

Turners
Falls Dam

Poet's Seat Tower

10

9
French King
Bridge

Greenfield

Turners
Falls

Millers
Falls

Erving

Orange

Shellburne

Deerfield

Features on or near the Connecticut River

0   1   2   3   4
Miles

North
↑

Conway

New
Salem

Mt Sugarloaf
State Reservation   11   8

South
Deerfield

Sunderland

Goshen

Whately

Leverett

Pellam

Quabbin
Reservoir

Williamsburg

9

Amherst

Hatfield

Florence

9   Elwell State Park   12

NORTHAMPTON   13

Skinner
State Park
Mount Holyoke   12

Mass Audubon
Arcadia Sanctuary   13

Mt Tom State
Reservation   14

Easthampton

Granby

HOLYOKE   Holyoke Dam   14

Westover
Airport

**● Conte National Fish and
Wildlife Refuge sites:**

7   Wissatinnewag Unit
8   Mount Toby Unit
9   Hatfield Oxbow Wetlands Unit
10 Dead Branch Division
11 Westfield River Division
12 Fort River Division
13 Mill River Division
14 Mount Tom Unit
15 Honey Pot Unit
16 Fanny Stebbins Unit

Westfield

Chicopee

Wilbraham

Monson

SPRINGFIELD

○ Location of photos in this
Introduction section.

15

East
Longmeadow

Hampden

Longmeadow

MASSACHUSETTS

16

CONNECTICUT

Suffield

Enfield

Somers

Stafford

Granby

Stafford
Springs

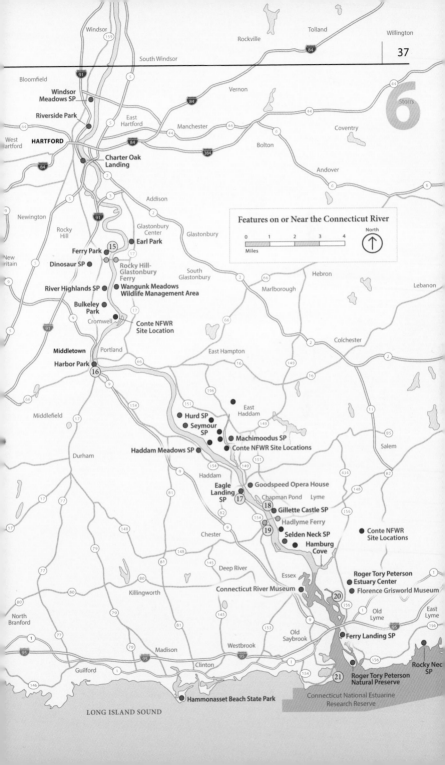

Features on or Near the Connecticut River

Miles
0   1   2   3   4

North

The Connecticut River

15 Map location, p. 37

Looking north across the Connecticut River from Rocky Hill, Connecticut's Ferry Park, on September 3, 2021. This was the day after Hurricane Ida passed over Connecticut and raised the level of the river 10 feet or more. Ida drenched Connecticut with nine inches of rain in 48 hours and created flash flooding across the state and into central New England.

The oddly textured look of the river surface is caused by huge mats of the invasive water weed *Hydrilla verticillata* that were dislodged by the floodwaters. *Hydrilla* was first noticed in the Connecticut River watershed only in

2016, and the infestation has spread with stunning speed. The US Army Corps of Engineers calls *Hydrilla* "the world's worst invasive aquatic plant."

The current infestation of *Hydrilla* in the Connecticut River extends from the river mouth at Old Saybrook, Connecticut, to at least Agawam, Massachusetts, and the weed spreads farther every year. Dense infestations of *Hydrilla* shade or crowd out all other native aquatic plants, cause major swings in dissolved oxygen levels, increase water temperatures, and reduce the diversity and abundance of fish populations.

The Connecticut River

16 Map location, p. 37

A view north from Middletown, Connecticut's Harbor Park, with the Arrigoni Bridge in the distance. An older and now disused railroad bridge sits near the Arrigoni Bridge, with its swing section open.

This portion of the Connecticut River is interesting for several reasons. At Middletown the river turns sharply to the east and exits New England's Central Valley lowlands. This is because of the large traprock ridges just west of Middletown, which are far too high and tough for the river to flow over or erode through (see p. 67).

Middletown is also the upriver beginning of The Straits area, where the Connecticut is squeezed into a narrow bedrock channel just 800 feet wide (see pp. 68–69). This very narrow channel creates what geologists call a hydraulic dam. The dam acts to slow the river flow and raises the river level significantly in times of flood.

The Connecticut River

17 Map location,
p. 37

Eagle Landing State Park, the Goodspeed Opera House, and the East Haddam Swing Bridge, Connecticut.

The glories of the Connecticut River estuary area include the many historical and cultural institutions and museums that line the river down to Long Island Sound. Banker William Henry Goodspeed built the Goodspeed Opera House (opposite bank) in 1877. The venue was never designed for operas but instead featured performances of the time's popular musicals and music reviews. Although the opera house faded into disuse in the early twentieth century, it was revived in the early 1960s by the Goodspeed Musicals group.

 The theater is now famed for its light comedic productions and the number of shows it has sent on to Broadway success.

There isn't much to Eagle Landing State Park—it's mostly just a big grassy parking lot with docks for river tour boats. But these docks are vital for the tour boats that run Bald Eagle watches in winter and spring and the famous Tree Swallow cruises in September. Both are superb Connecticut River wildlife spectacles not to be missed.

The Connecticut River

(18) Map location, p. 37

Gillette Castle and the view south over the upper Connecticut River estuary, East Haddam, Connecticut.
The rough fieldstone Gillette Castle is more oddly extravagant than beautiful, but it offers magnificent views over
the lower Connecticut River and its landscape. Here the Connecticut follows a series of faults in the bedrock, but
the river is much wider and even more tidal here than it is north of The Straits area just past Middletown, Connecticut (see pp. 68–69). The landscape is asymmetrical: it is far higher and rockier on the eastern (closer) side than on
the distant western bank. Gillette Castle perches on one of the highest promontories east of the river.

All the major rivers that enter Long Island Sound are tidal for two reasons: rivers that flow to the ocean are always influenced by ocean tides. The coastal rivers in Connecticut are also tidal because they are all drowned river valleys, land that was flooded by the 400-foot sea level rise at the end of the Wisconsinan Glacial Episode. But tidal rivers are generally not salty until they are near the coast. Here the Connecticut River is always fresh and does not show any brackishness for another six miles down to Essex, Connecticut, and there the water is slightly salty only

The Connecticut River

(19) Map location, p. 37

Dawn on the Connecticut River at Chester, Connecticut.
Among the most remarkable things about the Connecticut River is how it escaped the fate of most large rivers, which generally have major ports and lots of urban development near their mouths. The terminus of New England's longest and most historic river has no port and relatively light development because of the treacherous sandbars near the river mouth at Old Saybrook. Even with modern dredging techniques the Connecticut fills its estuary with so much silt that only relatively small, shallow-draft vessels can navigate the river.

Matthew Male

We owe the current beauty of the Connecticut River estuary and riverine landscape to the Ice Age glaciers. The Wisconsinan ice sheet (p. 71) produced so much glacial till, sand, and silt that 20,000 years after the ice melted back, the river is still full of sediments. Much of the Ice Age sediment flowed into Long Island Sound and now fills about half the basin of the Sound. Without those sediment layers, the Sound would be twice as deep as it is today.

Photograph courtesy of Matthew Male.

The Connecticut River

20 Map location,
p. 37

The view east over the vast tidal cattail marshes of Lord Cove, on the east bank of the Connecticut River in Lyme, Connecticut. In the lower flow levels of late summer, the river here can be moderately brackish, with saline levels of 0.5–5.0 parts per thousand in the main river channel. However, freshwater flows from Deep Creek, Lord Creek, and other smaller streams limit salt intrusion into the m___ ___ ___ at most times of the year.

The cattails here are almost entirely Narrow-Leaved Cattails (*Typha angustifolia*), which tolerate brackish waters well. This area was once threatened by the invasive Common Reed (*Phragmites australis*), which typically moves in and overwhelms native emergents like cattails. However, local efforts to eradicate large stands of Phragmites have been successful, and the marshes are now once again dominated by native aquatic plants.

The Connecticut River

21 Map location,
p. 37

The mouth of the Connecticut River at Old Saybrook, Connecticut.
Here the Outer Bar Channel between the breakwaters passes the nearer Lynde Point Lighthouse and the farther Saybrook Point Lighthouse. As wide as the view is in this photo, it shows only the western half of the river mouth. East (to the left), the shallow, shifting sandbars make navigation too uncertain even for smaller craft.

An estuary is a body of water that is partially salty for some portion of the year. Estuaries are the most productive and biologically essential environments on coastlines. They provide food and shelter to the young of most major game fish, food fish, and waterfowl (p. 344). The surface waters of the lower Connecticut River are rarely brackish

Gregory

north of the I-95 Baldwin Bridge, about three miles upstream from the river mouth. But salt water is heavier than freshwater, so there is often an extension of deep salt water under the fresh surface water, and this deep salty water may extend as far as five miles north of the river mouth.

The brackish estuary of the Connecticut River extends north from Old Saybrook about six miles upriver to Essex, Connecticut (p. 349). The river is primarily responsible for Long Island Sound's brackish water. At an average annual flow rate of 18,400 cubic feet per second, the river provides 70 percent of the freshwater entering the Sound. This volume of freshwater significantly lowers the average salinity, particularly in the Sound's Central Basin.

The view north from the French King Bridge, in Gill, Massachusetts. Here the Connecticut Riv-
er runs directly through the Eastern Border Fault, which forms a steep gorge. The gorge marks
a significant geological divide. The rocks of the west side of the river (left) are part of the same
Jurassic brownstones and conglomerate rocks that fill the Central Valley. To the right (east),
the rocks are Paleozoic metamorphic rocks of the Bronson Volcanic Arc Terrane (see p. 54).

THE RIVER LANDSCAPE

The Connecticut River is a great highway that leads animals and people into the interior of a complex landscape. The river is the circulatory system and lifeblood of much of the ecology of central New England. Seeming accidents of geology had profound effects on the land we see today: the north-south orientation of valleys and rivers in the crumpled and corrugated New England landscape determined the destinies of plant, animal, and human populations throughout central New England. For much of its length, the Connecticut River does not run through a river valley—the Central Valley of New England is a valley that happens to have a great river in it. The ocean's nutrient wealth was once transported hundreds of miles into northern forests through migratory river fish. One of North America's largest lakes appeared and disappeared in this region but left behind a legacy that shapes human and natural history today.

This geologic history has mostly been fortunate for New England but has also created paradoxes. The Ice Age stripped the landscape of all living things 25,000 years ago. Yet 7,000 years ago, Native Americans lived in forests and freshwater environments that were almost unimaginably rich and biologically complex by today's standards. The glaciers devastated the land but also left a wealth of freshwater habitats. The lesson here is simple: whether your focus is fishing, bird-watching,

A view of the river looking south from the heights of Gillette Castle in East Haddam, Connecticut. The lower portion of the Connecticut River south of Middletown runs through a narrow bedrock canyon called The Straits, then follows a series of fracture zones between the Bronson Volcanic Arc and Iapetus Terranes, and finally is bordered by Avalon Terrane rocks south of Essex, Connecticut (see overleaf).

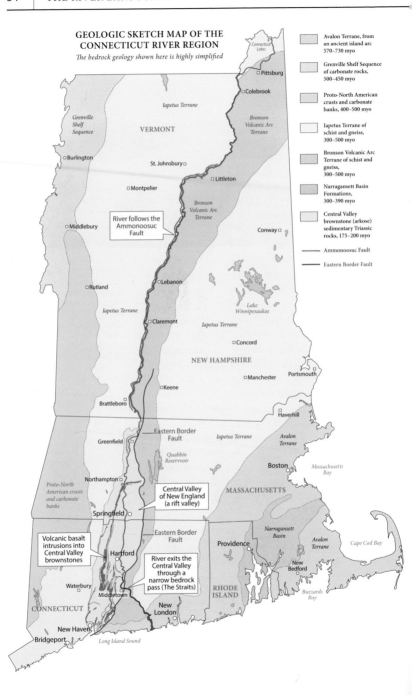

GEOLOGIC SKETCH MAP OF THE CONNECTICUT RIVER REGION

The bedrock geology shown here is highly simplified

Avalon Terrane, from an ancient island arc 570–730 myo

Grenville Shelf Sequence of carbonate rocks, 500–450 myo

Proto-North American crusts and carbonate banks, 400–500 myo

Iapetus Terrane of schist and gneiss, 300–500 myo

Bronson Volcanic Arc Terrane of schist and gneiss, 300–500 myo

Narragansett Basin Formations, 300–390 myo

Central Valley brownstone (arkose) sedimentary Triassic rocks, 175–200 myo

— Ammonoosuc Fault

— Eastern Border Fault

Connecticut Lakes

Pittsburg

Colebrook

Iapetus Terrane

Grenville Shelf Sequence

VERMONT

Bronson Volcanic Arc Terrane

Burlington

St. Johnsbury

Littleton

Montpelier

Bronson Volcanic Arc Terrane

Conway

River follows the Ammonoosuc Fault

Middlebury

Rutland

Lebanon

Lake Winnipesaukee

Iapetus Terrane

Claremont

Iapetus Terrane

Concord

NEW HAMPSHIRE

Keene

Manchester

Portsmouth

Brattleboro

Haverhill

Eastern Border Fault

Greenfield

Iapetus Terrane

Avalon Terrane

Quabbin Reservvoir

Boston

Massachusetts Bay

Proto-North American crusts and carbonate banks

Northampton

Central Valley of New England (a rift valley)

MASSACHUSETTS

Springfield

Eastern Border Fault

Narragansett Basin

Avalon Terrane

Cape Cod Bay

Volcanic basalt intrusions into Central Valley brownstones

Hartford

Providence

River exits the Central Valley through a narrow bedrock pass (The Straits)

New Bedford

Waterbury

Middletown

RHODE ISLAND

Buzzards Bay

CONNECTICUT

New London

New Haven

Bridgeport

Long Island Sound

hiking, boating, or simply appreciating the natural history of one of America's great waterways, you can't understand what you see on today's Connecticut River without some knowledge of the geologic past.

The geologic history of New England's Central Valley

New England, particularly the Connecticut River region, has a long and intricate geologic history that stretches back more than 750 million years. The whole story of the bedrock history of New England is beyond the scope of this guide, which concentrates on the significant events that formed New England's bedrock and the relatively recent geologic history of the areas surrounding the Connecticut River during the most recent Ice Age. What follows is a highly simplified view of the major elements that converged over the past 500 million years to form the New England and Connecticut River we know today.

A spectacular 10-foot-tall S-fold in metamorphic rocks along Route 9 in Higganum, Connecticut, attests to New England's complex and dramatic geologic past. Multiple continental collisions and mountain-building events shaped our landscape.

The modern science of geology is founded on the theory—and fact—of plate tectonics. The giant, long-lived cores of continents slowly drift over the earth's surface, occasionally colliding to form new mountain ranges and squeeze old oceans out of existence, only then to break up again, creating new oceans and sometimes new continents. These massive geological events are momentous in retrospect, but most titanic geologic events occur at the rate of inches per year over many tens of millions of years. We mostly notice instantaneous events such as volcanoes, earthquakes, and floods in our human time frame. However, plate tectonics' almost invisible, undramatic forces and steady erosion over geologic stretches of time are the most essential factors in creating a landscape.

The Connecticut River's bedrock geology story goes back about half a billion years when the ancient Iapetus Ocean separated the continental cores of what later became North America, Africa, and parts of Europe (see pp. 56–57). At its most basic level, the bedrock of New England is composed of five major terranes: the Iapetus, Avalon, Bronson Volcanic Arc, and Central Valley Terranes and the ancient North American Plate. A terrane is a broad region in geology

The massive granite gneiss formations that make up much of the coast around the Connecticut River mouth originated in the Japan-like Avalonia archipelago of islands (see the diagrams). The boulders we see along the Connecticut coast today were moved and jumbled by the Wisconsinan Glaciation ("Ice Age") about 20,000 years ago. But the granite itself is far more ancient and was formed by volcanoes in the Avalonian Islands as much as 730 million years ago.

that shares a common bedrock origin and structure. Five hundred million years ago, these five terranes were arrayed across the ancient Iapetus Ocean, where the protocontinents of North America and Africa were drifting toward each other in a way that would eventually squeeze the Iapetus Ocean out of existence. In the Iapetus Ocean, there were two chains of volcanic islands between the continental plates. Geologists call the larger island chain Avalonia (often described as a Japan-like chain), composed of volcanic rocks over 700 million years old. The younger, smaller Bronson Volcanic Island Arc lay between Avalonia and the proto–North American Plate.

By 250 million years ago, the continental plates of proto-Africa and proto–North America collided, forming the supercontinent of Pangaea. The old Iapetus Ocean disappeared as a water body but left behind the rock of its ocean floor. The rocks of the old Iapetus Ocean floor, Avalonia, and Bronson Volcanic Arc formed bands of bedrock terrane between the continental plates.

After existing intact for about 100 million years, the supercontinent of Pangaea broke apart starting about 200–175 million years ago. The breakup may have been because the sheer size of the supercontinent trapped the earth's internal heat like a thermal blanket. The warming raised and stretched the crust of central Pangaea until it thinned and finally cracked apart. This

500 million years ago: Iapetus Ocean and the Avalonia and Bronson Island Chains

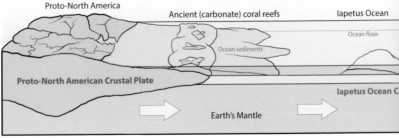

Proto-North America

Ancient (carbonate) coral reefs

Iapetus Ocean

Ocean floor

Ocean sediments

Proto-North American Crustal Plate

Iapetus Ocean C

Earth's Mantle

Distance ~800–1,000 miles

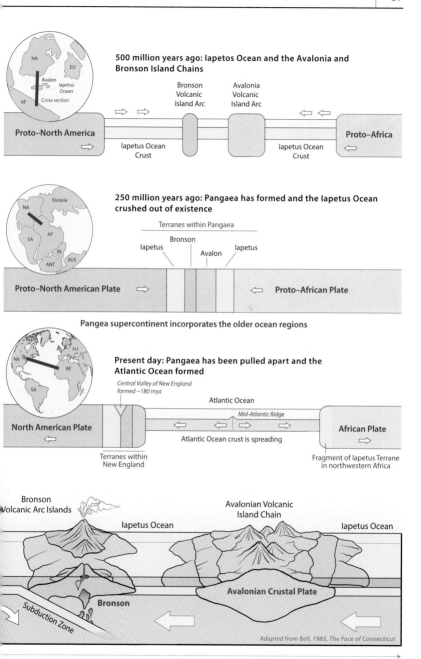

500 million years ago: Iapetos Ocean and the Avalonia and Bronson Island Chains

NA · EU · Avalon · Iapetus Ocean · Cross section · AF

Bronson Volcanic Island Arc

Avalonia Volcanic Island Arc

Proto–North America

Iapetus Ocean Crust

Iapetus Ocean Crust

Proto–Africa

250 million years ago: Pangaea has formed and the Iapetus Ocean crushed out of existence

Eurasia · NA · AF · SA · IN · AUS · ANT

Terranes within Pangaea

Iapetus · Bronson · Avalon · Iapetus

Proto–North American Plate

Proto–African Plate

Pangea supercontinent incorporates the older ocean regions

Present day: Pangaea has been pulled apart and the Atlantic Ocean formed

EU · NA · AF · SA

Central Valley of New England formed ~180 mya

Atlantic Ocean

Mid-Atlantic Ridge

North American Plate

Atlantic Ocean crust is spreading

African Plate

Terranes within New England

Fragment of Iapetus Terrane in northwestern Africa

Bronson Volcanic Arc Islands

Iapetus Ocean

Avalonian Volcanic Island Chain

Iapetus Ocean

Subduction Zone

Bronson

Avalonian Crustal Plate

Adapted from Bell, 1985, The Face of Connecticut

Jon Chica

Brownstone is familiar to residents of the Northeast as the classic building material commonly used to create late nineteenth-century homes and commercial structures in many cities in New York and New England. Brownstone was once widely quarried in Connecticut and New Jersey. One of the largest brownstone quarries was located on the Connecticut River in Portland, Connecticut. The flooded remnant of the Portland quarry is now the Brownstone Adventure Sports Park.

drifting apart of the elements of Pangaea was the beginning of the earth's continental and ocean structure that we know today.

The formation of New England's great rift valley

In the late Triassic Period (200 million years ago), the breakup of Pangaea produced giant tension cracks near the edge of the North American Plate as it pulled away from the African Plate. The early Atlantic Ocean was born in the growing divide between North America's east coast and Africa's northwestern coast. New England's Central Valley is one of those great tension cracks, or rift valleys, in the earth's crust. As the east and west sides of the new valley pulled apart along fault lines, the valley floor dropped down, eventually by several thousand feet below the land surface on either side (see below). After the deep faulting and drop of the valley floor, the Central Valley entered a 50-million-year period dominated mainly by erosion. The lowlands gradually filled with brick-red sand eroded from the then-mountainous highlands on the east and west sides of the valley. The sandy sediments eventually hardened to become the brownstone for which the Central Valley is famous. All was not quiet, though—at least three episodes of violent volcanic activity interrupted the slow process of erosion that filled the Central Valley with brownstone.

The uplifting and breakup of the continental pieces of Pangaea created volcanic activity that periodically invaded the rift valleys along the new Atlantic Coast of North America. This vulcanism was the source of the traprock ridges found in New England's Central Valley

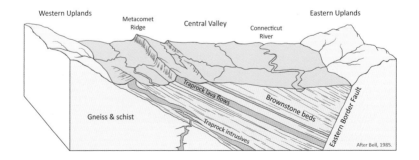

Western Uplands
Metacomet Ridge
Central Valley
Connecticut River
Eastern Uplands
Traprock lava flows
Brownstone beds
Eastern Border Fault
Gneiss & schist
Traprock intrusives
After Bell, 1985.

today. In the early Jurassic (200 million years ago), the faults that created the rift valley penetrated the crust so deeply that they activated pools of traprock (basalt) magma, which formed huge subterranean chambers of rock within the brownstone sediments of the Central Valley. The traprock magma pools also periodically vented to the valley surface, forming vast lava lakes across the valley floor. These volcanic eruptions at the ground surface did not produce conical volcanoes such as Mount Vesuvius or Mount Saint Helens. Where the traprock lava reached the valley's surface, the highly liquid magma spread across the ground as fissure eruptions of flood traprock basalts. The magma layers cooled to form thick layers of hard traprock that are far more durable than the brown sandstone surrounding them. The magma flows could be as much as 400 feet thick. These horizontal slabs of basalt are the origin of most of the traprock ridges we see today in the Central Valley. There were three separate eruptions of magma over a period of about 600,000 years. After each eruption, erosion filled the valley with yet more red-brown sediment from erosion of the edges of the rift valley, burying the old basaltic lava intrusions on the valley floor.

Thus, the basalt or traprock ridges within the Central Valley originated from two types of volcanic eruptions: massive underground domes of magma that never reached the valley's ancient surface and basalt lava floods across the valley floor. Most of them are formed from the ancient flood eruptions; downward slippage along the Eastern Border Fault caused the old horizontal traprock layers to tilt over time. Erosion of the softer brownstone sediments surrounding the plates then exposed the layers above the landscape. The Hanging Hills of Meriden, Higby Mountain in Meriden, and the Metacomet Ridge that extends north from southern Connecticut to central Massachusetts are all formed from tilted basalt plates. A few major basalt landmarks in the Central Valley originated as underground magma chambers that were later exposed by erosion. The fine-grained basalt that cooled slowly underground is diabase, a related form of traprock. Mount Carmel at Connecticut's Sleeping Giant State

Michael Marsland

East Rock in New Haven, Connecticut, is one of the many traprock (basalt) ridges that dot New England's Central Valley in Connecticut. The Hanging Hills of Meriden, Connecticut, are the largest traprock formation in the Central Valley. It was the size and height of the Hanging Hills that forced the Connecticut River to turn eastward and out of the Central Valley and into its present course past Middletown, Connecticut.

West

East

The tilted west-to-east profile of New Haven, Connecticut's West Rock is typical of Central Valley traprock formations (see diagram, p. 58). The tilt is caused by downward slippage along the Eastern Border Fault.

Park and New Haven's famous East and West Rocks were formed from deep reservoirs of diabase basalt magma. This form of traprock ridge gradually emerged from deep burial as the surrounding brown sandstone eroded, creating the New Haven–area mountains we know today.

The Eastern Border Fault along the eastern edge of the Central Valley was an active geologic fault until about 50 million years ago. Movement along this fault is responsible for the distinct forms of the Central Valley traprock ridges, with cliffs that mostly face southwest and more gently sloping eastern slopes. Since the earliest formation of the Central Valley, the valley floor has been slipping downward along the Eastern Border Fault, resulting in valley sediment and basalt layers that tilt downward toward the east by as much as several thousand feet. Immediately east of the Eastern Border Fault, the bedrock has also been uplifted by hundreds of feet. This slippage along the Eastern Border Fault is why the east side of the valley in Connecticut has much more relief than the west side, with high ridges including the Saltonstall Ridge and Totoket Mountain east of New Haven, Higby Mountain in Meriden, and the long series of traprock ridges that run north of Portland.

The brownstones of the Central Valley have preserved hundred of dinosaur footprints from the late Triassic and early Jurassic periods (about 200 million years ago). The footprints preserved by the Dinosaur State Park in Rocky Hill, Connecticut, were mostly made by the 20-foot-long early Jurassic dinosaur *Eubrontes*.

Ancient life in the Central Valley

The Central Valley is famous for its dinosaur foot-prints, found in many locations throughout the valley, from central Massachusetts south to central Connecticut. The best-known dinosaur footprints were laid down in early Jurassic times by small and medium-sized bipedal dinosaurs such as *Dilophosaurus* and *Podokesaurus* and by primitive crocodiles such as *Stegomosuchus*. The Central Valley climate when the tracks were laid was a tropical monsoon environment, where hot, dry summers alternated with cooler rainy seasons. The sediment beds the dinosaurs knew were originally a yellow color, but these sandy sediments became tinted with red-brown as the iron content within them oxidized. In early Jurassic times, the edges of the Central Valley were rugged mountain ranges, far taller than the eroded stumps visible today. The eastward tilting of the valley floor due to the Eastern Border Fault created a series of shallow early Jurassic lakes that ran north-south on the eastern side of the valley, and these ancient lakes became a source of fossil fish and other aquatic life. Because few tracks from herbivorous dinosaurs have been found in the valley, paleontologists speculate that the carnivorous dinosaurs such as *Dilophosaurus* were primarily fish eaters, feeding in the shallow Central Valley lakes. Unfortunately, despite the abundance of dinosaur tracks, fossils of larger animals

Dinosaur State Park in Rocky Hill, Connecticut, is the best place to learn about the fascinating geologic history of New England's Central Valley and its famous dinosaur footprints.

The ancient Central Valley in the early Jurassic wasn't just a home to dinosaurs. Shallow lakes and wetlands filled much of the southern end of the valley. The Connecticut and Massachusetts valley sediments preserved the remains of many fish species, including the four-inch *Semionotus* shown here. Fossil from Dinosaur State Park.

A group of predatory **Coelophysis** dinosaurs roam across the floor of the Central Valley in the Late Triassic, about 200 million years ago. Millions of years of erosion have softened the profile of New England's Central Valley, but this ancient rift valley was once at least as steep and rugged as East Africa's famous rift valley is today. The dry-tropical environment was much warmer than today, because this section of what was then Pangaea was located on the equator.

are rare in the Central Valley. The area's shallow lakes and streams were well oxygenated, and therefore large dead animals were likely to decay rapidly without fossilizing. In contrast, smaller animals such as fish were more likely to be quickly and entirely buried by lake-bottom sediments and therefore were fossilized more frequently.

A long, quiet period of erosion

As the newly formed Atlantic Ocean continued to widen in the Late Jurassic and Cretaceous Periods (160–66 million years ago), the early dramatic events that formed and shaped the Central Valley gradually faded. The Connecticut River region and the rest of the East Coast of North America entered a 50-million-year period dominated by the quiet but powerful forces of erosion; atmospheric water combines with carbon dioxide to produce carbonic acid in raindrops, a natural weathering agent that slowly erodes even the hardest rocks. On average, erosion wears away rock at a rate of about two inches every thousand years. Although this doesn't sound like much, when you multiply that erosion rate by 50 million years, even high granite mountains can be reduced to low hills on the landscape. The once-rugged mountain chains on the east and west sides of the Central Valley wore down to the modest hills we know today; most of their former substance washed down into the Central Valley, where they complexly buried most of the old traprock intrusions. Over millions of years, these sandy sediments in the Central Valley were transformed by the heat and pressure of

In the broad view from New Haven, Connecticut's West Rock you can still see the ancient flat peneplain of New England that formed over 50 million years of quiet erosion. A period of uplifting about 10 million years ago initiated the erosion that produced the major outlines of the hills and river valleys today. The landscape may look complex from up close, but from a high vantage point, you can see that the old peneplain still dominates the landscape. The few exceptions are the basalt ridges such as West Rock and East Rock (on the far horizon at left).

East Rock

Downtown New Haven

West   East

deep burial into the relatively soft, easily worked red-brown sandstone known as brownstone.

By early Cenozoic times (about 60–50 million years ago), most of New England was a heavily eroded, largely featureless plain that sloped gently to the shores of the young Atlantic Ocean. Geologists call these ancient flat and heavily eroded landscapes peneplains. The essentially flat New England peneplain probably had sluggish tidal rivers that meandered across it, much like the rivers on the broad coastal plain of the mid-Atlantic states of Virginia and North Carolina. Hills and valleys still existed in New England's bedrock, but the rocky forms of the bedrock were deeply

Exposed brownstone beds along the Route 40 Mount Carmel Connector in North Haven, Connecticut. These brownstone layers show the eastward tilt of sediments in the Central Valley, due to slippage along the Eastern Border Fault (see p. 58, bottom).

Ten million years ago, the uplifting of the crust under New England produced the gently rolling hills and river valleys we see today. The uplift invigorated ancient rivers, and the flowing waters eroded the flat peneplain landscape into roughly the contours visible today.
View toward Northampton from the summit of Mount Holyoke, Massachusetts.

The Deerfield River at Shelburne, Massachusetts (below). The early ancestors of the major tributaries of the Connecticut River, such as the Deerfield, White, Westfield, and Farmington Rivers, all formed during the period of crustal uplift 10 million years ago.

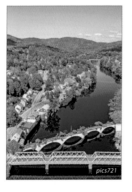

buried under a thick blanket of eroded sediments. The effects of the old peneplain can still be seen in New England. The immediate hills and valleys seem dominant in close views of local landscapes. Still, when you are high up and can get broad views of the landscape, it becomes evident that most of the hills are the same height and that only singular features such as traprock ridges disturb the overall evenness of the view.

Formation of the early Connecticut River

About 10 million years ago, the bedrock under New England was uniformly uplifted by changes in the underlying geology of the North American Plate and the earth's mantle beneath. For several million years, the crust of northern New England was uplifted by as much as 2,000 feet, and the crust of coastal New England was uplifted by hundreds of feet. As the land rose and sloped, languid rivers that had been slowly eroding the coastal plain became rushing torrents that cut deeply into the soft sediments of the landscape. The more vigorous river flows created deep river valleys that gradually eroded their way down through harder rocks. Over a relatively short period, what had been a very flat peneplain landscape was transformed into the more familiar hills and valleys of today's central New England.

The newly invigorated rivers began to consolidate into drainage networks controlled by the underlying bedrock valleys and fault lines. It was at this time that the ancestral Connecticut River formed. Regional rivers such as the Farmington River, the Westfield River, the Deerfield River, and the rivers of northern New England coalesced into the early Connecticut River, which ran in much the same fault channels and valleys as today's river. There are some ironies here: without the rifted Central Valley, there would have been no soft brownstones created in the age of the dinosaurs from sediment eroded from ancient mountains. The valley filled with sediment, but then the soft brownstone was re-eroded after uplifting millions of years later, restoring the valley to its place in the center of New England—just in time to see the birth of the modern Connecticut River.

At this time of renewed rapid erosion, the ancestral Connecticut River created two formations critical to its run to the sea. In the area between what is now Mount Tom and Mount Holyoke in Massachusetts, the river eroded its way down through the soft brownstone sediments that had buried most of the Holyoke-area traprock ridges. It then continued cutting down through the newly exposed traprock to create the Holyoke Water Gap between Mount Holyoke and Mount Tom (see Thomas Cole's painting, pp. 120–21). Farther south, in what is now Middletown, Connecticut, the river took a sharp bend to the east and out of the Central Valley and flowed southeastward to meet the Atlantic Coast. The ancestral Connecticut River could not have continued south of Middletown within the Central Valley because the traprock ridges of Mount Higby and the Hanging Hills of Meriden were too high and massive to surmount or erode. Instead, the river cut east through lower bedrock valley areas just north of Middletown. The final 25 miles of the Connecticut River now flow through a narrow bedrock canyon between Middletown and Old Lyme, Connecticut (see below, red circle). South of Old Lyme and Essex,

Mr. Matté

Higby Mountain is the massive traprock ridge that you see to your left as you drive south on I-91 just north of Meriden, Connecticut. It was the sheer size of Higby Mountain and the other ridges of the Metacomet Range that forced the Connecticut River out of the Central Valley and east to its present course through The Straits (see below and overleaf). *Photo: Mr. Matté, via Wikimedia.*

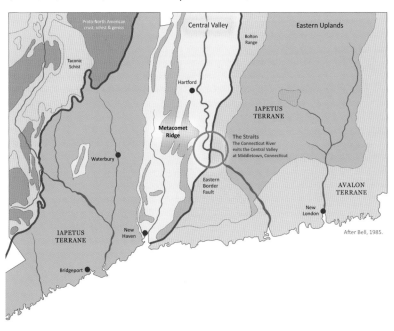

The Straits region of the Connecticut River just south and east of Middletown, Connecticut. Here the Connecticut River passes out of New England's Central Valley and enters a narrow bedrock canyon where the river is squeezed into a strait only 800 feet wide. The Straits constrains and slows the flow of the Connecticut River in a phenomenon known as a hydraulic dam. North of The Straits the partially dammed river has created the rich floodplains between Hartford and Cromwell, Connecticut. In times of flood the slower river flow through The Straits also benefits the tidal marshes in the Connecticut River estuary area by buffering the force of floodwater.

See *A Field Guide to Long Island Sound* for more information on the geology of Connecticut and the Long Island Sound coast.

Connecticut, the river widens into broad, brackish salt marshes as it enters Long Island Sound.

Although this uplift and erosion during the early Cenozoic Era restored the familiar contours of New England's landscape, deep erosion of surface sediments also erased much of the evidence we might have had about the climate and biology of the region 8–10 million years ago. After the erosion caused by the uplift of the land, multiple glacial periods during the Pleistocene Epoch (2.5 million to 11,000 years ago) further wiped the landscape clean of ancient sediments and fossil records. However, farther south in the unglaciated parts of the Atlantic Coast, we have evidence that the climate during this time was temperate and that New England during the Pleistocene was covered with the same kinds of mixed hardwood forests visible in the landscape today.

The Wisconsinan Ice Age

Over the past 2 million years, there have been many glacial episodes or "ice ages"* at intervals of approximately 100,000 years, interspersed with warmer interglacial periods. We are in such a warmer interglacial period and have been for about 11,000 years since the last glacial period ended. Glacial episodes begin with a subtle cooling trend in the earth's environment. In cooling periods, snow fell each year and did not entirely melt away in summer, and every year the snowfields expanded across the northern landscape. Bright white snow reflects a lot of sunlight. That, combined with the cooling effect of large expanses of snow, creates an accelerating cycle of regional cooling and yet more snow accumulation. Science isn't entirely sure why the earth enters long-term cooling weather trends from time to time, but the best current theory involves the oval orbit of the earth around the sun, which wobbles slightly in roughly 100,000-year cycles. These slight but important variations in the oval orbit (called Milankovitch cycles) can combine with subtle changes in the angle of the earth's rotational axis to produce periods where the earth receives slightly less solar energy than average. The variation in sunlight is subtle, but it only takes a few colder-than-average years to initiate a glacial episode. Over the past million

*When people refer to the Ice Age in New England, they usually mean the Wisconsinan Glacial Episode, 85,000–16,500 years ago, but the term "Ice Age" is ambiguous. There have been multiple ice ages in our region over the past 2.6 million years.

Peak of the Wisconsinan Glacial Period, 25,000 years ago

The Laurentide Ice Sheet. At its maximum extent during the Wisconsinan Glacial Episode 25,000 years ago, the Laurentide Ice Sheet, a single, massive glacier, covered most of northeastern, eastern, and north-central North America. Ice also covered much of northwestern North America, Europe, and Asia. It may be easiest to think of the Wisconsinan Glaciation as a giant extension of the polar ice cap.

years, known ice age cycles have roughly matched the 100,000-year periods of Milankovitch cycles, lending strong evidence that variations in the earth's orbit drive glacial cycles. However, some climate scientists dispute the theory.

The Wisconsinan Glacial Episode—popularly known as New England's Ice Age—began with a global cooling cycle that started about 150,000 years ago, at a time interval roughly predicted by Milankovitch cycles and previous glacial periods. It is called the Wisconsinan because the first major studies of this glacial period were conducted in Wisconsin. The continent-sized ice sheet that formed in this glaciation is called the Laurentide Ice Sheet, named for the Laurentian region of northeastern Canada, where the ice was thought to have originated. The massive Toba supervolcano eruption in Sumatra 74,000 years ago also accelerated the global temperature drop during the Wisconsinan glaciation. Climate scientists estimate that the Toba eruption lowered global average temperatures by 5–6

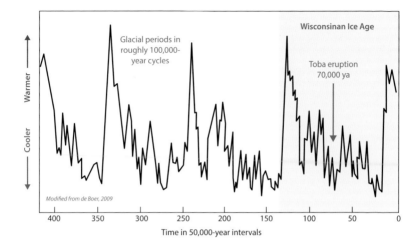

Warmer ← → Cooler

Glacial periods in roughly 100,000-year cycles

Wisconsinan Ice Age

Toba eruption 70,000 ya

Modified from de Boer, 2009

400 350 300 250 200 150 100 50 0

Time in 50,000-year intervals

There have been many ice ages over the past several million years of earth's history. The Wisconsinan Glacial Episode was the most recent ice age in New England.

degrees Fahrenheit, causing a global volcanic winter that may have lasted at least five to 10 years. During the volcanic winter, temperatures in the subtropics would have hovered near freezing most of the year, with hard freezes lasting all year in temperate latitudes.

The Laurentide Ice Sheet reached northern New England about 100,000 years ago and retreated from the northern reaches of the Connecticut River by about 13,000 years ago (see the ice retreat lines on the map, p. 76).

At the peak of the Wisconsinan Episode 25,000 years ago, the Laurentide Ice Sheet blanketed New England (see pp. 71) and reached as far south as the middle of present-day Long Island. In most places, the ice sheet was thousands of feet thick, and the landscape of the New England region resembled today's central Greenland. All of New England's mountains were under the ice sheet, including Mount Washington, the region's highest peak. At the glacial maximum, so much of the earth's water was bound up in glacial ice that the sea level was 400 feet lower than it is today, and a large area of dry land extended south and east of the present-day coasts of Long Island and New England. This ice-free land resembled northern Canada's spruce taiga forests and tundra today. It provided a refuge area where many of the plant and animal species in our area today could survive. These species began to repopulate New England when the ice sheet started to retreat about 24,000 years ago.

After the glacial maximum 25,000 years ago, the climate began to warm, and the Laurentide Ice Sheet began to retreat across the landscape. Glaciers cannot flow backward—glaciers retreat by melting away. On average, the Laurentide Ice Sheet retreated across New England at a rate of about 150–250 feet per year. The warming trend of the climate was not perfectly uniform, and there were times during the glacier's retreat when the climate cooled again for hundreds of years, leaving recessional moraines as lines of great boulders and glacial till on the landscape.

The rocky soils of New England

As the ice receded 20,000–15,000 years ago, the Connecticut River Valley resembled a wet moonscape of exposed bedrock, considerable barren glacial till, and countless meltwater streams draining the land. Large bergs of remnant ice dotted the land, the largest of which later became kettle ponds and small lakes as the ice finally melted away. The Laurentide Ice Sheet was a single glacier, but it had many individual streams or lobes within the general mass of ice. One ice stream, the Connecticut Valley Lobe, flowed through the Central Valley, plucking great quantities of rock from the valley's upland sides and leaving vast masses of sand, silt, and clay as a thick layer of muddy paste on the valley floor. The enormous weight of the flowing glacier "lodged" or forced quantities of this so-called lodgment till into every nook and crack of the bedrock, and lodgment till is responsible for both the soft, rolling character of today's upland and valley lands and the great fertility of New England's upland soils.

In most areas, the glacier also left a superficial layer of stony ablation till lying over the deeper lodgment till. In the warming climate after the peak of the Wisconsinan Glaciation 25,000 years ago, the ice sheet began to melt or "ablate," leaving behind tremendous quantities of rocks, sand, and silt that were held within the body of the ice. Ablation till is also associated with terminal and other glacial moraines, lines across the

Glacial ice is nothing like the clear, clean ice cubes in your freezer. Glaciers are full of rocks, giant boulders, sand, and fine silt. Here two modern glaciers (top and bottom of picture) on Washington State's Mount Rainier are so full of rock debris that you can hardly tell where the rock ends and the ice begins.

landscape where the glacier dumped rocky debris as it melted away.

The wide assortment of pulverized minerals in lodgment till make soils derived from it very fertile. The high silt and clay content allow lodgment till to hold quantities of water without significant surface runoff. The great amount of sand and gravel in some lowland or riverine soils doesn't hold rainwater or snowmelt, and minerals may be quickly leached from these soils. The trade-off for farmers is that glacial lodgment soils are full of stones. In pre-European times these glacial stones were buried deep under the leaf litter of soils created by 10,000 years of forest growth, but as colonial and early American farmers cleared the upland landscapes of New England for pastures and farming, the lodgment soils were exposed to more frost-heaving and weather erosion, both of which brought the load of glacial stones to the surface.

Not all Central Valley soils were ideal for farming. Particularly up in the northern sections of the Connecticut River, the rich lake-bottom soils of Glacial Lake Hitchcock were often interrupted by sand and gravel deposits called eskers, left behind in long strands across the valley by glacial meltwater streams that flowed under the rotting ice in the valley.

Postglacial uplift and rebound of the land

The enormous mass of the Laurentide Ice Sheet was such a burden that the crust of New England sank hundreds of feet under the weight of ice. Parts of northern Vermont and New Hampshire were pressed down almost 1,000 feet lower than before the Wisconsinan Glacial Episode (see the crust depression numbers in blue, p. 76). This elastic downward bend in the earth's crust slowly began to rebound as the glaciers melted. However, the crustal rebound was much slower than the ice melting rate, and the crustal rebound rate had important effects on the formation, size, and lifespan of the glacial meltwater lakes formed as the ice retreated. Crust rebound also affected the course and rate of flow of streams and rivers in the region. For example, glacial lakes in northern New England lasted much longer than they might have otherwise because

Layered glacial moraine till that was part of the earthen dam across the Connecticut River between Rocky Hill and South Glastonbury, Connecticut. This glacial till dam created Glacial Lake Hitchcock.

the normal southward slope of the crust was distorted by the crustal depression.

Melting and crustal rebound proceeded more quickly in the central Massachusetts and Connecticut regions, eventually tilting the land seaward from north to south. This new slope accelerated the speed and downcutting of the Connecticut River and its tributaries, widening and deepening river valleys and cutting through the glacial till. New regional drainage systems emerged similar to the courses of modern rivers and streams.

Glacial Lake Hitchcock

One of the most significant features in the glacial and human history of the Connecticut River evolved as the Wisconsinan Glaciation ended. Glacial Lake Hitchcock (see map, p. 76) was a vast fresh meltwater lake extending through the entire Central Valley and into Vermont and New Hampshire. The lake drained over 15,500 years ago but left behind a flat lake bed containing the richest soils in New England. The Pioneer Valley of Massachusetts and Connecticut's Central Valley areas north of Rocky Hill are still the region's most significant farming and agricultural areas, all based on the lake bed soils from the late Ice Age. Both

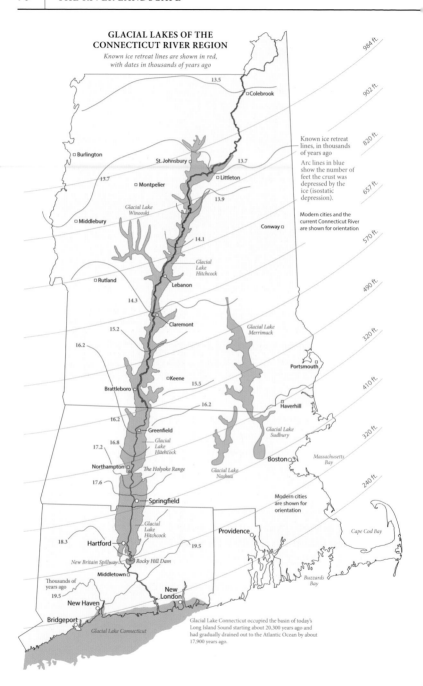

GLACIAL LAKES OF THE CONNECTICUT RIVER REGION

Known ice retreat lines are shown in red, with dates in thousands of years ago

984 ft.

902 ft.

820 ft.

657 ft.

570 ft.

490 ft.

320 ft.

410 ft.

320 ft.

240 ft.

Known ice retreat lines, in thousands of years ago

Arc lines in blue show the number of feet the crust was depressed by the ice (isostatic depression).

Modern cities and the current Connecticut River are shown for orientation

Colebrook

13.5

13.7

Burlington

St. Johnsbury

Littleton

13.7

Montpelier

13.9

Glacial Lake Winooski

Conway

14.1

Middlebury

Glacial Lake Hitchcock

Rutland

Lebanon

14.3

15.2

Claremont

Glacial Lake Merrimack

16.2

Keene

15.5

Portsmouth

Brattleboro

16.2

Haverhill

16.2

Greenfield

Glacial Lake Sudbury

16.8

Glacial Lake Hitchcock

17.2

Northampton

The Holyoke Range

Glacial Lake Nashua

Boston

Massachusetts Bay

17.6

Springfield

Modern cities are shown for orientation

Glacial Lake Hitchcock

18.3

Hartford

19.5

Providence

Cape Cod Bay

New Britain Spillway

Rocky Hill Dam

Middletown

New London

Buzzards Bay

Thousands of years ago

19.5

New Haven

Bridgeport

Glacial Lake Connecticut

Glacial Lake Connecticut occupied the basin of today's Long Island Sound starting about 20,300 years ago and had gradually drained out to the Atlantic Ocean by about 17,900 years ago.

Native American and later European settlers were quick to take advantage of the extremely fertile and stone-free soil left behind by the glacial lake. Some of New England's earliest permanent human settlements were along the Connecticut River in the old lake bed area. Native Americans had used the fertile soil for agriculture for centuries before Europeans arrived. The early valley towns of Northampton, Holyoke, Springfield, Windsor Locks, and Hartford were all created on the sites of long-established Native American farming villages. (See "Environmental History" for more on this topic.)

Glacial Lake Hitchcock filled much of the Central Valley for 2,500 years, between 18,000 and 15,500 years ago, as determined by lake sediment layers and radiocarbon dating. The lake was formed by an earthen dam of sandy sediments and meltwater deposits created by an earlier and short-lived glacial lake, Glacial Lake Middletown. This dam across the course of the Connecticut River held back the river near today's riverside site of the TPC River Highlands golf course in Rocky Hill, Connecticut. The water did not spill over the Rocky Hill dam during the lake's life. Instead, the lake drained through a small spillway west of Rocky Hill, in a channel now occupied by today's small Mattabesset River that runs southeast between New Britain and Cromwell, Connecticut.

Large sediment and sand deposits from the old Rocky Hill dam still exist on the western and eastern sides of

The remains of the huge earthen dam of glacial till that created Glacial Lake Hitchcock can still be seen on both sides of the Connecticut River in Cromwell and Rocky Hill, Connecticut (west side), and in a till quarry in South Glastonbury (east side). The quarry is shown below. On the river's west bank in Cromwell, much of the ground under the well-known TPC River Highlands golf complex is glacial till from the ancient dam.

Dividend Pond and the surrounding Dividend Pond Park in Rocky Hill, Connecticut, sit atop the remains of the earthen dam that created Glacial Lake Hitchcock.

the river. On the west side of the river, the northern end of the TPC River Highlands golf course complex, the adjacent Mustard Bowl field, and Dividend Pond Park still show expansive areas of sandy open space and exposed sediments that are remnants of the glacial dam. Near the opposite, eastern bank of the river, there is a large sand quarry that taps the deep sediments remaining there.

Lake bottoms accumulate seasonal sediments that are often laid down in annual two-part winter-summer layers called varves. Each varve layer pair is roughly analogous to an annual tree ring. In the warmer months, active water flows and currents deposit thick layers of new silt, sand, and small pebble sediments on the lake bottom. In winter, the frozen lake surface creates still waters, and the lake bottom mainly receives thin layers of fine clay and silt. Geologists can use varve sequences to establish the age and lifespan of the lake, although most varve sequences are also paired with radiocarbon dating to make the measurements more accurate. Varve sediments sometimes contain enough ancient pollen and plant remains to establish the kinds of environments that surrounded ancient lakes.

Environments after the ice

Fourteen thousand years ago, New England's landscape was a muddy, barren ruin after the Ice Age glacier retreated. Bare bedrock outcrops stood above fields of glacial rubble, countless boulders were scattered on the landscape, and torrents of icy meltwater stripped loose sand and clay from the land. Without vegetation cover, winter winds created great sand dunes across the now-empty lake bottom of the former Glacial Lake Hitchcock. Some of these ancient dune fields are still visible near the Connecticut River near Longmeadow, Massachusetts.

Because of the Ice Age, the region's ecosystems are relatively young. New England's plants and animals began to arrive 14,000 years ago, and most of the hardwood trees returned in the past 8,000 years. However, pollen profiles from ancient bogs and lake bottoms show that some plant and animal life quickly returned

to postglacial southern New England and then spread to the rest of the ancient Connecticut River region. At first, the landscape was dominated by tundra vegetation of cold-adapted grasses, sedges, lichens, mosses, and low-growing shrubs such as Arctic Willow. As the climate moderated and soil conditions improved, low evergreens such as spruce and fir formed dwarfed Krumholz forests, much as can be seen near the summits of the White Mountains of New Hampshire today. Warmer times brought full-size taiga conifer forests of the kind seen in northern Canada today, and finally, by about 7,000 years ago, the forests of New England looked much as they did when Europeans arrived in the 1600s. In southern New England, the forests are currently dominated by oaks, hickories, and maples, with scatterings of coniferous trees such as White Pine and Pitch Pine. North of Massachusetts, the forest transitioned to a mix of coniferous and northern deciduous trees, including spruces, firs, birches, and pines.

Varved (layered) clay deposits from Glacial Lake Hitchcock have been used to reconstruct the history of the lake's water level, which was controlled by changes in the advance and retreat of glaciers during the last ice age. The varves also contain evidence of changes in the climate and environment, including shifts in precipitation patterns, the frequency of drought, and the timing of the onset and end of the growing season. *Photo courtesy of Anthony Zemba, CHMM, of a location in Suffield, Connecticut, just west of the Connecticut River.*

Mill River in New Haven, Connecticut. In this southern stretch of the Mill River near New Haven Harbor, the river is tidal for several miles. Most of the rivers that end at Long Island Sound are tidal, but that doesn't mean they are always brackish. Most tidal rivers are salty only near their mouth.

WEATHER AND CLIMATE

Weather is what is currently happening in the local atmosphere over relatively short periods. You chat about the weather on social media or at the grocery store. Along the Connecticut River, weather can be very localized because of New England's hilly topography, sheltered river valleys, low mountain ranges, and proximity to the Atlantic Ocean. Hartford, Connecticut, may get three inches of snow, while just 35 miles to the south, Old Saybrook, Connecticut, receives rain.

Studies of the climate reflect average conditions over years and often look at broader geographic regions that are covered by routine weather reports. Climate studies are also concerned with severe or unusual weather and with determining long-term trends in the number or severity of storms, heat or cold waves, precipitation patterns, and river or coastal flooding.

For the most part, central New England is graced with a temperate, well-watered climate, where typically two days in three are sunny or at least partly so. It tends to be cloudier in the northern reaches of Vermont and New Hampshire, where the Connecticut River lies between the Green Mountains to the west and the higher White Mountains to the east. Mountain ranges and deep valleys complicate northern New England weather by creating rain or snow shadows. For example, the higher elevations of the Green and

Dam, First Connecticut Lake, in Pittsburg, New Hampshire. The young Connecticut River is heavily controlled, even just a dozen miles south of its source in the Fourth Lake. The Fourth and Third Connecticut Lakes are natural, although both are partially dammed by North American Beavers. The Second and First Connecticut Lakes are man-made reservoirs created by dams. The First and Second Lakes are not only a major recreational and tourist resource but help regulate the flow of river water during spring melts and heavy rainfalls.

Average temperature and precipitation profiles for central New England

White River Junction, NH – Average temperature and percent chance of precipitation

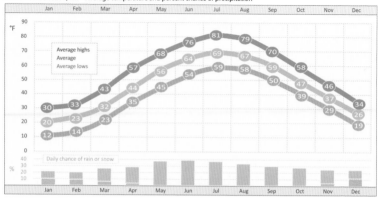

Springfield, MA – Average temperature and percent chance of precipitation

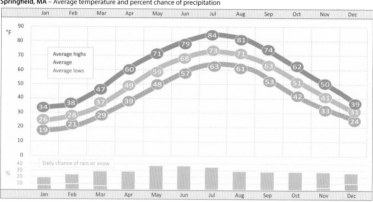

Old Saybrook, CT – Average temperature and percent chance of precipitation

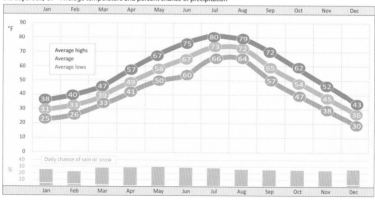

White Mountains receive about two to three times the total precipitation (rain or snow) than the Connecticut River Valley between the mountain ranges. In most years, precipitation in New England is reliable enough to sustain a richly forested landscape and permanent river and stream systems.

However, despite its ordinarily lush, green landscape, New England is increasingly suffering seasonal droughts, particularly in late summer and early fall. Most climate scientists credit the warming environment for these more frequent and severe dry spells, but New England has always had some droughts. In 1964–65, a regional drought was severe enough to cause widespread crop damage and federal emergency aid to farmers (see p. 96).

During drought conditions, trees may experience stress and produce fewer or less vibrant leaves. This can result in a less colorful and spectacular fall foliage display. However, drought is not the only factor that affects fall foliage; other factors such as temperature and light levels also play a role.

New England's Central Valley along the Connecticut River is generally sunnier, warmer, and less windy than the surrounding highlands and mountains, particularly in the river's northern reaches. However, air masses can stagnate in the valley from lack of wind, and the still air can magnify the surrounding temperatures. Both the Vermont state record high (105 degrees Fahrenheit) and the New England region's record low (−50 degrees Fahrenheit) were recorded in Connecticut River towns.

The diversity of climate and weather in New England is reflected in the US Department of Agriculture plant hardiness zone maps, which list five hardiness zones for New England, more than are found in any other equivalent-sized area of the United States.

New England is in the latitude zone of prevailing westerly winds,* and the air masses moving over the North American continent thus have the most significant influence on the region's day-to-day weather. This normal west-to-east movement of weather systems often follows predictable patterns of storm tracks (see p. 87). The Connecticut River empties into Long Island Sound, and although the Sound is not the ocean, the Atlantic Ocean does moderate temperatures in the tidal estuarine portion of the river south of Middletown, Connecticut.

*Winds are named for the direction they come from. Westerly winds come from the west.

The view west from New Hampshire's Weeks State Park, in the foothills of the White Mountains. The Connecticut River Valley is just below, with Vermont's Green Mountain range on the far horizon. The Connecticut River Valley and New England's Central Valley in Massachusetts and Connecticut generally have fair, sunny weather. But in the more mountainous northern range of the Connecticut River, skies are often cloudy, as the mountains drive the prevailing westerly winds upward, causing moisture in the air to condense into clouds. The White Mountains are notorious for highly variable weather. On Mount Washington, New Hampshire, your drive to the top may be foggy much of the way, and then suddenly the cloud layer parts and you can see for miles in bright sun.

The old Yankee saying that "if you don't like the weather right now, just wait a few minutes" is very true but a bit misleading. In general, the weather in central and southern New England is mild and moist most of the year. Compared to other sections of the country, this region has relatively few violent storms.
Middle Cove, Essex, Connecticut.

New England weather is also influenced by narrow bands of fast-moving upper atmospheric westerly winds, commonly called jet streams (see opposite). The polar jet stream, also called the polar vortex, above the northern hemisphere typically sits at the boundary between cold Arctic air and warmer air over North America. Because the temperature difference between warm and cold is most pronounced in winter, the polar jet stream's effect on North American weather is most apparent in winter. The polar jet stream acts as a partial barrier preventing icy Arctic air masses from descending into the United States. Occasionally, however, the polar jet stream waves or meanders, dipping well below its usual 50–60°N latitudes and bringing icy air masses across New England. The bitter cold wave of January and February 2015 made the "polar vortex" famous on cable news, but almost every year, the jet stream brings some cold spells as it dips southward into the United States, including New England. These variations in the position of the polar jet stream have become more frequent in the past two decades. Climate scientists speculate that the overall warming of the earth may be weakening the polar jet stream, causing it to wobble or meander more frequently in winter. These periodic blasts of Arctic cold remind us that climate change is complex and that the general warming of the atmosphere does not guarantee milder temperatures all year.

General weather patterns in New England

New England is blessed with four distinctive seasons, created primarily by variations in the amount of sunlight the region receives during the year. The earth's rotational axis is tilted 23.5 degrees to its orbital plane around the sun, so different latitudes receive varying amounts of sunlight over a year, depending on whether the tilt is toward (summer) or away (winter) from the sun. The sunlight hitting New England on the summer solstice (June 20–21) is six times greater than on the winter solstice (December 20–21). The spring and fall equinoxes each receive about half the sunlight that falls during the summer solstice.

Day-to-day and annual changes

The primary determinant of weather conditions is the insolation, or incoming solar radiation, present at any given day and time. The amount of sunlight is influenced by other weather conditions, such as cloud cover, precipitation, and winds, which can decrease or amplify the effects of solar heating. The amount of insolation is also influenced by ground cover. Forests,

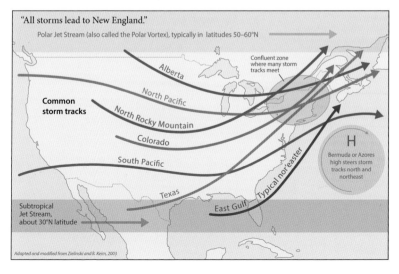

"All storms lead to New England."

Polar Jet Stream (also called the Polar Vortex), typically in latitudes 50–60°N

Confluent zone where many storm tracks meet

Alberta

North Pacific

Common storm tracks

North Rocky Mountain

Colorado

South Pacific

H

Bermuda or Azores high steers storm tracks north and northeast

Typical nor'easter

Texas

East Gulf

Subtropical Jet Stream, about 30°N latitude

Adapted and modified from Zielinski and B. Keim, 2003

vegetation, and farm fields absorb most of the solar radiation they receive and thus warm quickly once the sun has risen. Snow-covered ground is inherently cold from the snow and reflects up to 95 percent of the sunlight that hits the snow. Thus, once a blanket of snow covers the ground, the immediate area tends to stay cold for extended periods, even during milder weather.

In New England, the weather comes mainly from the west, flowing with generally westerly winds over the interior of North America. Thus, New England's weather is primarily continental, but there are important exceptions to this general pattern. Occasionally, in late summer and early fall, New England is hit by large low-pressure hurricanes and tropical storms that originate far to the south and generally follow the Atlantic Coast northward to strike coastal New England. Nor'easters are another form of a large low-pressure storm that can strike New England from the south and east at any time of year, although nor'easters are more common in the colder months (see pp. 91, 103).

High- and low-pressure weather systems

The final major components of New England weather are high- or low-pressure systems that generally arrive in New England from the west. These systems move along predictable tracks enough to have been recognized and named by meteorologists (see weather patterns, pp. 90–91, and storm tracks, p. 93). In general, high-pressure systems arriving from the north or west bring dry, cooler continental air for most of the year. In

A panoramic view of New Hampshire's White Mountains in winter. The tallest peak, Mount Washington (6,288 feet), is the peak on this page showing the observation towers of the Mount Washington Observatory.

Natalie Rotman Cote

winter, high-pressure systems from the north and west can bring clear skies and icy dry air into New England. In the fall, these cool high-pressure systems can be particularly important to the migration of birds, butterflies, and dragonflies, as the generally northwesterly winds sweep the fliers down along the Atlantic Coast flyway as they migrate southward. High-pressure systems that back into New England from the northeast can bring trouble, with rain or snow and icy air from the Arctic. The uniting of a northeastern high-pressure system and a winter nor'easter can bring the biggest snowfalls in the region. The notorious blizzards of 1888 and 1978 and Winter Storms Nemo (2013) and Juno (2015) were all wicked combinations of nor'easters that joined with high-pressure systems from the northeast.

Low-pressure systems arriving in New England from the west and southwest generally bring warmer but dreary weather and rain during the year's colder months and the hazy, hot, and humid days of summer. However, in spring, low-pressure systems arriving in New England from the south and southeast behind a cold front are helpful for birds migrating northward. The weather may be overcast and drizzly, but these lows from the southwest often bring a bonanza of songbirds into the forests, especially along the coast and the Central Valley (see p. 90).

Thick fogs are common in the deeper New England valleys, especially in late spring and early fall, when the days are warm but nights are much cooler.

NASA

A satellite view of Winter Storm Nemo (2013), a nor'easter blizzard that combined two low-pressure systems. A classic nor'easter storm developed over the southeastern Atlantic Coast and moved northward along the coast. Off Cape Cod the moisture-laden nor'easter collided with a very cold low-pressure system from the Midwest. As Winter Storm Nemo, the combined storms dumped 20–30 inches of snow from northern New Jersey and all of New England north to Nova Scotia.

Common regional weather patterns that affect weather and migration

High-pressure system to the northwest of New England

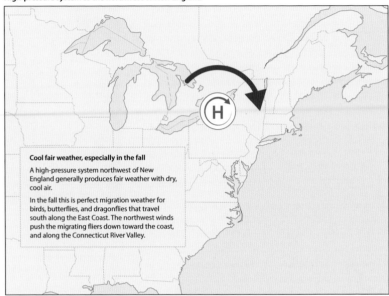

Cool fair weather, especially in the fall

A high-pressure system northwest of New England generally produces fair weather with dry, cool air.

In the fall this is perfect migration weather for birds, butterflies, and dragonflies that travel south along the East Coast. The northwest winds push the migrating fliers down toward the coast, and along the Connecticut River Valley.

High-pressure system to the southwest of New England

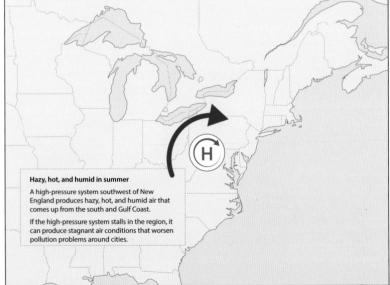

Hazy, hot, and humid in summer

A high-pressure system southwest of New England produces hazy, hot, and humid air that comes up from the south and Gulf Coast.

If the high-pressure system stalls in the region, it can produce stagnant air conditions that worsen pollution problems around cities.

Adapted and modified from Zielinski and B. Keim, 2003. New England Weather, New England Climate

Low-pressure system to the west or southwest of New England

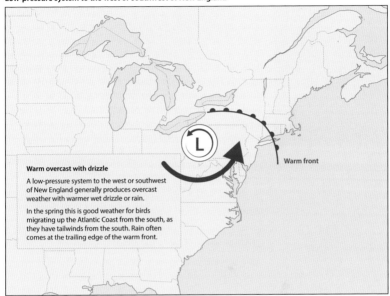

Warm overcast with drizzle

A low-pressure system to the west or southwest of New England generally produces overcast weather with warmer wet drizzle or rain.

In the spring this is good weather for birds migrating up the Atlantic Coast from the south, as they have tailwinds from the south. Rain often comes at the trailing edge of the warm front.

Warm front

Low-pressure system offshore — The classic nor'easter

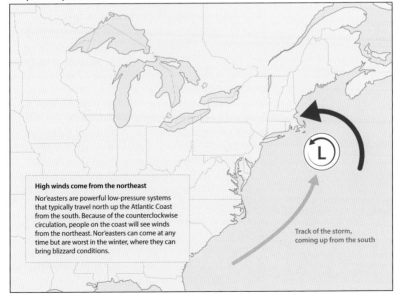

High winds come from the northeast

Nor'easters are powerful low-pressure systems that typically travel north up the Atlantic Coast from the south. Because of the counterclockwise circulation, people on the coast will see winds from the northeast. Nor'easters can come at any time but are worst in the winter, where they can bring blizzard conditions.

Track of the storm, coming up from the south

Black ice on a New Hampshire road. The moisture from mountain fogs can condense on cold road surfaces and quickly produce slippery, hazardous driving conditions.

Mountain valley fogs form when the rapid cooling of the highlands causes moist air to cool and flow down into valleys overnight. As the cold air sinks, it reaches the local dew point, and the water vapor in the air condenses as fog. Mountain valley fogs usually burn off as the sun warms the valley but may persist for days if the air is stagnant. In the colder times of the year, freezing fog is a danger, where moist air condenses at the freezing point, but tiny droplets of water vapor stay liquid until they hit a cold surface, such as a road, and form ice crystals that coat surfaces. Freezing fog can quickly form slippery black ice conditions on roadways and bridges, endangering drivers. In summer, evaporation or mixing fogs can form when cooler night air flows over warm ground such as farm fields and riverine wetlands. Steam fog also forms when the water temperature of ponds and rivers is higher than the cool overnight air. Evaporation fogs typically dissipate quickly after sunrise as the sun warms the air.

Year-to-year changes

New England also sees variations in weather from year to year. These days the most noticeable changes are in average temperature, which has been increasing steadily, particularly over the past two decades. If you are younger than age 44, you've never known a year that was colder than average. The 10 warmest years on record have all occurred since 2005. Unfortunately, the northeastern United States is one of the world's fastest-warming regions, warming 3.29 degrees Fahrenheit of average annual temperature over the past 120 years. Massachusetts is warming even faster, at 3.55 degrees Fahrenheit over the same period. By comparison, the average global warming is about 2 degrees Fahrenheit. This relatively rapid warming of New England will challenge the timber, maple sugar, and ski industries. In every decade since 1965, New England has lost nine snow-cover days due to less snowfall, more rain, and faster snowmelt. Connecticut's average temperature has risen 3.6 degrees Fahrenheit, double the average for the Lower 48 States. It is not yet clear why the northeastern United States is warming so quickly, but it may be due at least in part to the rapidly warming Atlantic Ocean off New England.

The best and most authoritative popular reference to New England's weather is *New England Weather, New England Climate*, by Gregory Zielinsky and Barry Keim (Hanover, NH: University Press of New England, 2003).

El Niño and La Niña weather patterns

In recent decades two worldwide weather phenomena are now understood to influence many weather factors across North America. El Niño, and its opposite, La Niña, are two poles in a massive weather pattern of ocean temperatures in the southern Pacific Ocean. The El Niño and La Niña patterns do not occur every year. Still, when they occur, the effects can be profound, particularly for winter weather in the United States. An El Niño event occurs when warm ocean waters off the northeastern Australian coast migrate eastward toward South America's west coast, where waters are relatively cool in an average year. As the warm pool of El Niño waters moves into the eastern Pacific, the trade winds off South America weaken (below, top). The unusually warm waters off the western South American coast trigger storms across Central America and the southern United States. The net effect of an El Niño pattern is a general warming of temperatures across the northern portions of North America. For example, some of the warmest Connecticut winter temperatures

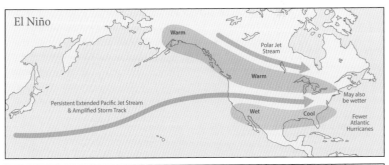

Adapted and modified from Zielinski and B. Keim, 2003. New England Weather, New England Climate.

on record occurred in the El Niño years of 1997–98, where temperatures averaged 5.7 degrees Fahrenheit warmer than average. In the same year, New Hampshire was 5.9 degrees Fahrenheit warmer than average. In more typical El Niño years, winter temperatures across New England averaged 1.4–1.8 degrees Fahrenheit warmer than average.

In the opposing La Niña weather pattern, the pool of warm tropical water stays in the western Pacific Ocean near Australia. La Niña's effect on US weather is less pronounced, but generally in La Niña years, most of North America will be cooler than average. Ironically, New England may also experience warmer and slightly wetter winters in La Niña years, along with cooler than average summers.

The United States generally sees a weak El Niño pattern about every three years and a strong El Niño effect once in about six to 10 years. La Niña patterns occur about once every three to five years.

Climate change in New England

Although it is difficult to blame the severity of any one storm on climate change, we now have deep and broad proof that climate change is driving up the number and severity of many kinds of weather events. Storms are becoming far wetter than in the past, with direct implications for riverine and freshwater environments in New England. Heavy downpours are increasing in size and frequency, with some of the most significant

Global temperature anomaly (compared to the 1951–1980 average)
Last nine years have been the warmest on record

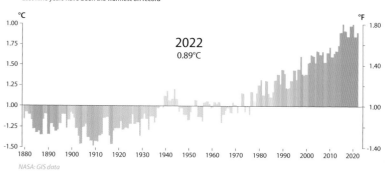

2022
0.89°C

NASA: GIS data

increases being recorded in the northeastern United States. A recent NASA-JPL study showed that for every 1.8 degrees Fahrenheit of warming, sea surface temperatures also increased, and the incidence of tropical storms (the origins of North America's hurricanes and most of its nor'easters) rose by about 21 percent. Based on current NASA projections, extreme storms may increase by about 60 percent by 2100. Nationwide since 1948, extreme precipitation events have increased by 24 percent.

The northeastern United States has warmed twice as much as the rest of the Lower 48. Climate modelers predict that this region could see 4–6 degrees Fahrenheit increases by 2100. This would give Hanover, New Hampshire, roughly the same climate that is experienced today in Richmond, Virginia, with all the ecological, economic, and societal disruption such warming would cause.

martin33

Human-made carbon dioxide emissions have grown to critical levels in recent decades. Although carbon dioxide levels have been rising since the widespread use of coal in the nineteenth century, fully half of the carbon in today's atmosphere was emitted in the past 30 years.

Climate change drives rising temperatures and shifting rainfall patterns in the Connecticut River region. Average annual precipitation in the Northeast has increased by 10 percent from 1895 to 2011, and precipitation from heavy storms has increased 70 percent since 1958. Projected climate changes for rivers include increased precipitation intensity, groundwater runoff, flooding, droughts, and drought-associated floodplain fires, as well as unpredictable changes in the seasonality of river flows. More frequent and powerful storms increase the likelihood of pollution from excess soil runoff, fertilizer runoff, and trash and human and animal wastes washed into rivers and reservoirs. General water pollution from runoff in urban areas can necessitate more water treatment or render river sources unusable for periods.

Droughts and climate change

Increasingly severe precipitation is not the only effect of climate change. Seasonal droughts are becoming common in central New England, particularly in the past decade (see p. 96). The droughts of 2002, 2017–18, and 2022 rivaled New England's most severe historical droughts and seem to be the harbingers of a new normal in which late summers bring sharply reduced

Drought in Massachusetts, 2000–2023

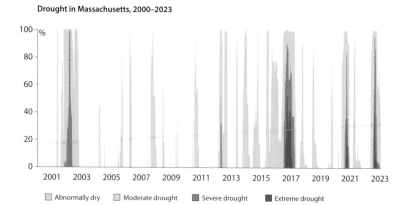

Abnormally dry | Moderate drought | Severe drought | Extreme drought

U.S. Drought Monitor

Occasional severe droughts occurred in New England's past, even before recent changes in the climate. The New England drought of 1965 was a severe dry spell that affected the northeastern United States, particularly Massachusetts, Connecticut, and Rhode Island, during the summer. The drought was caused by a combination of factors, including a lack of precipitation, high temperatures, and low humidity.

The drought of 1965 had a severe impact on agriculture: farmers were unable to grow crops, and many were forced to sell their livestock. The lack of rainfall led to an increase in wildfires, which burned thousands of acres of forest. The drought also led to a sharp decrease in the water levels of rivers and lakes, which had a devastating impact on fish populations.

stream flows and lower groundwater tables throughout the Connecticut River region. Water scientists now use the term "flash droughts" to describe these quick-onset summer and fall dry periods. Although dry conditions generally improve as the year ends, winter precipitation and snowmelt are becoming increasingly critical to groundwater and stream supplies. Summer and early fall drought conditions now often extend late into the year and early winter. Seasonal droughts damage crops and pasturelands and create domestic water supply problems when home wells run dry. In 2020, the US Department of Agriculture rated 90 percent of Connecticut and Massachusetts pasturelands as poor to very poor because of drought conditions.

Implications for human health

Warming increases transpiration and evaporation in freshwater environments managed for drinking water, with potential declines in river flow volume, reservoir levels, and water quality. One-third of Americans depend on rain-fed or seasonal freshwater streams and rivers for their drinking water.

Sewage overflows are more frequent after severe downpours. Warming can also affect changes in snowmelt volume and timing, complicating flood management and hydropower generation. Warming can cause or exacerbate harmful algae blooms in freshwater.

boophuket

Warmer average temperatures have a direct effect on human health as well. The Blacklegged Ticks that carry Lyme disease are active at temperatures above 45 degrees Fahrenheit, so warmer winters and early springs will lengthen the season when people are vulnerable to Lyme disease and other tick-borne and mosquito-borne diseases. Rising temperatures also have implications for respiratory diseases. Longer pollen seasons and increased ground-level smog and ozone in the warmer air can exacerbate acute and chronic respiratory conditions such as asthma. Recently, entomologists have seen an increase in the range and population of the Asian Tiger Mosquito, the most common carrier of West Nile virus.

Climate resiliency and natural environments

Healthy rivers and freshwater ecosystems can help build resilience against the increasing frequency of severe weather. Still, if we depend on natural environments, we need better protections to ensure that rivers and river water supplies are dependable. Riverine ecosystems and freshwater floodplain habitats trap floodwaters, retain moisture during drought periods, recharge groundwater supplies, filter pollutants, provide safe river and lake recreational facilities, and create habitats for fish and other wildlife.

Unfortunately, climate change is not the only factor that increases the damage that severe storms create in

Combined sewage overflow (CSO) systems
Although most municipalities along the Connecticut River have long since moved away from routinely dumping untreated sewage directly into rivers and streams, the problem of sewage outflows into the Connecticut River remains. Most cities use a combined sewage and stormwater drainage system (CSO). Raw sewage is normally treated before being released into rivers. However, when there is a heavy rainfall, stormwater often overwhelms the CSO, and a combination of raw sewage and stormwater enters the river. This is why you often see advisories against swimming in rivers after a heavy rainfall.

the Connecticut River area. The absorbent capacity of farmland and natural floodplain ecosystems were once robust buffers against flood damage. Modern drainage schemes often result in stormwater shunting into rivers and streams almost instantly. Where the land drains quickly, dangerous floods are practically inevitable. Poor zoning in flood-prone areas makes houses and commercial construction vulnerable to flood damage. Natural floodplains that once protected river communities from flash flooding are often buried under new neighborhoods, commercial zones, and shopping areas. Climate change is a significant challenge of our time. Still, old stream dams, poorly designed drainage, impermeable surfaces, and the removal of natural vegetation are often the most direct cause of storm damage along our rivers and streams.

We can design "green infrastructure" to work with and supplement natural riverine communities. Rain gardens, temporary stormwater storage, and restored floodplain vegetation can help replicate natural drainage and groundwater recharge in urban areas. These techniques prevent excess drainage from impervious surfaces such as streets, parking lots, and roofs and cut pollution from urban runoff. By removing old dams and restoring floodplains to give flooded rivers space to spread out, we can buffer the effects of more severe storms and floods.

Natural vegetation can be used to capture stormwater runoff. One way this is done is through the creation of rain gardens, which are landscaped areas planted with native vegetation that is well suited to absorb and filter water. In this case the rainwater runoff is mostly diverted into groundwater drainage and not into local storm sewers. Green roofs, which are covered in vegetation, can also slow down and absorb stormwater runoff. Preserving or restoring natural wetlands, riparian zones, and floodplain forests can also help to capture and filter stormwater runoff. In all these cases, natural vegetation acts as a sponge, slowing down and filtering the water before it reaches streams and rivers.

Pavel Iarunichev

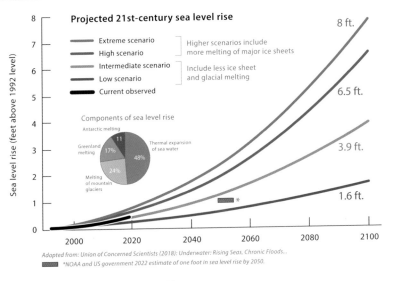

Projected 21st-century sea level rise

Adapted from: Union of Concerned Scientists (2018): Underwater: Rising Seas, Chronic Floods...
*NOAA and US government 2022 estimate of one foot in sea level rise by 2050.

Sea level rise in the Connecticut River estuary

Along the northern and inland stretches of the Connecticut River, sea level rise might seem to be a remote problem. Still, most of the river south of Massachusetts is already tidal, and the tidal portions of the river will move farther upstream in the coming decades. The Connecticut River south of Middletown, Connecticut, is an estuary (detailed later in the chapter "The Connecticut River Estuary") and is directly tied to the tides and sea level of Long Island Sound and the Atlantic Ocean. The river north of Middletown is currently tidal up to Windsor Locks, Connecticut, which has a two-foot tide. Tidal rivers are not salty for most of their length. Saltwater intrusion into the Connecticut River is rare north of Haddam, Connecticut (p. 349). However, the daily rhythms of tides are directly connected to the flow rate and river water level for the 50 miles between the river mouth at Old Saybrook and the shallows of Enfield Falls at Windsor Locks.

Climatologists estimate that we will see at least a foot of sea level rise by 2050—and perhaps far more than that if the earth continues to warm at the current pace. The rising sea level will be directly reflected in rising river levels throughout the current tidal region. Rising sea level is already affecting the estuarine portion of the Connecticut River, with significant erosion along the brackish marshlands near the mouth of the river and saltwater intrusion into formerly freshwater riparian areas. Suppose Connecticut's experience proves to be similar to sea level rise along the rest of the Atlantic Coast. In that case, we will see freshwater environments converted to salt marshes, "ghost forests" of trees killed by saltwater intrusion, increased salt in groundwater and well systems, and increased flooding of human infrastructure near the river.

Managing impervious surfaces and stormwater drainage

Stormwater is rainwater or sudden snowmelt that runs over the ground, usually resulting from falling on impervious urban and suburban surfaces such as streets, parking lots, building roofs, and other nonabsorbent surfaces. Runoff water in these settings picks up many pollutants: oils, other chemicals, diesel grit, and animal waste. Such runoff is rare in natural environments because there most water soaks into the ground, and the ground helps filter any contaminants. In most developed areas, water is quickly channeled into storm drains and sewers and then directly into rivers and streams. This runoff boosts the chance of flooding in severe storms, increases river pollution, and does

Rain gardens are landscape features designed to capture and filter runoff from rain or snowmelt and return it to groundwater instead of funneling it into sewer systems. Rain gardens are typically shallow basins with well-draining soils and vegetation that can tolerate both wet and dry conditions.

auntspray

nothing to recharge groundwater supplies, especially in drought conditions. Most cities and towns along the Connecticut River still have integrated stormwater and sewage systems. In severe runoff situations, the volume of stormwater overwhelms the sewage system, and raw sewage flows into rivers. In addition to containing many pollutant chemicals, sewage-contaminated stormwater disease may contain microorganisms that can cause Covid-19, flu, diarrhea, dysentery, hepatitis, methicillin-resistant *Staphylococcus aureus* (MRSA), and other diseases.

Green infrastructure uses rain gardens to capture and channel stormwater into areas with natural soil and vegetation. Plants blunt the force of the stormwater flow, and water is absorbed into the ground instead of being shunted into street drainage. Natural floodplains are also preserved and used as storage buffers to contain and then slowly release floodwater. Better building techniques can minimize stormwater flows, including using permeable paving blocks instead of asphalt and rain barrels or other temporary storage solutions to contain excess stormwater for short periods. These techniques for urban and suburban areas are less effective than simply preserving natural environments. Still, they help slow stormwater runoff and channel as much water as possible into groundwater absorption and away from storm drains.

Extreme weather

For those living near a river, the potential for flooding can be the most anxiety-provoking of all weather events. Even if the river stays within its normal banks, a river in flood can be terrifying to watch. The roaring water flows with such speed and ferocity that the ground trembles even well away from the banks. Moving water is unbelievably strong—even just eight to 10 inches of swiftly flowing water can sweep large adults off their feet.

The Connecticut River is no stranger to high-water disasters. Severe flooding in the Connecticut River Valley in 1913, 1927, and 1936 and the Great Hurricane of 1938 brought devastation and death all along the Connecticut River. The floods of 1936 were

At street level the massive impervious surfaces of building roofs and parking lots may not seem to be an issue for stormwater, but drainage from these structures forms a big percentage of urban stormwater runoff into streams and rivers.

Green infrastructure such as roof gardens can help capture and divert routine levels of rainfall into evaporation from vegetation, reducing the water volume that goes straight into sewers. By acting as insulation, green roofs can also save energy for the building. All the greenery from (ideally) native plantings also provides pollinators and other wildlife with new habitat in urban areas.

A flood level sign at 120 Hockanum Road, in Hadley, Massachusetts, records flood levels from the nearby Connecticut River. The notorious river floods of 1936 and 1938 were particularly devastating. The ground level below this sign is at least 10 feet above the normal river level.

particularly severe. A large snowpack combined with an unusual series of mid-March rainstorms sent eight to 25 inches of water into rivers already full of ice and snowmelt. The Connecticut River flooded from northern New England to Long Island Sound. Just two years later, the Great Hurricane of 1938 brought record flood levels to the Connecticut River, along with devastating winds. More than 700 people died in the winds and flooding of this hurricane, and in some forests, you can still see the damage wrought by the storm in ancient fallen trees now almost rotted away. More than half the White Pines in central New England are believed to have been destroyed in a single day, as were three-quarters of Sugar Maples and most fruit orchards.

The New England states, federal government, and US Army Corps of Engineers responded to the epic floods of the 1930s by building seven flood control dams on the main Connecticut River tributaries. There are now 65 major dams along the length of the Connecticut River watershed. Large hydropower dams on the river's main stem help control the river's overall flow rate, but even the modern dam and flood control infrastructure does not guarantee an end to flooding in major storms. In 2005, more than 50 homes were destroyed along the Cold River tributary near Bellows Falls, Vermont. In August 2011, Tropical Storm Irene brought torrential rain into a Connecticut River region that was already saturated from a series of major rainstorms over the spring and summer of 2011. Irene created the worst flooding seen in New England since 1936. Vermont and western New Hampshire were hardest hit by the storm. As Irene passed over the northern stretches of the Connecticut River, it unleashed four to six inches of rain in just a few hours and as much as eight inches of rain in the White Mountains. Several Vermont towns received over 10 inches of rainfall in under 24 hours. Normally placid streams became raging torrents as the water came out of the mountains and entered the major tributaries of the Connecticut River, creating catastrophic flash flood damage throughout the Connecticut River Valley in Vermont and New Hampshire. In Massachusetts, the Westfield River rose 20 feet in just a few hours, and the Deerfield River rose over 15 feet simultaneously. The storm wrecked the year's harvest season over much of New England, and erosion stripped massive amounts of sediment from farm fields and developed areas without natural ground cover (see below). Measurements after the storm showed that the Connecticut River at Thompsonville, Connecticut, was running at 64 times the usual flow rate.

Nor'easters

Nor'easters are storms that typically originate in the Gulf of Mexico as warm, moist, low-pressure systems that are steered northeast across the south-central United States by the prevailing jet stream winds. Eventually, the storms track north-northeast, paralleling the Atlantic Coast. The region's predominant west wind patterns also create a weak but large low-pressure area east of the Appalachian Mountains. Meteorologists call the low a lee trough, as it sits in the lee behind the mountains. This lee trough of low pressure sitting over the Atlantic Coastal Plain can help draw the Gulf-area storms north along the Atlantic Coast. Nor'easters are particularly likely when a large high-pressure system sits over the Bahamas area, as this forces the storms off their usual eastward track and toward the northeast.

With climate change, storms are getting much wetter. Nearly a week after 2011's Tropical Storm Irene hit New England the Connecticut River was spewing millions of tons of muddy sediment into Long Island Sound. Irene's unusually heavy rainfall devastated farmlands within the Connecticut River's watershed, and stripped many farms of all their topsoil. Estimates of the Connecticut River flow at Thompsonville, Connecticut, reached 128,000 cubic feet per second (cfs), or 64 times the normal flow of about 2,000 cfs. The turbidity (muddiness) of the river water, measured at Essex, Connecticut, was 50 times higher than before the storm.

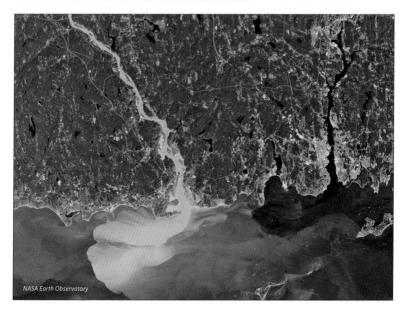

NASA Earth Observatory

Although a nor'easter can appear at any time of year, these storms are more common in the cold months between October and March. They can bring devastating winds, large coastal storm surges, and blizzard conditions to New England and the Canadian Maritime Provinces.

As a low-pressure system, a nor'easter circulates in a counterclockwise motion and can be pictured as a circular clock face for points of reference (see below). As the storm tracks along the coast, the counterclockwise winds from about 5 o'clock to 10 o'clock blow freely across the ocean and pick up speed and moisture. Observers along the coast will experience high winds coming onto shore from the northeast direction—hence the name "nor'easter." In a powerful nor'easter, the winds coming off the ocean can pile up large waves and hurricane-like storm surges of up to 20 feet on ocean shores, flooding coastal communities and causing shoreline erosion. Winter nor'easters also bring snow.

The largest recorded blizzards along the East Coast were nor'easters, such as the famous blizzards of 1978 and 1996, which dumped two to three feet of snow along large sections of New England in just a few hours. Winter Storm Nemo in February 2013 was a

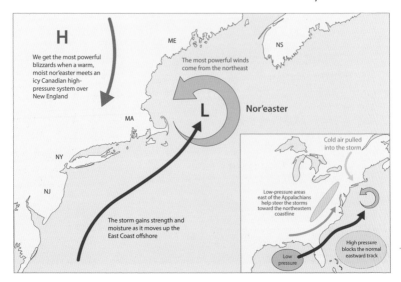

H

We get the most powerful blizzards when a warm, moist nor'easter meets an icy Canadian high-pressure system over New England

ME

NS

The most powerful winds come from the northeast

L   **Nor'easter**

MA

NY

NJ

The storm gains strength and moisture as it moves up the East Coast offshore

Cold air pulled into the storm

Low-pressure areas east of the Appalachians help steer the storms toward the northeastern coastline

Low pressure

High pressure blocks the normal eastward track

classic blizzard-generating nor'easter. A massive, moist, low-pressure system traveled north along the Eastern Seaboard and met another low-pressure system coming east out of the central United States. This collision triggered a blizzard that dumped record snowfall amounts over New England. Several back-to-back winter nor'easters created record snows across central New England in early 2015, where Winter Storms Juno and Linus helped break snowfall records. Boston recorded its highest snowfall record in 2015, with 109 inches. Severe nor'easters don't just bring snow. The winds and waves from nor'easters accelerate erosion along the coast and can make long-lasting changes, particularly in barrier islands, sandspits, and coastal cliffs.

f11photo

Hurricanes

Hurricanes are tropical cyclones typically born as low-pressure systems off the west coast of Africa that track westward across the Atlantic. The low-pressure systems gain heat energy and moisture from the tropical midocean and arrive on the American side of the Atlantic with storm-force winds and heavy seas. As they approach the Atlantic Coast, the north-tracking hurricanes gain additional energy from the hot Florida Current at the base of the Gulf Stream, and almost every year, these tropical storms hit parts of the East Coast. In New England, these summer and fall storms are the warm-weather counterparts to winter nor'easters and are a significant factor in creating flood conditions. Although direct hits from major hurricanes are unusual on the relatively cool coastlines of New England and Long Island, over the past 110 years, 69 tropical storms and hurricanes have tracked over southern New England (see illustration, p. 107). The Great Hurricane of 1938 was much more devastating to the Connecticut River area, but it is 2011's Tropical Storm Irene that most current river-area residents remember with a shudder. Irene's catastrophic rains and floods were a harbinger of more recent tropical storms and hurricanes along the East Coast.

In 2021, Hurricane Ida dumped over nine inches of rain on the New England states in just a few hours. Ida caused 96 deaths and at least $75 billion in damages from the Gulf Coast to the Northeast, making it the fifth-costliest storm on record. The United States had 18 billion-dollar weather disasters in 2022, including storms and droughts. Hurricane Ian alone caused $113 billion in damages all along the East Coast, particularly in Florida and the southeastern coastal states. Scientists have linked all these storms and droughts to the warming environment and climate change. Thanks to climate change, these storms often travel more slowly, and their major punch is from huge amounts of rain, not high winds.

Flooding on the Connecticut River at the historic Rocky Hill car ferry. Hurricane Ida (2021) delivered as much as nine inches of rain in the Connecticut River watershed in 24 hours. The ferry closed for a week, until the river subsided to normal levels. The nation's oldest continuously operating ferry service connects Rocky Hill on the western bank of the Connecticut River with Glastonbury on the eastern bank.

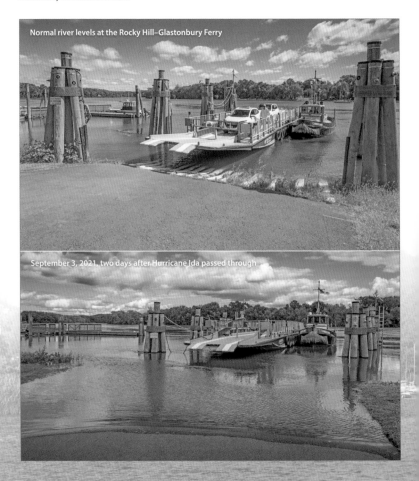

Normal river levels at the Rocky Hill–Glastonbury Ferry

September 3, 2021, two days after Hurricane Ida passed through

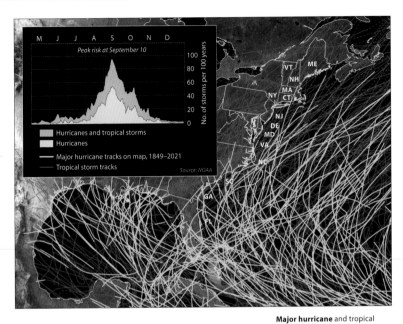

M J J A S O N D

Peak risk at September 10

No. of storms per 100 years

Hurricanes and tropical storms
Hurricanes
Major hurricane tracks on map, 1849–2021
Tropical storm tracks

Source: NOAA

Major hurricane and tropical tracks from 1849 to 2021. Off the Atlantic Coast, note the general pattern of a large arc, approaching the United States from the southeast and then typically making a sweeping turn toward the northeast around Cape Hatteras, North Carolina. New England has been hit many times, but hurricanes usually degrade into tropical storms before they hit the Connecticut River region.

Calves Island Channel, Old Lyme, Connecticut.

Environmental History

Craig Zerba

After 11,000 years of Indigenous Peoples history and more than 400 years of inhabitants from Europe and the rest of the globe, New England presents us with a uniquely humanized American landscape. The soft, domesticated contours of the familiar New England wilds don't easily fit into romantic notions of unspoiled wilderness. Steeped as it is in human and ecological history, with deeply layered cultural associations and great beauty, nature in New England is neither a determining force nor a passive victim. It sometimes seems that New England's landscape was designed to teach us that people are never outside the natural world and that looking for a pristine wilderness today is a fool's errand.

The goals are necessarily modest in this chapter. Whole shelves of books have been written about the environmental history of New England, and you'll find many of the best ones listed in "Further Reading." This guide focuses on the Connecticut River's natural world and its associated freshwater environments. But a contemporary field guide can't simply be a catalog of the *what* without reckoning with something of the *why:* Why are things the way they are, and how did we get here from our past?

Bear in mind that we look back at our history from the perspective of the twenty-first century, after at least

"**A succession of New England villages,** composed of neat houses, surrounding neat school-houses and churches, adorned with gardens, meadows and orchards, and exhibiting the universally easy circumstances of the inhabitants, is, at least in my own opinion, one of the most delightful prospects which this world can afford."

Rev. Timothy Dwight, 1796, describing New England, in *Travels in New England and New York,* vol. 1 (1821).

Opposite: A replica of Adriaen Block's tiny ship *Onrust* that sails daily in the warmer months from the Connecticut River Museum in Essex, Connecticut. Block and his crew made several voyages on the *Onrust,* including one in 1614 where they sailed up the Connecticut River and established a trading post on the site of present-day Hartford, Connecticut.

100 years or more of environmental consciousness. The founders and builders of colonial and American New England were proud of the enormous work it took to transform an indifferent natural world into the civility and prosperity of classic New England towns and rural landscapes. Our busy ancestors often saw the environmental compromises they made very clearly but thought of those hard choices as justified for the greater civic good.

Precontact inhabitants of the Central Valley

When the glaciers retreated from New England about 15,000 years ago and the climate warmed, Paleo-Indian hunter-gatherers likely moved into what was then a harsh, cold landscape in the mid-Atlantic region, similar to that of the Canadian Maritime provinces today. Radiocarbon-dated evidence of human activity in the area dates back to 10,200 years ago, and other evidence indicates that people were in the region before then. At that time, the sea level was 150–200 feet lower than it is today, and early people probably moved into coastal areas on what is now the continental shelf east and south of the current Atlantic Coast, but the Atlantic Ocean has long since submerged evidence of their settlements.

Indigenous Peoples in the Connecticut River region used fire extensively to remove undergrowth in favorite game-hunting areas and to clear land for planting crops. With patches of open grassland, the fire-cleared woodland edges were especially appealing to White-Tailed Deer, a significant game animal for Native Americans. However, because Indigenous populations were relatively small and scattered, the overall ecological impact of their settlements, agriculture, hunting, shellfish gathering, and fire use was environmentally benign compared to what came after Europeans arrived. Except near large villages and permanent settlements along the coast, and besides commonly using fire to clear forest undergrowth, Native American land use in the millennium before European contact made relatively few widespread or long-term changes in the natural environments of central New England.

NATIVE AMERICAN AND EARLY ENGLISH SETTLEMENTS IN THE CONNECTICUT RIVER REGION

Early English settlements were largely located on or near the sites of existing Indigenous Peoples towns and villages

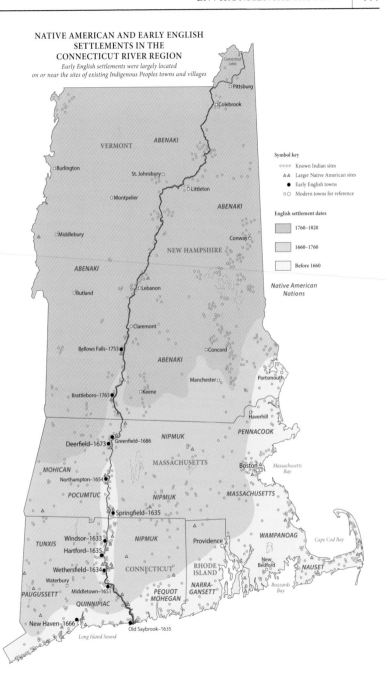

Symbol key

○○○○ Known Indian sites
△△ Larger Native American sites
● Early English towns
□○ Modern towns for reference

English settlement dates

▨ 1760–1820
▨ 1660–1760
□ Before 1660

Native American Nations

Connecticut Lakes
□ Pittsburg
□ Colebrook

ABENAKI

VERMONT
□Burlington
St. Johnsbury□
□Montpelier
□Littleton

ABENAKI

△ □Middlebury
Conway○
NEW HAMPSHIRE

ABENAKI
□Rutland □Lebanon

□Claremont

Bellows Falls–1753 ●
□Concord
ABENAKI
Manchester□
Portsmouth
Brattleboro–1763 ●
□Keene
Haverhill
PENNACOOK
Deerfield–1673 ●
Greenfield–1686
NIPMUK
△
MOHICAN
MASSACHUSETTS
Boston □
Massachusetts Bay
Northampton–1654 ●
POCUMTUC
New Bedford
NIPMUK
MASSACHUSETTS
Springfield–1635 ●
NIPMUK
WAMPANOAG
Cape Cod Bay
Windsor–1633 ●
NIPMUK
Providence
TUNXIS
Hartford–1635 ●
RHODE ISLAND
NAUSET
Wethersfield–1634 ●
CONNECTICUT
NARRA-GANSETT
Waterbury
Buzzards Bay
Middletown–1651 ●
PAUGUSSETT
QUINNIPIAC
PEQUOT MOHEGAN
● New Haven–1666
Old Saybrook–1635
Long Island Sound

Native American land use

Intensive Native American development along the Connecticut River began about 1,000 years ago, with villages and agriculture along the floodplains of the Connecticut River. Rivers were the main highways for movement and commerce. Large villages of 800–900 people were located in particularly good areas, such as the large and fertile river meadows in the Hartford, Connecticut, area and similar habitats along the Connecticut River in the Central Valley of Massachusetts. Many Indigenous villages and townsites along the Connecticut River were the foundation of early European forts and trading posts. Old Saybrook, Hartford, Springfield, Holyoke, and Northampton were all sites of Indigenous towns long before Europeans arrived (see p. 111).

At the time of first European contact, most Native Americans living in southern New England generally lived in small villages. Men hunted wildfowl, deer, and other game. Women and children tended small mixed farm fields of maize (American corn), beans, sunflowers, and squash, often supplemented with nuts, berries, and other gathered foods. The smaller Indigenous villages were often seasonal and located to take advantage of food resources. Warm-season villages were usually located near rivers and streams where migratory fish were abundant or near the coast to take advantage of large populations of oysters and other shellfish.

Population estimates for Native Americans near the mid-Atlantic Coast during European contact are rough and typically derived from early explorer accounts. The Indigenous Peoples population of New England in 1600 was about 70,000–100,000 people, with about 80 percent of that population in the southern New England area, where Indigenous Peoples practiced agriculture.

Native American agriculture

Paleo-Indians began farming in New England about 7,000–10,000 years ago, as the climate became more temperate. Native American swidden agriculture was a sophisticated mix of crops grown in fields created by burning small forest areas or in natural clearings.

Ashes from the burning provided natural fertilizers. Indigenous women planted a mix of corn, squash, sunflowers, and beans, where the corn and sunflower stalks made natural stakes for the bean and squash vines. As a legume, the bean vines provided a natural source of soil nitrogen. Squash vines covered the ground, suppressing weed species and helping to keep the ground moist. In this swidden style of agriculture, the Native Americans used a farm field for several years and then prepared a new field and left the old field fallow to recharge the nutrients in the soil.

It is a myth that the Indigenous Peoples commonly used fish to fertilize their fields. Indigenous women farmers did not catch and carry large quantities of heavy fish to their fields, and fish would stink and attract nuisance animals into the farm fields. English settlers near the coast adopted the practice of using bulk-caught fish such as shad and menhaden to boost the productivity of cornfields that were exhausted from too many crop cycles. Whole fish or ground fish meal provided a nutrient boost for a crop or two, but the fish quickly turned the soil oily and rancid, and the practice died out.

The Indigenous Peoples of New England did not keep domestic animals and rarely needed to fence their farm fields. Although early European settlers also adopted Native American swidden farming techniques (along with the native crop species), Europeans kept domestic animals. The cows, pigs, and sheep left to range freely created problems in areas with unfenced farm fields. European settlers quickly reverted to European farming and animal husbandry, with single-species fields of corn or wheat fenced off from marauding domestic pigs. Crop damage to unfenced Indigenous fields was an early and persistent source of tension between Native American villagers and their European neighbors.

Epidemics and disease

As Europeans began contact with the peoples of the Americas in the 1500s, they introduced diseases that immediately began to devastate Indigenous populations along the Atlantic Coast. Native Americans did not practice animal husbandry (a significant source of

*The long, complex history of the American Indian or Native American peoples of New England is beyond the scope of this guide. For more information, I recommend these books:

Changes in the Land: Indians, Colonists, and the Ecology of New England, by William Cronon, rev. ed. (New York: Hill and Wang, 2003). The best book on Indians, colonists, and their relationship to the natural world of New England.

Connecticut's Indigenous Peoples: What Archaeology and Oral Traditions Teach Us about Their Communities and Cultures, by Lucianne Lavin (New Haven: Yale University Press, 2013).

The Saltwater Frontier: Indians and the Contest for the American Coast, by Andrew Lipman (New Haven: Yale University Press, 2015).

Indian New England before the Mayflower, by Howard S. Russell (Hanover, NH: University Press of New England, 1980).

animal-to-human pathogens) and were long isolated from Eurasian diseases. Thus Native Americans had little genetic immunity to smallpox, measles, influenza, and other diseases common among the crews of early exploration and fishing vessels. Epidemics ran rampant through Indigenous populations, sometimes wiping out settlements within days, leaving empty villages full of corpses. The social infrastructure—food, medicine, clothing, commerce, religion, and social activities—quickly collapsed in such circumstances. Whole cultures, languages, and belief systems vanished within a few decades of first contact with Europeans.

In 1616–17, coastal New England Indigenous villages suffered an especially virulent smallpox outbreak, and bubonic or pneumonic plague killed an estimated 70–90 percent of coastal inhabitants. A similar epidemic decimated Indigenous villages in the Connecticut Valley in 1633. Weakened by disease and depopulation and quickly overwhelmed by thousands of settlers from Europe, the Indigenous Peoples of New England were marginalized and forced into separate communities. Most of those communities and reservations were later dismantled by legal maneuvers.

Early European settlements

New England's first European inhabitants settled along the coasts, where protected natural harbors, vast salt marshes, and open, fire-modified woodlands awaited them. After the first major settlements at Plymouth and later in Boston, the sheer volume of people arriving from England began to outstrip coastal resources. The colonists shifted their focus to the rich natural meadows and deep, stone-free soils of the Central Valley of New England.

Today's major cities and towns were founded mainly in the same locations as the major Native American villages on the coastline and along the Connecticut River (see p. 111). The first English settlements along the Connecticut River were tightly knit, almost communal towns. The initial goal of settlers was simple subsistence and collective defense. After King Philip's War in 1675–76 largely vanquished Native Americans as a regional military force, English settlements began to expand, and independent farmsteads became the norm in the Central Valley and its nearby uplands. Settlement of the northern Connecticut River Valley was slowed by a series of border disputes between New France and New England and their Native American allies. However, after 1700, English settlements quickly expanded northward from Massachusetts.

The first lands settled were flatlands beside the Connecticut River. The critical importance of riverine meadows on the ancient Lake Hitchcock lake bed is still preserved in modern riverside place-names: The Meadows (Northampton), Longmeadow, Windsor Meadows, North Meadows, South Meadows, Wangunk Meadows, and Haddam Meadows, to name a few. Even the common Massachusetts place-name "Hampton" is derived from Saxon words for "field or farm by the bend of a river," and Northampton's nickname is "The Meadow City."

The Central Valley between Rocky Hill, Connecticut, and Greenfield, Massachusetts, quickly became the primary agricultural center of New England. Settlers produced a variety of crops and domestic animals as insurance against weather and crop diseases. The economic unit was the family farm; initially, the goal was

These replicas of early Colonial rough-hewn, thatched-roof houses are probably good representations of the way early European settlements on the Connecticut River must have looked. Basic shelter and collective self-defense were the priorities. Classic "colonial-style" frame houses weren't common until well into the 1700s. Houses at Plimoth Patuxet Museums, Plymouth, Massachusetts.

Andreas J

The Pioneer Valley of Massachusetts, looking south from the top of Mount Sugarloaf, in South Deerfield, Massachusetts. This area was formed as a rift valley in the Triassic Period, 220 million years ago, as Pangaea pulled apart and the Atlantic Ocean began to form. Much later, during the Wisconsinan Glacial Episode, a giant freshwater lake formed as the ice sheet melted. Glacial Lake Hitchcock filled all the lowlands shown here, and over 2,500 years, the vast lake left a deep layer of rich lake-bed sediments across the valley.

Lake Hitchcock drained away 15,500 years ago, but its legacy profoundly influenced the history of New England. Early European settlers were drawn to the ideal farming conditions on the lake bed, and the Pioneer Valley was born in the late 1600s.

Broadleaf Plantain
Plantago major

Annual Ragweed
Ambrosia artemisiifolia

simply sustenance and survival. Cattle, swine, sheep, goats, and poultry provided insurance against crop failure and valuable material for barter. Isolated from the major New England towns along the coast, inland colonists generally exchanged food and goods through barter. Most trading boats with manufactured goods made only one or two voyages a year up the river from Long Island Sound.

Land use was primarily driven by European-style animal husbandry. Grazing animals required large amounts of open, grassy acreage, which was quickly becoming scarce by the late 1600s, forcing new populations of farmers deeper into the New England landscape in search of fresh pastureland. Ironically, most fields of native grasses were quickly destroyed by livestock, which trampled and compacted the ground and cropped off native plants that were poorly adapted to grazing animals.

As native plants died out, introduced European grasses and herbs replaced them, and thus began the explosion of alien weed species that continues to this day. The European weed species that came over with seeds and agricultural supplies from England were well adapted to compacted soil and close-cropping from grazing animals. Some native plants were preadapted to pastoral areas, such as Annual Ragweed. Populations of ragweed radically expanded in the 1600s, so much so that ecologists who study pollen in lake-bed mud cores to determine the mix of ancient plant species now use the sudden abundance of ragweed to date the first European settlements in an area. Native Americans were well aware of this sudden change in local plant species. They called the non-native Broadleaf and English Plantains "white man's foot" because plantains always followed the arrival of English settlers.

In 1700, about 80,000 English settlers lived in the Central Valley between New Haven, Connecticut, and Northfield, Massachusetts. By 1776, an observer wrote that the land between New Haven and Hartford was "a rich, well-cultivated Vale thickly settled and swarming with people.... It is though you were still traveling

along one continued town for seventy or eighty miles on end."

Conversion from barter to a cash economy

In the late 1700s, economic pressures built to convert traditional subsistence farms to raising commercial crops that could be sold for export to other parts of the region and country. Local merchants and grain millers were impatient with the local barter economy and increasingly demanded cash for finished goods and farm supplies. The older trade, barter, and goods exchange systems gave way to a cash-based economy where merchants paid cash for crops or gave short-term loans to commission specific crops. As river-based transportation systems improved, farmers in the Central and Pioneer Valleys began to shift toward crops that could be sold for cash and transported out of the region to the rapidly growing cities and familiar trade ports along the American coast. These changes effectively converted the Central Valley economy from subsistence farming and local exchange to cash-based resource extraction, especially of corn and timber.

Settlers initially planted familiar European crops such as wheat, but the cool, moist environment of the Connecticut Valley is marginal for wheat crops. Wheat

The Connecticut River
looking north toward Hartford, Connecticut, in the 1840s. In the seventeenth and eighteenth centuries, the Connecticut River was an important transportation route for goods and people. The river was used to transport goods such as lumber, food, and raw materials, and it also served as a highway for people traveling from Hartford to other parts of New England. The river was so important that Hartford was often referred to as "The Riverport."

Black Stem Rust on Wheat
Puccinia graminis

View from Mount Holyoke, Northampton, Massachusetts, after a Thunderstorm— The Oxbow, *by Thomas Cole.*

Cole painted the scene in 1836, and The Oxbow is considered one of the masterpieces of the Hudson River School. Cole depicted the Oxbow when it was still a part of the main stem of the Connecticut River. Four years after Cole finished his painting, the river broke through the narrow neck of the Oxbow, and the Oxbow became a lake tied to the river by a narrow channel, much as it is today. The painting depicts a sweeping vista of the Connecticut River Valley, with the rolling hills, forests, and clouds dramatically lit by the aftermath of a thunderstorm. Today you can recapture Cole's viewpoint by visiting the Summit House atop Skinner State Park, overlooking the Connecticut River in Hadley, Massachusetts.

Metropolitan Museum of Art

Larry Allen Peplin

quickly developed rust fungus (Black Stem Rust) and other diseases, and most farmers abandoned wheat as a major crop. In an increasingly cash-based economy, corn proved to be a versatile and easy-to-grow crop, with one great drawback—corn quickly exhausted soil nutrients, and after just a few years, corn yields from a field would drop sharply. Continued productivity required early fertilizers such as potash from burned wood, so corn crops encouraged more deforestation in the Central Valley and the surrounding uplands.

The stony soils of New England

It's a myth that early New England farmers faced impossibly stony soils. The "stony soils of New England" resulted from the deforestation of upland woodlands. Upland soils were not very rocky when Europeans first colonized New England, and early hill-country farmers had little trouble with stones in their fields. Most early farms were started in lowland areas around Hartford or the Pioneer Valley of western Massachusetts, where the ancient lake-bed and riparian soils were naturally stone-free. As farming expanded into higher ground, hillside forests were cleared, and farmers found deep, rich forest soils that were also relatively stone-free.

For 8,000–10,000 years before the arrival of Europeans, the virgin forests of New England produced a thick layer of forest soil and leaf mold, completely undisturbed by human activity except for river and coastal areas close to permanent Indigenous Peoples settlements. The Laurentide Ice Sheet destroyed the native New England populations of earthworms. Still, as the post–Ice Age climate warmed, these forest soils were worked and enriched by growing populations of ants, grubs, millipedes, mice, and other digging animals. The roots of trees were also important for converting the raw glacial till under the forest into rich soils. As plant roots grow, they move soil, leaving spaces within the soil when they die. As animals and roots worked the forest soils, the rock-filled rubble of the glacial ablation till sank further and further every year. Over thousands of years of undisturbed activity, the upland forest created a thick blanket of incredibly fertile soil over the stony rubble the glacier left behind. Forested land can remain frost-free well into the winter, even

For a fascinating environmental history of New England, as seen in its stone walls, see Robert M. Thorson's *Stone by Stone* (New York: Walker, 2002).

Atlantic Salmon

American Shad

Hickory Shad

Alewife

Blueback Herring

in parts of northern New England. A thick blanket of snow combines with deep forest ground littler and soil to keep soils from freezing so deeply that frost-heaving pushes up glacial stones. Studies in New Hampshire's Hubbard Brook Forest showed that snow-covered forest soils rarely froze more than a few inches deep, except in years with little snow cover. In contrast, exposed lawns and hayfields froze more than 24 inches deep in winter.

We may owe a quintessential feature of New England's landscape to deforestation: stone farm walls. Removing forest cover on upland slopes exposed the ground to greater frost-heaving, raising millions of stones from deep in glacial soils up to the surface. While clearing the stones from their fields, farmers made a virtue of necessity by building walls and foundations from the glacial stones. Most stone walls were not built as territorial markers but as linear stone-dumps at the edges of fields. But by the mid-1800s, stone walls became necessary because deforestation had made long wood logs far too expensive for farm walls.

Mill dams and anadromous and catadromous fish

Anadromous fish are born in freshwater rivers, run down to the sea to mature in marine waters, and then return to the rivers of their birth to breed. Some New England anadromous fish survive the spawning migration upriver and then return to the sea after breeding. Early colonial accounts of river fish show that Atlantic Salmon, Striped Bass, Atlantic Sturgeon, American Shad, Alewives, Blueback Herring, American Eels (catadromous), and Sea Lampreys were migratory in great numbers on the Connecticut River. Salmon, shad, and eels once reached deep into the northern river and its tributaries. The extent of the spawning runs on the northern river is known only from sporadic accounts, as northern New England was sparsely settled before 1800. Striped Bass and Alewife spawning runs probably didn't reach beyond northern Massachusetts. Early colonists disliked salmon as a commodity fish that was too common to value as a significant food source. Shad was actively disdained as food and considered suitable only for fertilizing exhausted cornfields. Ironically,

river fishing became an important business only in the decade of 1780–90, just before the first major Connecticut River dams were built. Although the general principles of anadromous fish migration and spawning were broadly understood by the late eighteenth century, the interest in improving river navigation with dams and canals won out over the interests of the relatively small Connecticut River fishing industry.

Larger dams and riverside dikes were initially built to support the newly fashionable riverside cargo canals of the late 1700s. In the era before steam-powered railroads, canals promised to solve the problems of moving bulk goods over long distances. Merchants north of Hartford believed that dams, locks, and canals paralleling the river would allow cargo boats to pass over the low rapids north of Enfield, Connecticut. These smaller dams and locks were designed to allow migratory fish to pass through in their spring migrations. As the political power of manufacturers increased, the dams, locks, and canals became increasingly higher and more robust, and accommodating river fish became a minor concern to the mill owners. The problem was particularly pressing on the Connecticut River, which crosses a series of bedrock faults beginning at Enfield. The faults create

The current dam at Turners Falls, Massachusetts, was rebuilt and raised five feet in 1970. The Turners Falls Pool of impounded water behind the dam extends 22 miles north to the Vernon Dam in Vermont. The section of dam shown above feeds water into the Turners Falls Canal. The canal parallels the old river course and was built in its present form in 1869 to supply mill power to factories. The canal now feeds the Cabot Power Station hydroelectric dam at the south end of the canal, where it rejoins the Connecticut River.

Turners Falls, Massachusetts, and the French King Bridge

Turners Falls and its eponymous dam played a central role in two key events in the environmental history of the Connecticut River: the end of major anadromous fish runs in the river north of Massachusetts and the beginning of the water-powered American Industrial Revolution.

The town of Turners Falls was founded in the 1790s around the building of a transportation canal bypassing the local Connecticut River rapids. Railroads quickly made the canal irrelevant. In 1867, factory owners rebuilt the old canal to supply hydropower to cutlery and paper factories along the industrial canal. The canal was further rebuilt and refurbished in the early 1900s to support hydroelectric power generation at the Cabot Power Station.

North

0   .25   .50   .75   1

MILE

The magnificent French King Bridge is a three-span steel cantilevered arch bridge that opened to traffic in 1932. The bridge spans a chasm created by the Eastern Border Fault, connects the towns of Gill and Erving, Massachusetts, and supports Massachusetts State Highway 2A, a major transportation route through north-central Massachusetts. The unusual name is derived from French King Rock just north of the bridge, once a navigation hazard to river traffic. The rock is rarely above water now because of the water impounded by the Turners Falls Dam.

63

2A

Connecticut River

French King Rock,
may be submerged
in high water

Millers River

Turners Falls
Airport

2A

63

Atlantic Salmon

American Shad

2A

The original wooden Turners Falls Dam of 1794 effectively killed off Atlantic Salmon on the Connecticut River and severely damaged American Shad runs as well. The basics of anadromous fish biology were understood even then, but the small Connecticut River commercial fishery was no match for the urge to industrialize manufacturing on the river, and the fish disappeared.

rapids that cargo barges and larger sailing vessels could not navigate.

In 1794, the first significant dam that blocked the main stem of the Connecticut River was built in Turners Falls, Massachusetts. The dam was part of a larger project to bypass a series of rapids and create the Turners Falls Canal, which opened in 1798. These structures ended the Atlantic Salmon run on the Connecticut River and effectively ended the American Shad run on the Connecticut River north of Turners Falls. However, some shad still managed to get north to the dam at Bellows Falls, Vermont, where the shad spawning run ended in 1802 after the Bellows Falls Dam was completed.

With the loss of the Atlantic Salmon and other massive anadromous fish runs, the freshwater systems of central New England lost a major element of their nutrient circulatory systems, whereby the myriad riches of the Atlantic Ocean were annually transported upstream by adult breeding fish to enrich freshwater ecosystems deep within the New England hills. The bodies of the adult fish and the eggs and fry of young salmon, shad, and river herring fed both wild predators and the Native American inhabitants, and marine nutrients fertilized the whole Connecticut River ecosystem.

The new dams had a direct effect on human health. As dammed waters backed up into previously dry areas, local mosquito populations exploded, bringing malaria and other diseases to places that had never seen the disease. When some of the first Central Valley commercial canals and dams were constructed in Holyoke, upstream residents near Northampton quickly complained of mosquitos and illnesses they had never before experienced.

The Industrial Revolution in New England's Central Valley was due to four factors that coalesced to produce great wealth at the cost of significant environmental damage. A more sophisticated banking system made capital available for complex manufacturing projects, local resources for iron, copper, and brownstone for building, hydropower from the narrower river in Massachusetts, and a rural

population ready to abandon marginal farms and try something new.

An aerial view of Holyoke's industrial canal system.

Thomas Jefferson imposed an embargo on manufactured goods from England just before the War of 1812, which drove up demand for local finished goods throughout the region. In particular, paper goods and finished cloth were in short supply, and merchants began to look at old riverside grain mills as potential small factory sites. After the war's end in 1815, there was a drive toward larger mills and factories using hydropower from the larger tributaries of the Connecticut River. In the early 1800s, the main stem of the Connecticut was too large for the modest scale of mill engineering and available capital. As the potential for hydropowered manufacturing became obvious, factory owners' plans became more ambitious. Mills were built to supply paper, wood products, and small manufactured goods, including pulleys and candles. Copper and iron mines provided the raw materials for light manufacturing of brassware, household hardware, pistols, and rifles. The great forests of New England provided the raw material for paper mills.

The New England mill towns

Holyoke was America's first planned industrial city, built around a dam designed to harness the power of

Northampton, The Oxbow, and Holyoke

The Oxbow

The Oxbow Lake is a former circular meander of the Connecticut River that was cut off from the river by a flood in 1840. With a long history of seasonal flooding, low-lying areas near the Connecticut and Mill Rivers still occasionally see high water. However, the presence of the oxbow pond and the wetlands surrounding it help buffer the effects of high water. The Oxbow is a popular destination for wildlife watching, fishing, and boating.

Hulberts Pond and the Mill River, Mass Audubon Arcadia Wildlife Sanctuary

Hulberts Pond is a dilation of the Mill River, and popular fishing and boating are just off the Oxbow Lake. The adjacent Mass Audubon Arcadia Sanctuary is one of the best spots in the region for birding and observing freshwater wildlife.

Wikimedia Commons

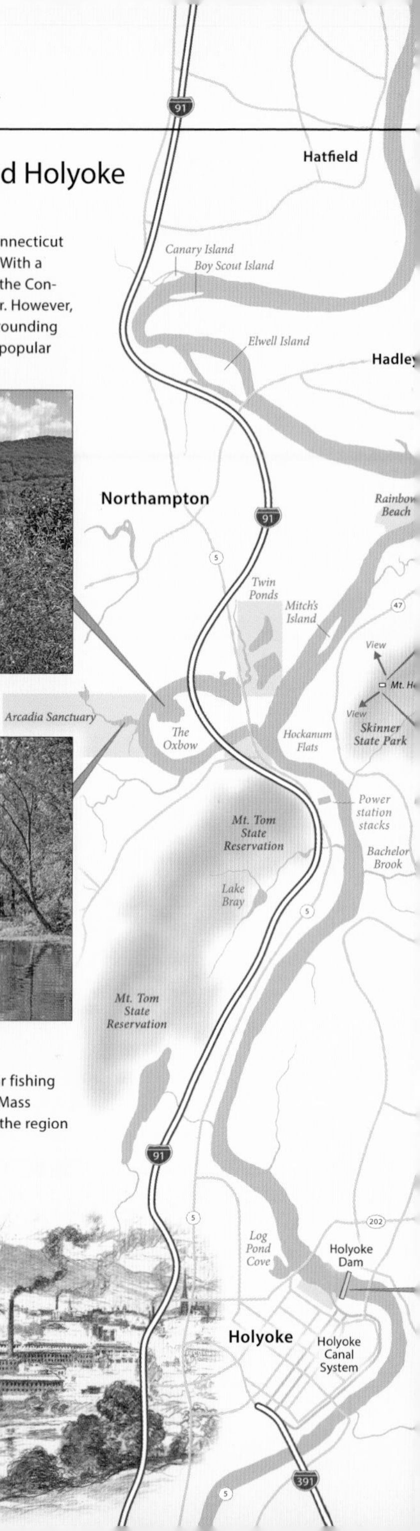

Hatfield

Canary Island
Boy Scout Island

Elwell Island

Hadley

Northampton

Rainbow Beach

Twin Ponds

Mitch's Island

View

Mt. He

View

Arcadia Sanctuary

The Oxbow

Hockanum Flats

Skinner State Park

Power station stacks

Mt. Tom State Reservation

Bachelor Brook

Lake Bray

Mt. Tom State Reservation

Log Pond Cove

Holyoke Dam

Holyoke

Holyoke Canal System

Amherst

The view north from the Mount Holyoke Summit House

The first English settlers arrived in this area of the Pioneer Valley in the 1660s and established the town of Northampton in 1664. During the colonial period, Northampton was an important center of trade and commerce and was known for its fertile farmland, sawmills, and gristmills. In the late eighteenth and early nineteenth centuries, Northampton became a center of progressive reform movements, including the abolition of slavery and women's suffrage.

Mount Holyoke Range

Mount Holyoke Range State Park

Mount Tom from the Holyoke Range

In a case of life imitating art, the view in Cole's masterpiece *The Oxbow* (pp. 120–21) became the inspiration for the Summit House Hotel, built atop Mount Holyoke in 1851. Today the hotel building is part of Skinner State Park, and the hotel veranda still offers a magnificent view over the Pioneer Valley, Mount Tom, and the Oxbow Lake.

Holyoke, The World's Paper City
Drawing, opposite page, by artist Vernon Howe Bailey, 1920. Bailey captures Holyoke at the peak of its industrial era.

The Holyoke Dam

Holyoke, Massachusetts, has a rich and complex environmental history that reflects the wider history of New England and the United States. During the nineteenth and early twentieth centuries, Holyoke was a rapidly growing industrial city with a canal system powered by the vast water resources of the Connecticut River. After multiple early failures at damming the Connecticut River resulted in success, the city became home to a thriving textile industry and was a hub of transportation and trade, with a network of canals, railroads, and roads connecting it to the rest of the region.

a 57-foot fall of rapids across the Connecticut River. In 1847, Boston financiers created the first successful version of the Holyoke Dam (an earlier version failed), forcing the river into a system of parallel canals lined with more than 25 textile and paper mills. As mills expanded, so did Holyoke's population, which doubled to 10,000 in 1860–70. By 1880, 22,000 people lived in Holyoke, which had far outstripped its ability to supply the growing population with clean water and safe sewage disposal. In 1863, Holyoke's annual mortality rate was 33 per 1,000, the highest in New England. Dysentery, typhoid fever, measles, diphtheria, scarlet fever, and tuberculosis were the primary drivers of the high death rate. All were due to overcrowded housing, polluted drinking water, and primitive open-drain sewage lines that ran directly into the Connecticut River.

Although the river had been dammed with locks at Turners Falls since 1798, in 1868, the town of Turners Falls was redesigned as a small industrial center, with a hydropower canal diverted from the river. Turners Falls had paper mills and other factories until early in the twentieth century and was also a significant site for managing logs shipped downriver from Vermont and New Hampshire. The expansion of sheep farming in New Hampshire and Vermont in the mid-1800s led to the establishment of woolen mills throughout the Connecticut River region. Many of the earliest large-

The Turners Falls Canal, also historically known as the Montague Canal.

scale riverside manufacturing plants were designed to produce woolen yarn and finished woolen cloth.

Manufacturing cities such as Hartford, Springfield, Holyoke, Turners Falls, and Bellows Falls were simultaneously prosperous and squalid. The development of new riverside factories and mills far outpaced municipal planning or governmental controls. The little environmental mitigation that was done was usually late and responsive only to life-threatening crises such as disease epidemics. Many observers from the 1850s and later noted pollution problems and tried to alleviate the problems through early pollution laws. But the net effect of most nineteenth-century governmental responses was ineffectual compared to the onslaught of factory wastes and municipal sewage. In the war between the Connecticut River and mercantile boosterism, the river lost almost every battle.

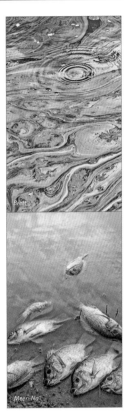

A decline in the rural New England countryside began between 1819 and 1830 when a combination of factors made small central New England farms uneconomical. The marketplace Panic of 1819 damaged global markets and particularly hit commodity farmers. The completion of the Erie Canal in 1825 made farm goods from western New York and the Great Lakes states far more accessible for East Coast markets. This caused commodities prices to fall sharply and ruined many central New England merchants and farmers. Unlike the small, stony, and often irregular plots of New England farms, the large, flat, stone-free, and inexpensive fields of the Ohio Valley and Midwest were perfect for newly invented mechanical plows, planters, and harvesting machinery. The creation of the first overland railroad in 1829 sealed the fate of small New England farms, which could not compete with western states bringing grains and produce to market through rail networks.

Deforestation

In the seventeenth and eighteenth centuries, the average New England household required 30–40 cords of firewood per year, or about as much wood as an acre of mature woodland could supply. The adoption of more efficient Franklin stoves cut the needed firewood to

10–15 cords, but this still meant that a farm required a woodlot of 20 acres or more to be fully self-sustaining. Although wood was also used for building, firewood for heating consumed about 18 times the wood used for construction. In the colonial period from 1600 to 1800, New England used more than 260 million cords of firewood. Colonial New England winters were bitter. This was the time of the Little Ice Age (1100–1900), when average temperatures were far lower than today.

Deforestation of the Central Valley and the surrounding upland hills accelerated in the late eighteenth and early nineteenth centuries. As the soils of valley farms were intensively cropped, they needed fertilizers and other soil amendments to stay productive. Valley forests were burned to create potash, which could be used as a fertilizer or as an ingredient of soaps, glass, or gunpowder sold by farmers to generate cash.

Burning and clear-cutting land for farming combined with logging to supply timber mills led to rapid declines in the forest cover of the Connecticut River region. From 1820 to 1860, Massachusetts, Vermont, and New Hampshire went from 60 percent forest cover to 40 percent coverage. Vermont lost forest cover rapidly until the 1870s, when just 35 percent of the

Clear-cut near Morey Pond, in Wilmot, New Hampshire. Clear-cutting of a forest destroys much of the forest soil through compaction and later erosion. In winter, exposed soil freezes as much as two feet below the surface, killing much of the soil microfauna. Trees can regenerate in decades, but it can take many more decades for the forest soil to recover.

state remained forested. During the mid- to late 1800s, the primary resource moving down the Connecticut River was logs to feed the paper mills of Bellows Falls, Turners Falls, and Holyoke. In 1876 alone, the Holyoke Lumber Company sent 6 million feet of logs down the Connecticut River to Central Valley manufacturers.

The general effect of deforestation was to make local temperature extremes even greater. Without tree cover, summers were hotter and winters much colder. River and stream flooding became more severe during the spring snowmelt, as barren, exposed ground froze deeply and thawed slowly, leading to much greater and faster runoff from hillsides. Rainfall was much more likely to simply run off the newly exposed ground, and observers as early as 1797 noted that the Connecticut River was much more likely to flood than in previous years. Excess sediments from runoff increased the sedimentation rate of ponds, lakes, and streams five-fold in the colonial era. Floods became more common because heavy rainfall quickly drained from barren land and into streams and rivers.

By the late 1800s, more than half the native forests of southern New England had been cut down and re-placed by farmland, grasslands for haying, pastureland, and the development of towns and cities. Many cut trees were not intended for either firewood or building material. Due to the heavy demand for fertilizer to feed corn crops, many woodlots were simply burned to the ground, and the cooled ashes were collected for potash (potassium) destined for cornfields. Many other forests were cut to produce charcoal to feed the furnaces of iron mines that developed in central New England in the 1700s. Huge piles of cut trees were covered with dirt and set alight to burn slowly in smothered, low-oxygen conditions to yield charcoal. You can still encounter the 200-year-old remains of huge charcoal piles in northern Connecticut and western Massachu-setts forests. Luckily for New England forests, furnace operators began switching to coal in the early 1800s. Not long afterward, the discovery of huge iron deposits in Minnesota and Wisconsin ended iron smelting in New England.

Virtually every forest near the Connecticut River in central New England has been clear-cut twice since 1620. Most have been clear-cut three times. White Mountain National Forest.

Eastern White Pines
Pinus strobus

By the 1870s, New England farms were being abandoned wholesale. Deserted farmhouses and barns became the norm in the countryside. People moved to urban areas for greater opportunities in the new factories or moved west to continue farming under better circumstances. You can follow the changes by looking at land records of the times after 1860. In 1860, only 27 percent of the land in Connecticut was forested. By 1910, forests had recovered to 45 percent coverage; by 1955, over 63 percent of Connecticut was forested. By 2004, Connecticut forests covered about 60 percent of the landscape, but under heavy suburban development pressure, that figure had fallen to 55 percent by 2019. One prominent beneficiary of abandoned farm fields was the Eastern White Pine, which quickly colonized open fields. The sheer number of mature, roughly 130-year-old White Pines in today's New England landscape shows how quickly and entirely many older farming areas were abandoned in the late 1800s. Young White Pines quickly spread their branches to form thick, rounded shapes that effectively shade out competing tree species. We might have even more White Pines on old farm fields today if not for the horrific effects of the Great Hurricane of 1938. Even far inland, a huge percentage of trees were felled by this hurricane, and the White Pine is both New England's tallest tree species and one of the weakest under wind stress.

The forestry industry that began life as simple clear-cutting of whole forests increasingly became a profession that managed forests for stainability and maximum utility of a precious resource. Both Harvard and Yale Universities established forestry schools in the early 1900s, and Yale's graduate university program has now evolved into the Yale School of the Environment. Once a profession that mainly thought about board feet of lumber, foresters began to think ecologically about whole forests and watersheds as natural systems. Unfortunately, it would take another half-century before the new concepts of environmentalism and watershed-wide management would translate into effective legislation.

"The world's most beautifully landscaped cesspool"

As living and sanitation standards improved in the middle of the nineteenth century, personal water usage became a critical limiting factor in the growth of cities and towns throughout New England. For example, per capita water use in Boston grew from five gallons per day in 1840 to over 70 gallons per day in the 1870s. The sheer volume of contaminated household and toilet water combined with growing industrial wastes in rivers created a health crisis. There was a widespread belief that natural waterways would always neutralize contaminants—"the solution to pollution is dilution." But nutrient-rich sewage and other contaminants cause algal blooms that sharply limit the ability of rivers to oxygenate and neutralize pollutants. Caustic chemicals killed the aquatic bacteria critical to breaking down organic wastes and sewage. Waterborne diseases such as cholera became a threat to river water supplies.

Fish conservationists saw large masses of Alewives and shad killed by contaminants or lack of dissolved oxygen in the polluted water. Livestock and humans were often sickened by drinking river water. In the Connecticut River estuary and other coastal regions,

For more information on the history of industrialization, resource extraction, and pollution of the Connecticut River region, I recommend these excellent books:

Reasonable Use: The People, the Environment, and the State, New England, 1790–1930, by John T. Cumbler (New York: Oxford University Press, 2001).

Second Nature: An Environmental History of New England, by Richard W. Judd (Amherst: University of Massachusetts Press, 2014).

bearok

The Connecticut River at Hanover, New Hampshire. For long stretches of its course, the Connecticut River is more like a long, narrow lake than a river. Three miles south of here, the Wilder Hydroelectric Dam at West Lebanon backs up the river for 45 miles to the north. The Hanover region is typical of many places along the Connecticut: public access sites are limited. This area is fortunate to have the Montshire Museum of Science on the west bank of the river in Norwich, Vermont. The tower of the museum building is just barely visible in the trees at the center of the photograph. The Montshire offers beautiful hiking trails along the river.

SeanPavonePhoto

New highways and efficient train service made the glories of the New England landscape conveniently available to population centers such as the New York City region and Boston.

shellfish beds were closed down to control outbreaks of typhoid and cholera. In nineteenth-century New England states, the concept of "reasonable use" governed the public and private use of common water sources. Everyone had common rights to use rivers, streams, and lakes for personal and commercial purposes. Over time, local governments began to restrict the gross contamination of waterways as a violation of reasonable use. They passed state regulations to control pollution and promote the development of sewage treatment of urban wastewater. Unfortunately, the new regulations did little to slow the decline of the Connecticut River.

Other environmental insults also took place: the spate of dam-building on the Connecticut River between the mid-1930s and the 1950s radically changed the nature of the river. The many main stem dams effectively converted stretches of the Connecticut River into a series of long, linear lakes, a very different biological environment from a flowing river.

Pollution remained rampant in the early to mid-1900s, as municipal sewer systems and industrial plants poured untreated waste into what most considered a watery waste dump. New Englanders engineered the relative security of a dammed, diked, and managed river but also got the "world's best-landscaped sewer" instead.*

Suburbanization and the automobile
In 1914, Henry Ford revolutionized the young automobile industry by introducing the Model T Ford, the first car that middle-class Americans could afford to own. By 1925, the Ford Motor Company was producing 9,000 Model Ts a day, and the increase in automobile ownership in the 1920s led to improved roads. The first parkways in Long Island, Westchester, and Connecticut date from the late 1920s and early 1930s. In the early 1950s, the Eisenhower-era Interstate Highway System Committee (dominated by Detroit carmakers) recommended that America's transportation needs be met almost entirely by cars and trucks. Construction of the US Interstate Highway System began with the Federal Aid Highway Act of 1956. We are still living with

*This infamous statement about the Connecticut River in the mid-twentieth century originated in a film from 1965 called *The Long Tidal River*, directed by Ellsworth S. Grant and narrated by his then-sister-in-law Katharine Hepburn. Hepburn's narration called the river "the world's most beautifully landscaped cesspool," and variations on the quotation have been widely used ever since.

Everett Collection

the consequences of this vast expansion of roads and highways at the expense of mass transit and railroads.

One of the first US highway projects to take advantage of the more powerful cars of the 1930s was the Merritt Parkway System. Built between 1934 and 1940 to alleviate traffic congestion on US Route 1 in swiftly urbanizing southwestern Connecticut, the Merritt Parkway was heralded on its opening as the "scenic gateway to New England."

In Connecticut, Route 5 long held its position as the main route north into Massachusetts, Vermont, and New Hampshire. Route 5 originated in the 1700s as the Upper Boston Post Road that ran from New Haven, Connecticut, north to Springfield, Massachusetts, and then east to Boston. Into the mid-1950s, Route 5 was the main road into eastern and northern New England, but since it was a local highway, it was relatively slowgoing by today's standards. As traffic volumes increased, Interstate 91 was built in sections that roughly paralleled the Connecticut River through the late 1950s into the late 1960s. Once I-91 was complete, you could travel north from New Haven to the Quebec border in less than seven hours. Western New England tourism and winter sports exploded in popularity.

The newly opened Merritt Parkway in Connecticut, above, and Robert Moses's Long Island Parkway System were two of the first US highway projects to cater to the more powerful cars of the 1930s.

John McGraw

What river?
Twentieth-century urban design in a nutshell: even today, Springfield, Massachusetts's most glorious natural asset is still largely walled off from the consciousness of the city. A rail line, an eight-lane highway, and a museum complex with its back to the water cut the city off from New England's longest and most important river.

The new parkways and highways created a demand for faster and more powerful cars. Larger gasoline engines, in turn, drove an increase in automobile exhaust, another primary source of excess nitrogen in the environment and acid rain from the polluted atmosphere. New transportation options allowed the rapid growth of affordable suburban housing in the 1950s and 1960s. The sprawling new suburban communities required yet more cars, and all those new lawns required millions of tons of fertilizer and hundreds of thousands of new sewer connections and septic fields.

Northeastern residents love to blame power plants in the Midwest for air pollution, acid rain, and excess nitrogen in the air. Yet New England's regional air-quality problems stem at least as much from vehicle exhaust fumes that originate locally in the metropolitan areas of Connecticut, eastern Massachusetts, and New York City. As raindrops wash pollutants from the skies, the rain increasingly falls on impervious, artificial surfaces and quickly runs into local sewers and storm drains. The excess nitrogen, acids, metals, carbon particulates, and other pollutants course into local rivers and streams. This runoff has contaminated the Central Valley rivers and, by extension, Long Island Sound.

Along with suburban sprawl came commercial development, leading to a dramatic rise in land covered by asphalt and cement pavements, parking lots, and building roofs. In the Central Valley, the flat, stone-free soils of the ancient Lake Hitchcock plains were highly attractive to developers. As real estate agents and developers often say, "What's best to farm is also best for building."

The lost, hidden river

Many of the best former farm fields and river meadows along the Connecticut River from Wethersfield, Connecticut, north to Northampton, Massachusetts, now sit under housing developments and commercial buildings built since the 1960s. Aside from the wild lands lost, the intensive development of the Central Valley over the past 60 years has damaged or destroyed the natural habitat buffers that once protected areas near the river from disastrous flooding. The upstream dams (an environmental problem in themselves) can do only so much good when much of the area near the main stem of today's Connecticut River is under impermeable surfaces, including building roofs, streets, and parking lots. Impervious surfaces drain stormwater directly into local streams and the major rivers. As many New England towns learned in Tropical Storm Irene in 2011, fast stormwater runoff can turn an ordinarily quiet stream into a raging river in flood within just a few hours.

Mark Lotterhand

Hartford, Connecticut.

By the mid-twentieth century, the Connecticut River was practically invisible to those living alongside it. Hidden from view by thin screens of riparian woods or by the factories that used the river as a flowing sump, the Connecticut River became a smelly eyesore (when it could be seen at all). From Hartford to Northampton, Interstate 91 became an almost impenetrable wall of concrete and support pilings that screened the river not only from view but from popular consciousness. It's hard to build a broad constituency for a natural resource that is both invisible to most people and a difficult place to visit, even for determined river advocates. Despite the development of the Silvio O. Conte National Fish and Wildlife Refuge in Massachusetts

SeanPavonePhoto

Over the past few decades Hartford has made significant progress in reopening the Connecticut River to the city and its people. The Mortensen Riverfront Plaza (1999), the Connecticut Science Center (2009), the restored Riverside Park, and local organizations like Riverfront Recapture have revitalized the riverfront and brought the river back to public consciousness.

and other hopeful developments, the problem of public access to the river still remains.

The Federal Clean Water Act of 1972

Although there were many efforts in the early twentieth century to raise public awareness of the destruction of the Connecticut River, by the mid-1960s, large stretches of the Connecticut River were what today would be called a Class D river: dirty, smelly, rife with pathogens and pollutants, and dangerous to both wildlife and human health. Even after passage of the Federal Water Pollution Control Act of 1948, improvements were modest. Not until this act was significantly overhauled as the Federal Water Pollution Control Act Amendments of 1972 did things change significantly for all of America's rivers, lakes, and coastal waters.

The Clean Water Act, as it is popularly known, was designed to restore and maintain the health and integrity of the country's fresh and coastal waters, which until the act was amended in 1972, were primarily governed by a patchwork of largely ineffective federal, state, and local laws. Since the passage of the amended Clean Water Act, gains in water quality across the United

States have been dramatic, particularly in limiting and prohibiting industrial pollution discharge and in encouraging and providing federal funds for developing secondary wastewater treatment of municipal sewage. However, even by the standards set by the Clean Water Act, its programs have failed to achieve the three critical aims of the law: "to make all U.S. waters fishable and swimmable by 1983; to have zero water pollution discharge by 1985; and to prohibit the discharge of toxic amounts of pollutants."

Continuing challenges

Even today, as many as half of the rivers and lakes in the United States violate state and federal water quality standards. Research shows that 70 percent of US lakes, ponds, streams, and rivers are impaired, as are about 70 percent of our coastlines. Much work remains to be done, particularly in protecting natural watershed lands from further development and in addressing the myriad non-point sources of water pollution that remain near freshwater lakes and rivers. "Non-point source pollution" describes the thousands of more minor but significant sources of water pollution that come from residential, commercial, and urban areas. Runoff from city streets contains oils, toxic chemicals, grit from diesel engines and brake linings, illegal dumping of household and automobile oils and lubricants, and so on. Household lawns, commercial building lawns, golf courses, parks, and farms all produce runoff of chemical pesticides and fertilizers. Poor management of construction sites and agricultural land produces excess runoff of soil and sediments, which cloud local rivers and lakes. Runoff from farm livestock operations, suburban neighborhoods, and cities contains significant bacteria and pathogens from animal and pet waste.

In the twenty-first century there is no "away." Much of what we throw away eventually ends up in our rivers and streams.

The designers of the Clean Water Act did not adequately foresee and manage the explosion of commercial and residential building since the early 1970s. While the worst of the mid-twentieth century's raw sewage and pollutant dumping has been prohibited, the pace of development in watersheds like the Connecticut River has outstripped society's ability to control the effects of wastewater treatment, stormwater containment, and non-point sources of pollutants.

Although it is unusual today to find untreated municipal sewage entering waterways, most of today's sewage systems are designed as combined sewer systems that mix stormwater runoff with industrial wastewater and treated sewage in a single system. During heavy rainfall, the combined systems are designed to overflow and discharge raw, untreated wastes into local streams, rivers, and coastal waters. These combined sewage overflows, or CSOs, have become a continuing and growing source of water pollution. CSOs are why local and state authorities commonly ban swimming in areas after a large rainstorm: these waters are temporarily polluted by sewage bacteria that have overflowed and bypassed water treatment plants.

Looking south along the Connecticut River from Hartford's beautiful Riverside Park, with its boat launch docks and facilities for rowing sports.

aerial-drone

A pond at Bauer Park, Madison, Connecticut, fed by a small forest creek. Although this pond has a large area free of floating plants, it's a pond and not a small lake because it is shallow and has submerged aquatic plants throughout.

PONDS AND LAKES

The basic facts of life in freshwater are the same for inhabitants of both streams and ponds—and more often than not, you'll find the same plants and animals in a range of flowing and still freshwater environments. Water quantity and quality, seasonal changes, and the tight relationship between dissolved oxygen and water temperature are universal challenges for aquatic animals. In a book that is nominally about a large river, it might seem obvious to start with river life, but life in rivers and streams is in many ways more physically complex, specialized, and demanding than life in still water.

Freshwater can seem endlessly abundant on a fair early summer day in New England. But on a global scale, the kinds of visible surface ponds, lakes, streams, and rivers we may take for granted are shockingly rare. Only 3.5 percent of the earth's total water supply is freshwater, and most of that is bound up in the polar ice caps or groundwater. Ponds, lakes, rivers, and streams account for less than 0.25 percent of global water supplies (see overleaf).

The water cycle describes the large water storage zones in the environment and how water constantly moves among these zones. The atmosphere, surface waters, and groundwater are freshwater storage zones. Gravity, solar heating, wind, local weather, and the activities of plants are the major motive forces in shifting

The Common Whitetail (*Plathemis lydia*) is found throughout the Connecticut River region. This species of dragonfly favors ponds and moist, swampy forest clearings.

Ponds & Lakes

All water on Earth

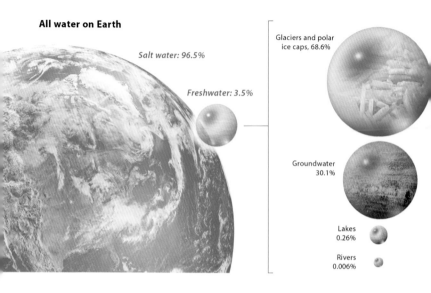

Salt water: 96.5%

Freshwater: 3.5%

Glaciers and polar ice caps, 68.6%

Groundwater 30.1%

Lakes 0.26%

Rivers 0.006%

freshwater from one zone to another. Within the local and regional water cycles, water can regularly change among liquid, solid (ice), and gaseous (water vapor) forms (see pp. 152–53).

Human activities modify both the quantity and quality of environmental water cycles. We dam rivers like the Connecticut to create reservoirs to supply our homes and businesses with water and electricity and to prevent flooding during major storms. Our domestic and industrial activities constantly introduce contaminants, pesticides, and fertilizers into the water cycle. Stormwater runoff from developed areas and agriculture carries sediment and pollutants into local waterways and the Connecticut River.

Transpiration and groundwater absorption are critical but normally invisible elements of the water cycle. As plants respire and use light and water to create photosynthesis, they "exhale" as much as 99 percent of the water they absorb through their roots. Tiny pores on the underside of leaves called stomata release water vapor into the air, where the water then returns to the atmosphere. Except in particular circumstances, streams, rivers, and lakes are fed mainly by groundwater that flows under the influence of gravity. Only a small percentage of water from a typical rainstorm directly reaches streams and ponds. Plant roots and soil absorb rainwater directly, and within hours almost all of the rainwater has transpired back into the atmosphere or absorbed into the groundwater. Groundwater reservoirs in a relatively moist environment such as New England are often vast, and the groundwater moves slowly through rock fissures and glacial soils deep beneath the ground surface. Depending on how porous the soil and bedrock are, it can take tens or even hundreds of years for groundwater to reemerge on the surface as it seeps into ponds, streams, and rivers.

The prominent exception to this normal rainwater cycle is during major rainstorms or sudden warming periods that melt the winter snowpack. If the soil and normal groundwater channels are already saturated with water (or frozen in winter), rain or meltwater will run directly from the land into ponds, streams, and rivers. Usually, this direct runoff just temporarily elevates ponds and stream levels. But in significant rainstorms, nor'easters, and hurricanes, so much rain running directly off the saturated ground and into local streams and rivers can cause catastrophic flooding. This is why preserving natural environments near streams and rivers is critical to flood control. Natural environments and soils act as giant sponges to buffer the effects of heavy rainfall. Roads, parking lots, storm sewers, concrete water drainage channels, and building roofs shed rainwater directly into local streams and rivers. The fast-flowing stormwater can turn a normally placid stream into a damaging flood within hours.

The local New England freshwater cycles of transpiration, evaporation, condensation, and precipitation are only a small part of the larger continental and global water cycles. These larger water cycles are now quickly evolving thanks to climate change, and new global patterns of drought and flood emerge almost daily. Even historically moist New England isn't immune to climate change: in the late summer of 2022, much of New England was in a moderate to severe drought.

Vera

Ponds & Lakes

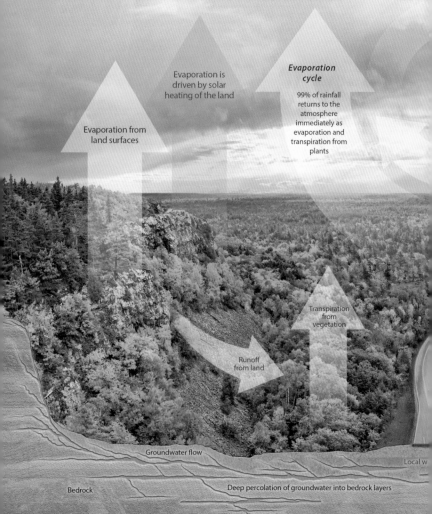

Solar energy
Energy from the sun is the ultimate power source for the wind and the water cycle

THE FRESHWATER CYCLE

Evaporation is driven by solar heating of the land

Evaporation cycle

99% of rainfall returns to the atmosphere immediately as evaporation and transpiration from plants

Evaporation from land surfaces

Transpiration from vegetation

Runoff from land

Groundwater flow

Local w

Bedrock

Deep percolation of groundwater into bedrock layers

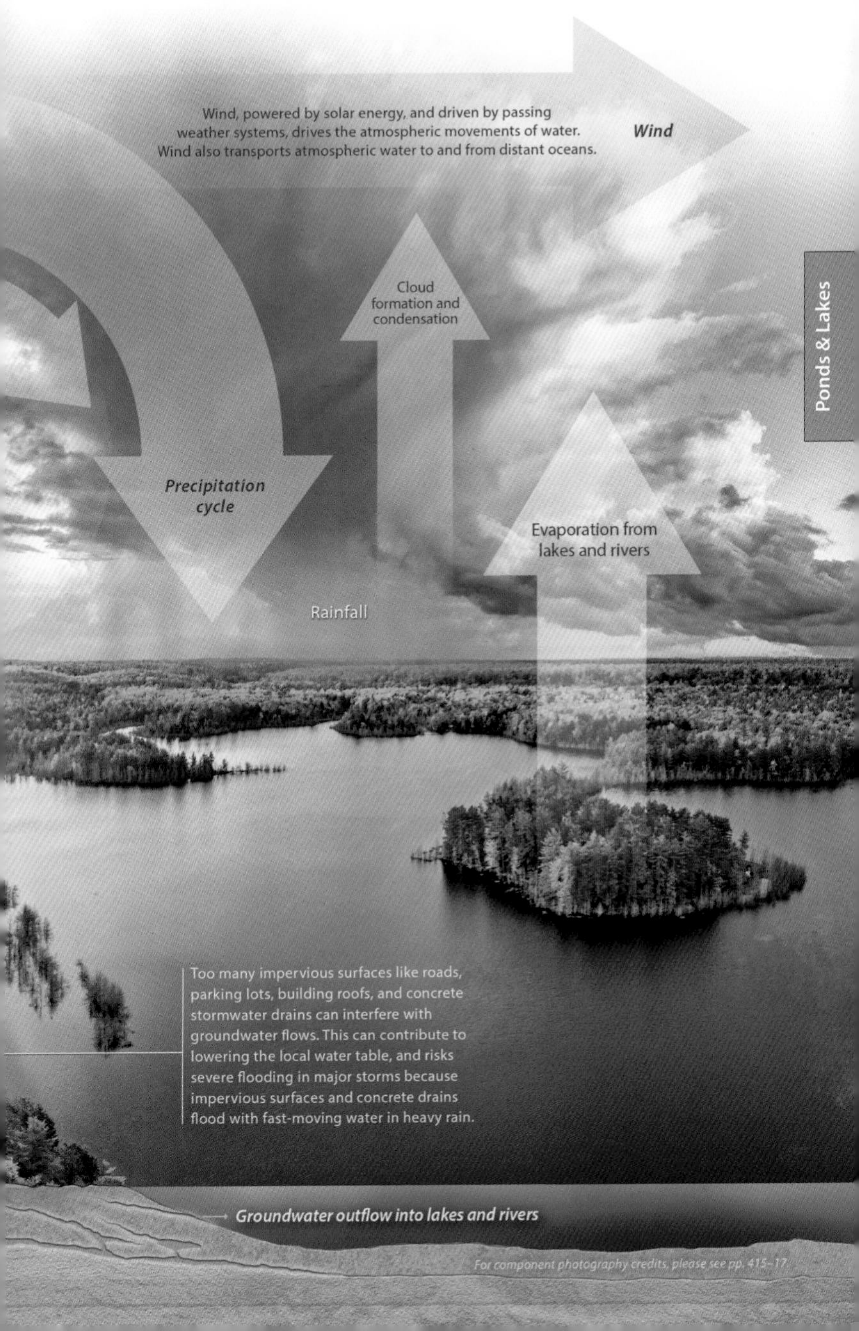

Wind, powered by solar energy, and driven by passing weather systems, drives the atmospheric movements of water. Wind also transports atmospheric water to and from distant oceans.
Wind
Cloud formation and condensation
Ponds & Lakes
Precipitation cycle
Evaporation from lakes and rivers
Rainfall
Too many impervious surfaces like roads, parking lots, building roofs, and concrete stormwater drains can interfere with groundwater flows. This can contribute to lowering the local water table, and risks severe flooding in major storms because impervious surfaces and concrete drains flood with fast-moving water in heavy rain.
Groundwater outflow into lakes and rivers

For component photography credits, please see pp. 415–17.

SEASONAL THERMAL STRATIFICATION AND CIRCULATION IN PONDS AND LAKES

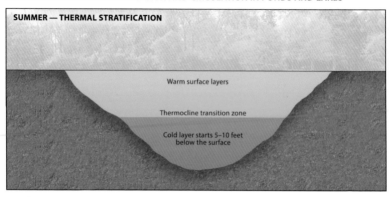

SUMMER — THERMAL STRATIFICATION

Warm surface layers

Thermocline transition zone

Cold layer starts 5–10 feet
below the surface

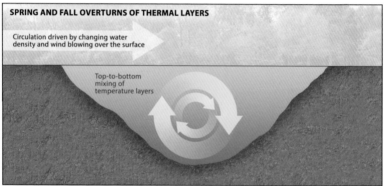

SPRING AND FALL OVERTURNS OF THERMAL LAYERS

Circulation driven by changing water
density and wind blowing over the surface

Top-to-bottom
mixing of
temperature layers

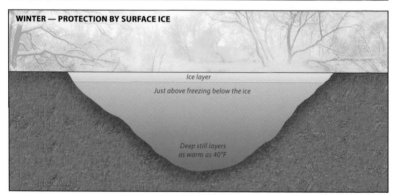

WINTER — PROTECTION BY SURFACE ICE

Ice layer

Just above freezing below the ice

*Deep still layers
as warm as 40°F*

Seasonal overturn is the mixing and circulating of water in lakes and ponds that occur through the seasons. This cyclical pattern of overturn is caused by temperature and density changes in the water column over a year. Seasonal overturn is critical for ponds and lakes. It helps distribute nutrients and oxygen throughout the water column, thereby providing a crucial energy source for the ecosystem.

Although rivers, lakes, and ponds didn't dry up and disappear in 2022, the weather pattern most adults in New England grew up with is clearly changing in unpredictable ways every year.

Seasonal changes in freshwater environments

In cool temperate environments such as central New England, all bodies of freshwater go through annual cycles of spring warming, summer heat, fall cooling, and winter freezing. Although these seasonal changes are primarily temperature cycles, the temperature is intimately linked with the level of dissolved oxygen saturation in water. Cool water can hold more dissolved oxygen than warm water, and the level of oxygen in the water is often what most directly controls the diversity and abundance of aquatic life.

Seasonality in freshwater ponds and lakes

Larger freshwater ponds and lakes are affected by seasonal variations that drive significant changes in the water column, moving nutrient-rich, deep cold waters to the surface and drawing surface waters downward to warm and oxygenate the dark bottom regions. Two critical physical characteristics of water make pond life possible. Because of its complex crystalline structure, frozen water is less dense than cold water, so ice floats. This counterintuitive fact is crucial because otherwise, ice would coat the bottoms of ponds rather than the surface, and it would be much harder for any pond life to survive the winter.

Valeriy Boyarskiy

Like most liquids, water becomes denser as it gets colder. But water reaches its highest density at 41 degrees Fahrenheit, still well above freezing. As water temperatures fall below 41 degrees, the near-freezing water is less dense than the waters above it, and the near-freezing water rises to the pond surface to form ice when the temperature reaches 32 degrees. These subtle but essential differences in water temperature and density drive seasonality in pond circulation. New England ponds and lakes typically have two overturning circulation events: spring and autumn. In spring, as the frozen pond surface warms from 32 to 41 degrees, the denser 41-degree water sinks, displacing the water deeper in the pond. This seasonal circulation is critical

Ponds & Lakes

A radiantly healthy pond in late summer. Good pond water is not free from algae; some algae are essential to a balanced and productive pond ecosystem. Here, the water is clear enough to support submerged aquatic plants throughout the pond. This pond is at a well-maintained nature center, so the water is not burdened with excess nitrogen and phosphorus from lawn runoff. In summer and early fall, shallow-water environments such as ponds are always vulnerable to heat and the low-oxygen conditions that warm water brings. Floating water lily leaves help provide shadows for fish and other wildlife, but most fish will retreat to the deepest water in the center of the pond to wait out the heat of the day.

However, even fortunately located ponds are vulnerable to pollution. Streams feed most ponds, and whatever has polluted the stream as it flows over the landscape will end up in the pond. Although few coal-fired plants remain in New England, smoke from distant coal-burning facilities brings a small but constant rain of heavy metals such as mercury and lead, in addition to carbon soot. The phase-out of regional coal-fired plants sharply reduced the acid rain and freshwater acidification problems of the 1960s through the 1980s, but general air pollution remains a threat to all freshwater environments.

Pond at the Flanders Nature Center, Woodbury, Connecticut.

to distribute oxygen and nutrients throughout ponds and lakes, which might otherwise become stagnant and lifeless in their bottom waters. In summer, deeper ponds and lakes stratify, with warm surface waters forming a distinctive layer above cold deep waters. In the autumn, the temperature layering begins to collapse as the surface waters cool and sink, and the fall circulation overturn begins.

Dissolved oxygen in freshwater

Atmospheric oxygen readily enters the waters of ponds and streams, where it becomes the dissolved oxygen critical to aquatic life. This is particularly true in small, active streams, where the shade-cooled shallow waters and constant splashing and water movement help the waters absorb atmospheric oxygen. Even in the more stagnant waters of ponds and lakes, wind drives small waves and water currents that bring fresh oxygen into the upper layers of the water column.

All plants and animals require oxygen for respiration and basic metabolic processes. In respiration, living cells use oxygen to process nutrient molecules and to support cellular energy cycles, growth, and maintenance. In respiration, living cells absorb oxygen and release carbon dioxide. In the sunlit part of the day, aquatic plants also produce oxygen as a byproduct of photosynthesis. This excess oxygen helps increase the level of dissolved oxygen in aquatic systems. But plants also require oxygen for respiration, so during the night, the respiration needs of both plants and aquatic animals reduce the dissolved oxygen level in ponds and streams.

Daily photosynthesis and respiration cycle in a pond, late spring through mid-autumn

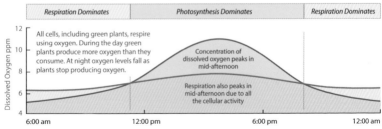

| Respiration Dominates | Photosynthesis Dominates | Respiration Dominates |

All cells, including green plants, respire using oxygen. During the day green plants produce more oxygen than they consume. At night oxygen levels fall as plants stop producing oxygen.

Concentration of dissolved oxygen peaks in mid-afternoon

Respiration also peaks in mid-afternoon due to all the cellular activity

Dissolved Oxygen ppm

12
10
8
6
4

6:00 am   12:00 pm   6:00 pm   12:00 am

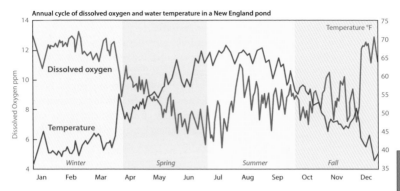

Annual cycle of dissolved oxygen and water temperature in a New England pond

The level of dissolved oxygen that water can hold is tightly linked to water temperature—cold water can hold more dissolved oxygen than warm water. Both ponds and streams show a distinct seasonal cycle in dissolved oxygen levels. In the cooler months, dissolved oxygen levels are higher, and in the warmth

Ponds & Lakes

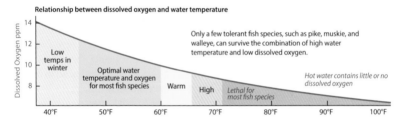

Relationship between dissolved oxygen and water temperature

of summer and early fall, dissolved oxygen levels are typically at their lowest points of the year.

The close link between water temperature and dissolved oxygen can turn deadly in summer. Small ponds and sunlit rivers can warm to the extent that dissolved oxygen falls to dangerous levels, particularly for most fish species. In New England, the smaller upland streams and rivers typically run through shady forests that help keep waters cool and well oxygenated. But larger rivers and small ponds are usually exposed to summer sunlight that can warm at least the surface water layers beyond what many fish and other aquatic animals can tolerate.

Excess nitrogen and phosphorus in freshwater systems

In pristine natural freshwater systems, nitrogen and phosphorus are essential but relatively scarce nutrients. Home gardeners will recognize nitrogen and phosphorus as essential elements in plant fertilizers. All living cells need both elements to grow and thrive, and the relative scarcity of nitrogen and phosphorus in clean, unpolluted waters limits aquatic algae and plant growth.

Unfortunately, in today's intensively developed central New England landscape, large amounts of nitrogen and phosphorus commonly enter freshwater in the runoff and stormwater from fertilized lawns, businesses, and farms. Sewage, animal wastes, and many home soaps and detergents are other common sources of excess nutrients. These high levels of nutrients drain from developed landscapes during rainstorms and enter ponds, lakes, and rivers, where they stimulate excess aquatic algae growth.

The excessive algae growth can quickly damage aquatic systems in several ways. Clouds of green algae limit the sunlight submerged aquatic plants need to thrive. Heavy surface mats of algae are unsightly and usually smell terrible, and they completely disrupt the lives of the many aquatic invertebrates, insects, fish, and other animals that depend on a clean water surface.

Eutrophication is a process by which water bodies, including small ponds, become enriched with excess nutrients, usually nitrogen and phosphorus, leading to the overgrowth of aquatic plants and algae. Small ponds are particularly vulnerable. This overabundance of nutrients can cause algal blooms, decreased water clarity, and most disastrous of all, little or no dissolved oxygen to support healthy aquatic life.

Worse still, excess algae growth can remove so much dissolved oxygen from the water that fish and other aquatic animals die from a lack of oxygen.

Excess algae growth limits the level of dissolved oxygen in two major ways. Like all living things, algae cells use oxygen and release carbon dioxide as part of normal cell metabolism. Although green algae do produce some oxygen as a result of photosynthesis during the day, at night, excess algae populations revert to oxygen consumption. They can quickly use up the dissolved oxygen in the water. As oxygen levels drop, large numbers of algae cells die, and the dead algae tissues then take up yet more dissolved oxygen as the algae decay. This downward spiral of excessive nutrients, the explosive growth of algae, and sharp drops in dissolved oxygen levels is called eutrophication. Eutrophication can happen in any freshwater or saltwater environment. Unfortunately, most of New England's freshwater systems show at least some degree of eutrophication from excess nutrient pollution.

Ecological succession

Ecological succession is one of those natural processes that are so familiar as to be practically invisible. Yet succession is a powerful phenomenon that transforms all environments over time, both aquatic and terrestrial. In New England, succession transforms barren ground into a young forest in a couple of decades or less (see pp. 162–63). Succession is the process where the species in a given area change over time, usually in a predictable sequence of plants and animals that are dominant for a time and then are outcompeted by other species. Eventually, the process of succession results in a more-or-less stable mix of species, or climax community, that continues over centuries. In central New England land environments, the climax community is an oak-maple forest. Given a few centuries, any barren dirt field in this region will transform itself through succession into a mature hardwood forest.

Ecological succession also operates in aquatic environments, although the process of aquatic succession is a bit less predictable and visible than the bare-field-to-forest type of succession on land.

Even on the scale of a human lifetime, all ponds and lakes are ephemeral and are always in transition to something new.

Many aquatic successional changes are driven by purely physical phenomena such as the buildup of silt in a pond. As a pond fills with sediment and becomes increasingly shallow, species that favor shallow water will outcompete species that require deeper water (see p. 164). We tend to notice ecological succession mainly through the changing mix of plant species, but succession also profoundly influences the mix of animal species around freshwater environments. For example, the ubiquitous presence of the White-Tailed Deer in contemporary New England is no accident. The White-Tailed Deer is adapted to live along the edges of forests, where open grassy or shrubby communities transition to deep woodlands. Ecologists call these successional transition zones ecotones. The modern pattern of suburban land development in New England has effectively created a giant forest-edge ecotone that stretches along the Connecticut River and the Central Valley from the shores of Long Island Sound north 125 miles to the cities and suburbs of southern Vermont and New Hampshire.

In this region, ecological succession in ponds, smaller lakes, and other wetlands is primarily driven by changes in the landscape since the ice of the most recent glacial period disappeared from most of New England by 16,000 years ago. As the vast ice sheet melted, countless small ponds and lakes were scattered across a landscape that was largely barren rock and glacial till. Most of these smaller wetlands quickly filled with sediment and over the past 10,000 years eventually became forests. Deeper lakes became shallow ponds

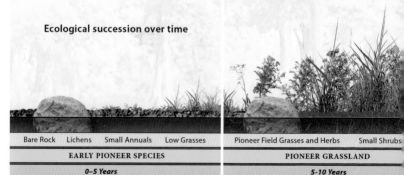

Ecological succession over time

Bare Rock	Lichens	Small Annuals	Low Grasses	Pioneer Field Grasses and Herbs	Small Shrubs
EARLY PIONEER SPECIES				**PIONEER GRASSLAND**	
0–5 Years				*5-10 Years*	

as they filled with silt, ponds became grass and shrub marshes, and the marshes gradually became swamps dominated by water-tolerant hardwood trees such as the Red Maple and Black Tupelo. Over hundreds of years, old drying swamps became forested land. Our current natural ponds and lakes are still undergoing a similar, if slower, siltation-driven transition from wetland to dry land.

Human activities have accelerated and distorted long-term succession in our wetlands, often by creating much more erosion that fills in wetlands. Land development and farming expose and mobilize large amounts of sediment, much of which eventually finds its way into local streams and ponds, hastening the filling of all wetlands. But most of the ponds and lakes in our current New England landscape are not natural. Most of the smaller ponds and lakes we see today are artificial creations of the eighteenth and nineteenth centuries, where small dams were used to create millponds to power grain mills and small factories. Well into the twentieth century, many dam-based ponds we see today were created or maintained solely for aesthetic enjoyment long after the original mills rotted

er Shrubs and Shade–Intolerant Small Trees

OW SHRUBS AND MATURE GRASSLAND

10–15 Years

Pioneer Tree Species and Young Forest Trees

PIONEER FOREST SPECIES

15–30 Years

Ponds & Lakes

Typical succession stages in a pond that fills with sediments over time

1 New pond with some submerged vegetation and little accumulated sediment.

2 Sediment from the feeder stream accumulates and vegetation thickens. The plant roots help capture sediment.

Sediment forms

3 The old pond is almost filled with sediment and has very dense submerged and emergent vegetation.

Sediment forms and deepens

4 The pond is completely filled, and swamp shrubs and trees move into the little water left in the center.

The last open water vanishes

Ecological succession in freshwater ponds is the natural change and development of plant and animal communities over time. Freshwater ponds are dynamic ecosystems that can change due to various factors, including variations in water levels, the introduction of silt and sand from feeders streams, changes in water chemistry, and the introduction of new species. The process of ecological succession in freshwater ponds typically begins with the colonization of a bare pond by pioneer species, such as algae and aquatic plants. These species can establish themselves quickly, adapting to grow in various environmental conditions. Over time, as the pioneer species die and decompose, they provide the nutrients and organic matter that support the growth of more complex plant and animal communities.

1 Open Water with Mostly Submerged Vegetation

2

D

Ponds & Lakes

...etation, Reeds, Sedges

3

Grassy Marsh, Becoming a Shrub Swamp

4

True Swamp, with Hardwood Trees

Many decades of time

As sediments finally fill the entire pond basin, many ponds evolve into a sluggish stream meandering through a maple swamp.

away. Most of the largest lakes in central New England are dammed man-made reservoirs designed to give our cities a predictable and safe water supply and sometimes to help with flood control. Because of all the dammed streams, we now have many more fresh-water ponds and lakes than we might have otherwise—but there's a tragic irony here. Our many dam-created ponds and lakes were responsible for the death of river migratory fish populations like the Atlantic Salmon and the American Shad because the dams blocked the breeding streams. See "Rivers and Streams" for more on migratory fish species and dams.

Definitions of lakes and ponds

Most biologists distinguish ponds and lakes less by overall size than by the depth of the water and the patterns of vegetation surrounding the water. In general, lakes are still-surface bodies of water deep enough (more than 15 feet) that rooted aquatic plants cannot grow near their centers. Some lakes are small but deep, with only a rim of aquatic vegetation near their shorelines. Ponds are shallower bodies of water with extensive edges of emergent aquatic plants and usually also have rich submerged aquatic vegetation growing across or almost across their centers. Marshes are very shallow bodies of water covered almost entirely by

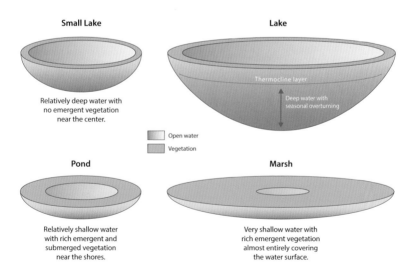

Small Lake

Relatively deep water with no emergent vegetation near the center.

Lake

Thermocline layer

Deep water with seasonal overturning

Open water

Vegetation

Pond

Relatively shallow water with rich emergent and submerged vegetation near the shores.

Marsh

Very shallow water with rich emergent vegetation almost entirely covering the water surface.

emergent vegetation, such as grasses and sedges. In later successional stages, aquatic shrubs such as Smooth Alder, Buttonbush, or Silky Dogwood may convert the grassy marsh to a shrub swamp (see pp. 304–5).

Food webs in ponds and lakes

Even small ponds and lakes in New England are remarkable engines of biological productivity and diversity, especially considering that most ponds are frozen over for at least three months a year. Ponds explode into a complex web of plant and animal interactions each spring using only light and warmth from the sun and water from streams or groundwater.

Ponds, at a glance. Note the heavy emergent vegetation around the pond edge, as well as floating water lilies almost all the way across the pond. This pond at Bauer Park in Madison, Connecticut, is only five to six feet deep in the center and has submerged vegetation all the way across the pond bottom.

Primary production in the pond food web is driven by photosynthesis and is composed of aquatic green algae, cyanobacteria (formerly called blue-green algae), and larger aquatic plants. Like all green plants, algae and cyanobacteria can produce complex carbohydrates and sugars through photosynthesis. During daylight hours, green plants release oxygen as a byproduct of photosynthesis, thereby helping to increase the dissolved oxygen levels in ponds. More complex green plants such as grasses, sedges, submerged aquatic plants, and emergent vegetation around pond edges also contribute to the base of the food web (see pp. 168–69).

In recent years the important role of biofilms in aquatic environments has received increased attention. Every surface underwater in ponds, lakes, and streams is coated with a complex living layer or biofilm composed of green algae, cyanobacteria, other types of bacteria, and fungi. Biofilms are hard to see with the naked eye, but anyone who has ever plucked an old leaf from a pond or stream has felt the slick, slimy biofilm coating on the decaying leaf. In sunlit areas of aquatic environments, the green algae and cyanobacteria in biofilms contribute directly to primary food production. But the bacteria and fungi in biofilms are also critical in the breakdown of dead plant and animal tissues and the recycling of nutrients in aquatic environments.

Lakes, at a glance. On a classic lake there is usually a relatively thin band of rich wetland and emergent vegetation on the shoreline, but the lake edge is sharply pronounced because the water depth drops off so quickly. The Second Connecticut Lake, in Pittsburg, New Hampshire.

Biofilms are also crucial in the seasonal recycling of pond nutrients. Frost kills off most tiny animals and plant leaves in the autumn. Biofilm bacteria and fungi

THE FRESHWATER FOOD WEB

Food webs in freshwater ponds are complex networks of interdependent relationships between the different species of plants and animals that inhabit these ecosystems. Food webs in freshwater ponds can also be influenced by other factors, such as the amount of sunlight reaching the water, the presence of pollutants, and the introduction of non-native species. For example, the introduction of non-native fish can disrupt the food web by competing with or predating on native species, which can lead to declines in the populations of native species and changes in the overall structure of the food web.

Biomass of Plants and Animals

NUTRIENT CYCLE
Nitrogen Cycle
Phosphorus Cycle

Decomposition

Nutrient recycling in freshwater ponds is the process by which nutrients are taken up by plants and other organisms, used for growth and metabolism, and then returned to the water column in a form that can be reused by other organisms. This cyclical process is an important component of the overall functioning of freshwater pond ecosystems, and helps to maintain the health and productivity of these ecosystems.

In freshwater ponds, primary producers, such as algae and aquatic plants, use sunlight and dissolved nutrients from the water to produce organic matter through photosynthesis. This organic matter is then consumed by herbivores, such as snails and water fleas, which are in turn consumed by carnivores, such as dragonflies and damselflies. As these organisms grow and reproduce, they release nutrients back into the water column in the form of waste products and dead organic matter.

These nutrients can then be taken up again by the primary producers, completing the cycle of nutrient recycling. This cycle is important because it helps to maintain the availability of nutrients in the water, which is critical for the growth and survival of the organisms in the pond.

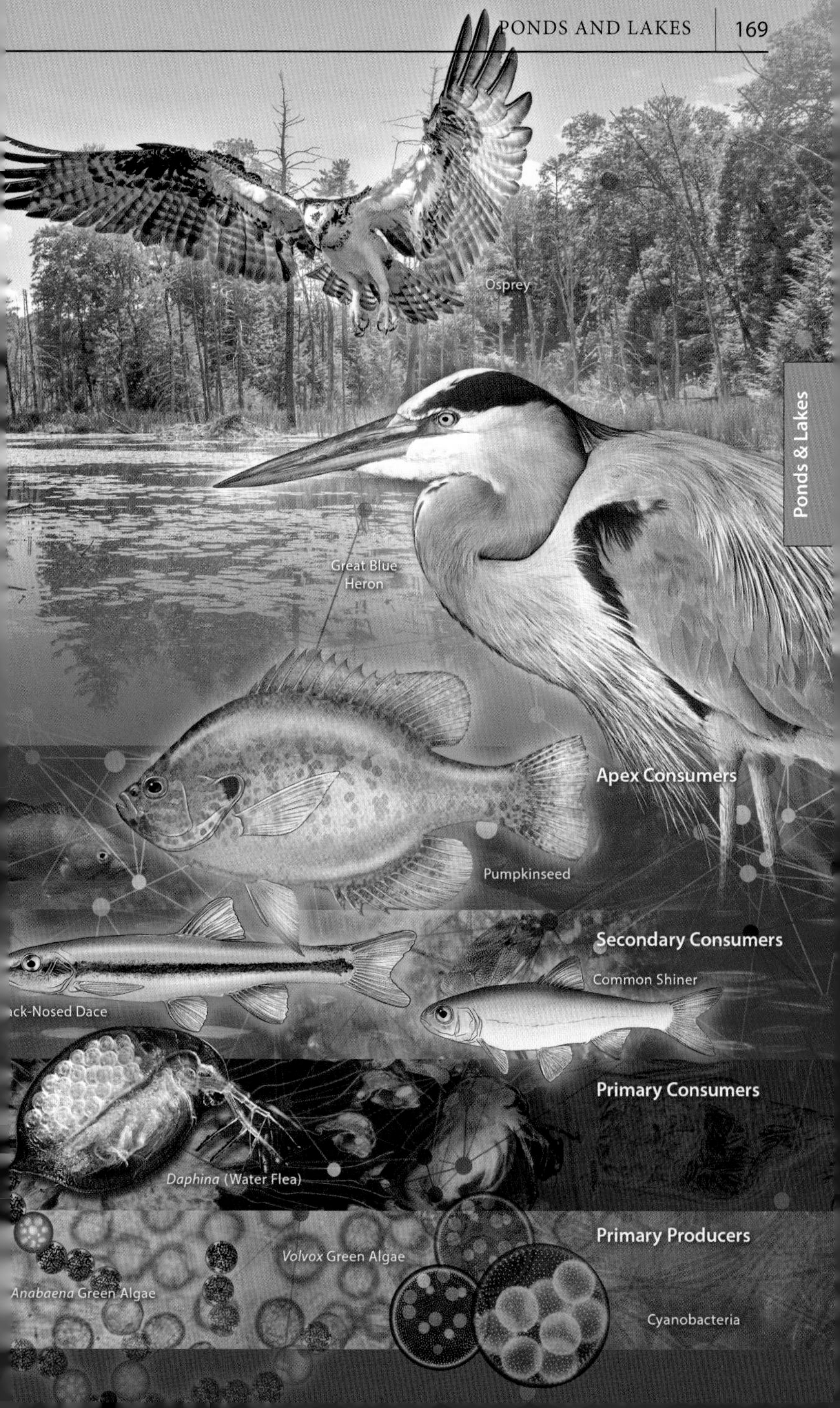

Osprey

Great Blue
Heron

Apex Consumers

Pumpkinseed

Secondary Consumers

Common Shiner

ack-Nosed Dace

Primary Consumers

Daphina (Water Flea)

Primary Producers

Volvox Green Algae

Anabaena Green Algae

Cyanobacteria

break up dead leaves and release their nutrients into the aquatic environment, aided by the chewing activities of small invertebrate primary consumers such as insect larvae, isopods, amphipods, and water fleas (*Daphnia*).

Many pond and stream animals feed directly on biofilms and aquatic algae, and these mostly tiny aquatic animals and insect larvae form the primary consumer elements of food webs. Larger, more easily seen insects, small fish, and tadpoles are secondary consumers. Finally, larger fish such as sunfish or bass, aquatic birds including the Great Blue Heron and the Osprey, and

White Pine

American Beech
Birch species

Idealized cross-section of a lake edge

Black
Gum

Red Maple

Mountain
Laurel

Ferns
Sumacs

Smooth Alder
Arrowwood viburnu

Goldenr
Ragwe

Highbush
Blueberry

Local water table

Dry upland forest

Moist Shore Edge

Wet Me

— Upland Zone —

— Riparian Zone —

mammals such as the Raccoon and North American River Otter form the apex or top level of the pond food web.

Plant zones in ponds and lakes

All New England ponds, lakes, and some river reservoirs behind dams are surrounded by a relatively predictable sequence of aquatic and semiaquatic plants that form distinctive zones. These plant zones often vary in size, mainly depending on the vertical profile of the shorelines. Most mature ponds and lakes have a gently sloping transition between dry forest uplands, the increasingly moist shoreline zone, and the shallow areas that typically lie underwater (see facing page). Some lakes and man-made reservoirs have such steep sides that there is not much of a vegetation zone. Still, in most pond edges, you can see distinct bands of marshy grasses and shrubs, emergent wetland grasses, submerged plants beneath the pond surface, and floating plants such as water lilies in the deeper water.

In smaller ponds, the water may be so shallow that the whole pond is vegetated, even in the deeper areas (see overleaf). This small pond in Connecticut's Machimoodus State Park is typical for central New England because it was created with a low dam, probably as a farm pond, about a century ago. The pond averages only two to four feet deep and receives sunlight for most of the day. Hence, there is a wide variety of emergent vegetation around the open water, and many White and Yellow Water-Lilies are present in the deeper water.

In addition to rich rims of pond edge vegetation, larger ponds (p. 176) usually show an even more

Tussock Sedge
Carex stricta

Common Cattail
Typha latifolia

Arrow Arum
Peltandra virginica

Pickerelweed
Pontederia cordata

Ponds & Lakes

Cattails
Wild Rice
Reedgrass

Arrow
Arum

Pickerelweed

Pond Lilies

Watermilfoil
Elodea
Coontail

Lake surface

Shallow Marsh   Emergent Plants   Submerged Plants   Open Water

Emergent Zone   Littoral Zone

Small Pond Habitat
Machimoodus State Park, East Haddam, CT

BLUEGILL
4–8 in.

PUMPKINSEED
3–6 in.

Yellow
Water Lilies

REDBREAST
SUNFISH
4–6 in.

Giant
Water Bug

Spotted
Turtle

Rusty Crayfish
An invasive species

For component photography credits please see pp. 415–17.

Ponds & Lakes

Belted
Kingfisher

Slaty
Skimmer

Water Strider

Buttonbush

Great
Egrets

Arrow
Arums

Blue Dasher

Bur-Reeds
and other mixed
sedge species

Eastern
Painted Turtle

American
Bullfrog

Bluegills

American Bullfrog
tadpoles

Northern
Watersnake

Common Duckweed
Lemnoideae sp.

**Water Shamrock or
Water Clover**
Marsilea quadrifolia

complex mix of submerged aquatic vegetation and a correspondingly wider variety of aquatic animal life. Coontail (Hornwort), Common *Elodea,* Northern Watermilfoil, and other submerged plants form a complex underwater landscape that offers small aquatic animals food and shelter from predators. Moderate-sized mats of green algae, floating plants such as Duckweed and Water Shamrock, and the leaves of water lilies form an underwater maze where tadpoles, young frogs, small turtles, small fish, and many insect larvae can thrive. The structural complexity of emergent, submerged, and floating vegetation is critical for young aquatic animals, which predators in the open water might otherwise pick off.

Large ponds can also sustain an enormously complex community of animals and plants too small to see with the unaided eye (p. 177, right side). These tiny plants and animals form the base of the pond food web, without which larger, more visible animals such as small fish, predatory insects, frogs, and aquatic birds could not thrive.

In the open water beyond the sheltered edges of large ponds and small lakes, a whole new complex of fish, turtles, birds, and mammals form the upper reaches of the aquatic food web. Powerful swimmers such as Northern Pike, Largemouth Bass, and Walleyes patrol the transition zones between the pond edge and the deep open water. Chain Pickerels often hide among submerged plants, waiting to ambush unwary small

Buffleheads are small diving ducks that are common on both freshwater and saltwater ponds and bays. Buffleheads are powerful underwater swimmers that eat insects and plants in freshwater and crustaceans and mollusks in salt water.

fish, tadpoles, and young ducklings. Larger ponds and lakes offer enough aquatic prey to attract larger predators including American Mink and North American River Otters. Mink and otters are more common than you might think, but both species are wary and secretive and avoid areas that hikers, fishers, and boaters frequent. In spring and fall migrations, many diving duck species, such as the Bufflehead, use larger ponds and lakes to rest and feed.

Wildlife of ponds and small lakes

Ponds and lakes surrounded by natural environments can be quite rich in wildlife. Lake and pond shores are inherently ecotones, boundaries between distinct environments. Natural ecotonal areas usually have abundant wildlife because they share plants and animals from both habitats: forest and lakeshore, for example, or marsh and lakeshore.

Although comprehensive guides to plant and animal groups such as wildflowers, wetland plants, insects,

gallinago_media

American Mink
Neovison vison

Ponds & Lakes

Bufflehead
Bucephala albeola

Pond Aquatic Habitat
Submerged plants and surface vegetation

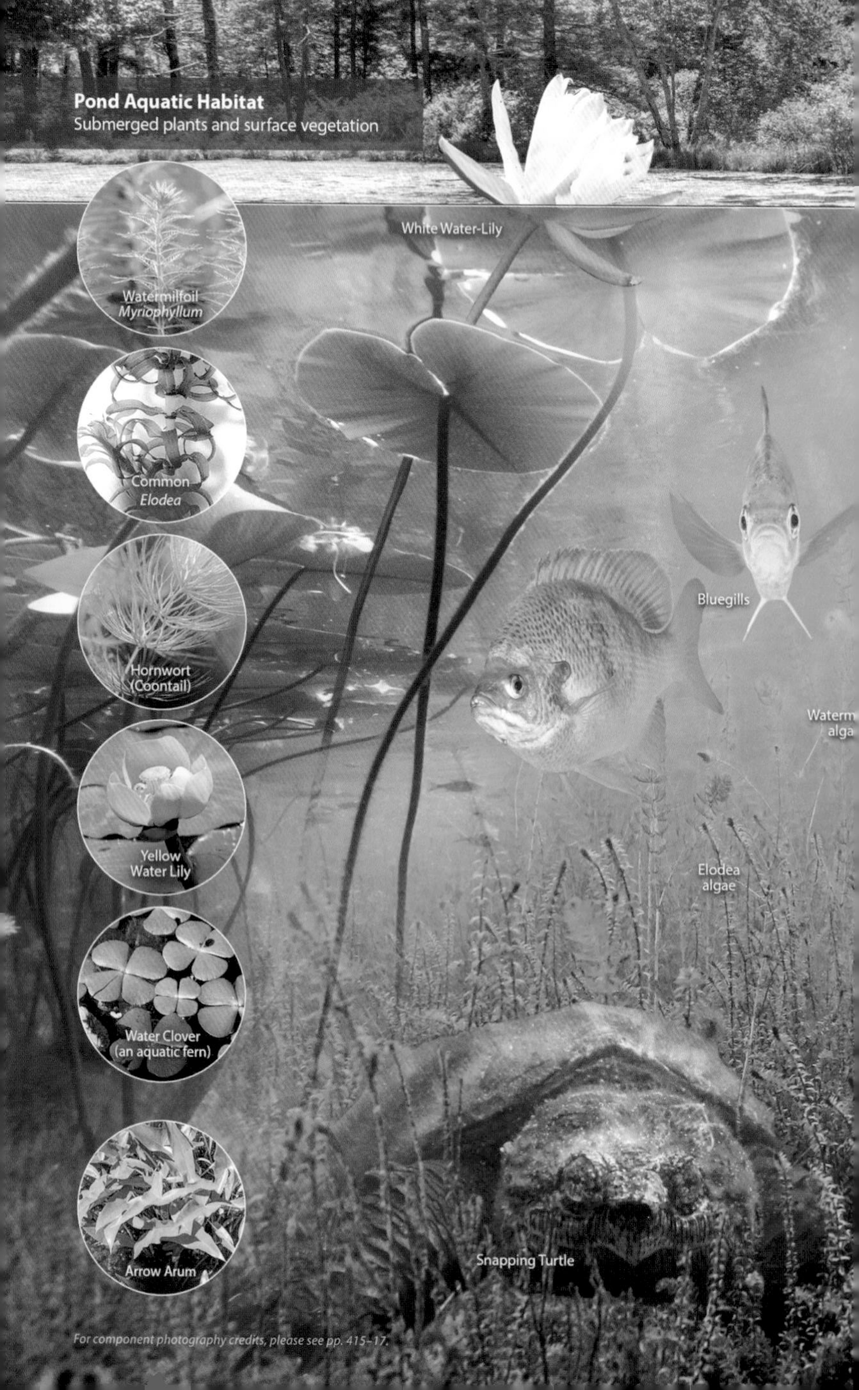
White Water-Lily
Watermilfoil
Myriophyllum
Common
Elodea
Hornwort
(Coontail)
Yellow
Water Lily
Water Clover
(an aquatic fern)
Arrow Arum
Bluegills
Waterm
alga
Elodea
algae
Snapping Turtle

For component photography credits, please see pp. 415–17.

Ponds & Lakes

American Bullfrog

Water Boatman

Giant Water Bug

Bullfrog tadpoles

Pond Surface Algal Mat Species

Algal mats on the pond surface

Spirogyra micro view

Closterium algae micro view

Chlorella algae micro view

Formerly called "blue-green algae"

Cyanobacteria *Gloeotrichia*

Cyanobacteria *Anabaena*

MICROSCOPIC ELEMENTS IN THE POND WATER

CRUSTACEANS

Daphnia

Cyclops

ALGAE

Pediastrum

Spirogyra

Euglena

Volvox

DIATOMS

Closterium

Larger, Deeper Open Water Environments
Large ponds with open water, lakes, and river reservoirs

Bald Eagle

Osprey

Bufflehead

Hooded Merganser

Common Goldeneye

River Otters

Largemouth Bass

Northern Pikes

For component photography credits, please see pp. 415–17.

Ponds & Lakes

Black Crappie

Yellow Perch

Lake Trout

Chain Pickerel

Walleye

other aquatic invertebrates, mammals, and birds are beyond the scope of this general guide, there are recommendations for guides to each group in "Further Reading." Here we'll concentrate on more common and visible pond plants and animals and field techniques to increase your success in viewing wetland animals.

Observing smaller pond wildlife

You should always approach pond or lake edges at a very slow pace, avoiding sudden noises or talking with companions. Often the first indication that you might have moved too quickly is the "plop" sounds of frogs hopping from their pondside perches and splashing into the water. Vertebrates such as fish, frogs, and turtles seem to recognize you as a fellow animal and potential predator, so approach the pond carefully and quietly and scan the area thoroughly before breaking cover and becoming more visible to pond animals. However, large insects such as dragonflies, various water bugs, and butterflies respond only to sudden movement and don't seem to distinguish humans from the rest of the pond environment. If you are still enough for long enough, it's not uncommon to have dragonflies perch on your binoculars or camera.

Chasing active fliers such as butterflies and dragonflies is pointless. Your sudden movements will only drive

Many dragonflies, such as the very common Blue Dasher (*Pachydiplax longipennis*) shown here, are perch hunters and habitually return to favorite prominent branches that give them a good field of view. For closer views or better photographs, watch the overall behavior pattern of pond dragonflies and then move closer to a favorite perch. You'll probably scare away the dragonflies at first, but if you are patient and still, they'll return very quickly.

the animals farther away, and all the thrashing and noise will scare away any other nearby animals. Patient waiting is a much better strategy, as whatever nearby flower or perch attracted the fliers in the first place will certainly attract other dragonflies or butterflies.

Wading out into a pond or lake edge to observe smaller aquatic animals isn't practical for most visitors to wetlands. That traditional kind of observation and collection can disrupt heavily visited park wetland environments. But there are techniques to help bridge that awkward gap between the pond and the shore. Most hikers and avid naturalists are also bird-watchers and own a pair of binoculars. Birds are the most popular form of wildlife because they are both easily visible and diurnal—that is, they are active during daylight hours. But binoculars are also perfect tools to observe many forms of small-to-medium-sized wildlife on the edges of ponds.

Many current roof prism 8 × 42 (or similar) binocular models can focus as close as four to six feet and are perfect for adding dragonfly, butterfly, and aquatic animal observation to your bird-watching routines. If you are buying a pair of binoculars for general use, go to a local birding, wildlife, or photography store and get expert advice. Test a range of models for brightness and viewing comfort, and pay particular attention to the minimum focusing distance of each model.

Large insect observation complements birding, as by midmorning on sunny summer days, most bird species have become less active, but butterflies, damselflies, dragonflies, and bees are just beginning their period of highest activity. Hence, as the midday bird activity fades, you can quickly shift to observing other pond wildlife. Butterflies are attracted to the wide variety of plants along pond edges and wet meadow areas and may also concentrate on exposed wet mud or damp pond banks. Carefully scan any flowers present, particularly for smaller species including skippers and bumblebees. On breezy days, try to favor the downwind shore of the pond, as the wind will carry butterflies and dragonflies across the water and concentrate them on the leeward shore. Many dragonfly species are

Avoid these older, Porro prism designs. While some older Porro models from reputable brands such as Nikon are of good quality, cheaper Porro prism binoculars will be dimmer and less sharp than current roof prism models. Older Porro prism binoculars also rarely focus as close as current designs, a big factor if you are interested in watching butterflies and dragonflies.

The most popular binoculars for wildlife watching are straight-tube roof prism designs. Midpriced or premium-priced roof prism designs offer sharp optics, reasonable brightness, and much better close focusing. However, a cheap roof prism binocular will *not* outperform one of the better Porro prism binoculars.

Cherry Pond, part of the Pondicherry Wildlife Refuge. Pondicherry is a significant part of the Silvio O. Conte National Fish and Wildlife Refuge of protected wildlife habitats all along the Connecticut River. Pondicherry is called "one of the crown jewels" of New Hampshire's landscape and is an important refuge for rare plant environments and wild animals of all kinds. The boreal forests, bogs, fens, swamps, marshes, ponds, and grasslands support a wide variety of bird life. Cherry Pond is critical as a migration way station for many kinds of waterfowl, and the surrounding forests are full of songbird migrants in spring and fall.

perch hunters who habitually return to their favorite twigs or branches near the pond edges. Be patient and still. If you scare a dragonfly away from its perch, it will almost certainly return, sometimes within seconds.

Spring mating season

Early to midspring can be a great time to observe pond life, since many frogs, salamanders, and snakes mate in the spring and are easy to find. For example, the American Toad and the Wood Frog are generally shy creatures that are inactive and hidden during much of the daytime. But in many early spring ponds, mating balls of American Toads are conspicuous throughout the day as multiple males try to mate with single females floating at the pond surface. You'll have to look more closely to spot the very common but more inconspicuous Northern Two-Lined Salamander adults: they are usually submerged as they mate and lay their gelatinous egg masses in vernal pools and streams. Wood Frogs favor the shallower areas of ponds or vernal pools in swampy wetlands and are often easy to spot because they call constantly.

Mating Northern Watersnakes are often easy to find as pairs entwine in the foliage around pond edges. The Northern Watersnake is nonvenomous, but because of its boldly patterned brick-red skin, this snake is sometimes mistaken for the Northern Copperhead. The copperhead is a venomous species that is much rarer and generally lives on rocky upland slopes and

This schedule of frog mating calls gives an approximate time range for each species, but many frog species call only for a few weeks each year. The exact timing for spring calling depends a lot on local weather and geography. The temperature in colder bottomland areas or sheltered valleys may cause frogs to call much later, and in warmer areas the frogs may call much earlier in their "scheduled" time window. It pays big dividends to check your favorite wetlands frequently so that you don't miss a mating event.

Schedule of Frog Calls in Spring and Summer

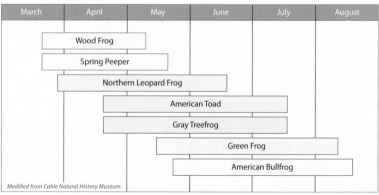

March	April	May	June	July	August
	Wood Frog				
	Spring Peeper				
	Northern Leopard Frog				
		American Toad			
		Gray Treefrog			
			Green Frog		
			American Bullfrog		

Modified from Cable Natural History Museum

Ponds & Lakes

in dry meadows, not along pond edges. The chances of encountering a venomous snake in a central New England wetland are slim. Always respect wild snakes, and never attempt to harm or move them.

Ponds in warm weather

In summer, most frog species are less visually conspicuous, but the very common Green Frogs and Bullfrogs are easy to spot if you are patient and quiet. When you slowly approach the pond edge, use your binoculars to scan the pond's edges, just above where the pond foliage meets the water. Adult frogs like to perch under the overhanging leaves along the pond edge, where they can more easily spot prey and jump into the water to escape predators such as herons. In ponds with water lilies, scan the surface near the lily flowers and leaves for the heads of frogs poking up above the surface. American Bullfrogs frequently bask in the warm surface water of ponds, using water lily leaves as both shelter and hiding places. Common dragonfly species such as the Blue Dasher and the Slaty Skimmer (pp. 208–9) often use floating water lily leaves as perches.

Always carefully scan pond and lake edges for larger birds such as the ubiquitous Great Blue Heron and the bright-white Great Egret (see p. 375). The black-

The Northern Watersnake (*Nerodia sipedon*) is a semi-aquatic snake found in North America, including parts of the northeastern United States, such as New England. It is a common species often encountered near bodies of water, such as rivers, streams, and lakes.

Northern Watersnakes are heavy-bodied snakes that can grow up to 5 feet in length. They have a distinct pattern of large, dark brown or black patches on a lighter brown or gray background.

Northern Watersnakes are generally non-aggressive and usually retreat into the water when they feel threatened. However, they will defend themselves if cornered and can deliver a painful but non-venomous bite.

**EASTERN
SCREECH OWL**
Megascops asio
Red morph

billed Snowy Egret is less common and looks like
a smaller Great Egret. But in freshwater wetlands,
the Black-Crowned Night-Heron is often the most
common if stealthy avian predator. Night-herons are
relatively short-legged; as their name suggests, they are
most active between dusk and dawn. During the day,
night-herons tend to perch on branches above or very
near water, so it is always worthwhile to scan pondside
trees for roosting night-herons. As you move along
lakeshores at dusk, you will sometimes hear the loud
"kwok!" of a night-heron driven off its perch by your
approach.

From the mighty Connecticut River down to the
smallest of our streams and ponds, there's no waterbird
more conspicuous or characteristic than the Belted
Kingfisher (pp. i, 234). The kingfisher's loud, rattling
call usually announces its presence near any water
containing small fish. The Belted Kingfisher's outsized
head and bill make it look larger than it is, as the bird
is only slightly larger than a Blue Jay. Kingfishers are
one of the few bird species that can truly hover in
place, which they do to spot small fish beneath the

pond or stream surface. They then fold their wings and make a headfirst dive into the water, usually emerging with a fish in their beak.

Although you might not think of owls as waterbirds, the Eastern Screech Owl is an aggressive hunter in all freshwater environments. These owls will enter the shallow water of ponds and streams in search of larger insects, frogs, crayfish, and whatever else they can capture. They are more common than most birders realize and are seldom found far from wetlands. If you want to see (or, more likely, hear) your first Eastern Screech Owl, quietly hang out at a favorite pond or stream as dusk turns to true darkness, about half an hour after sunset. The owl's high, wavering call is very distinctive at close range. But when filtered through trees with a breeze blowing, the call is sometimes hard to distinguish from a distant dog howl or a wailing siren. Wetlands also attract larger owls, including the Barred and Great Horned Owls. If you hear them calling, appreciate your good luck but give up on hearing screech owls that night. Barred Owls and Great Horned Owls will readily hunt the much smaller Eastern Screech Owl, and their calls will typically silence the smaller raptor.

Barred Owl
Strix varia

Ponds & Lakes

**BLACK-CROWNED
NIGHT-HERON**
Nycticorax nycticorax

*Brian E Kushner,
pferreira*

Great Horned Owl *(Bubo virginianus)*
The Great Horned Owl is an extremely adaptable predator, found in virtually all environments. Wooded wetlands are especially favored haunts for this owl, but these birds also hunt in marshes and along streams and will even take un-wary waterbirds from ponds and lakes. Even large raptors such as the Red-Tailed Hawk and the Osprey are potential prey, as are all other owl species. Great Horned Owls are one of the most nocturnal owls but can sometimes be spotted while roosting during the day, usually in trees with dense foliage, such as in larger Eastern White Pines. On nights well after sunset in winter you'll often hear Great Horned Owls calling, because these birds define their mat-ing territories and even lay their eggs in the dead of winter.

FRESHWATER GUIDES

For practicality and portability, a survey guidebook such as this one can't cover all of the thousands of plant and animal species in New England wetlands. For deeper dives into particular groups, including wildflowers, butterflies, and birds, see "Further Reading." The following pages present commonly found flora and fauna.

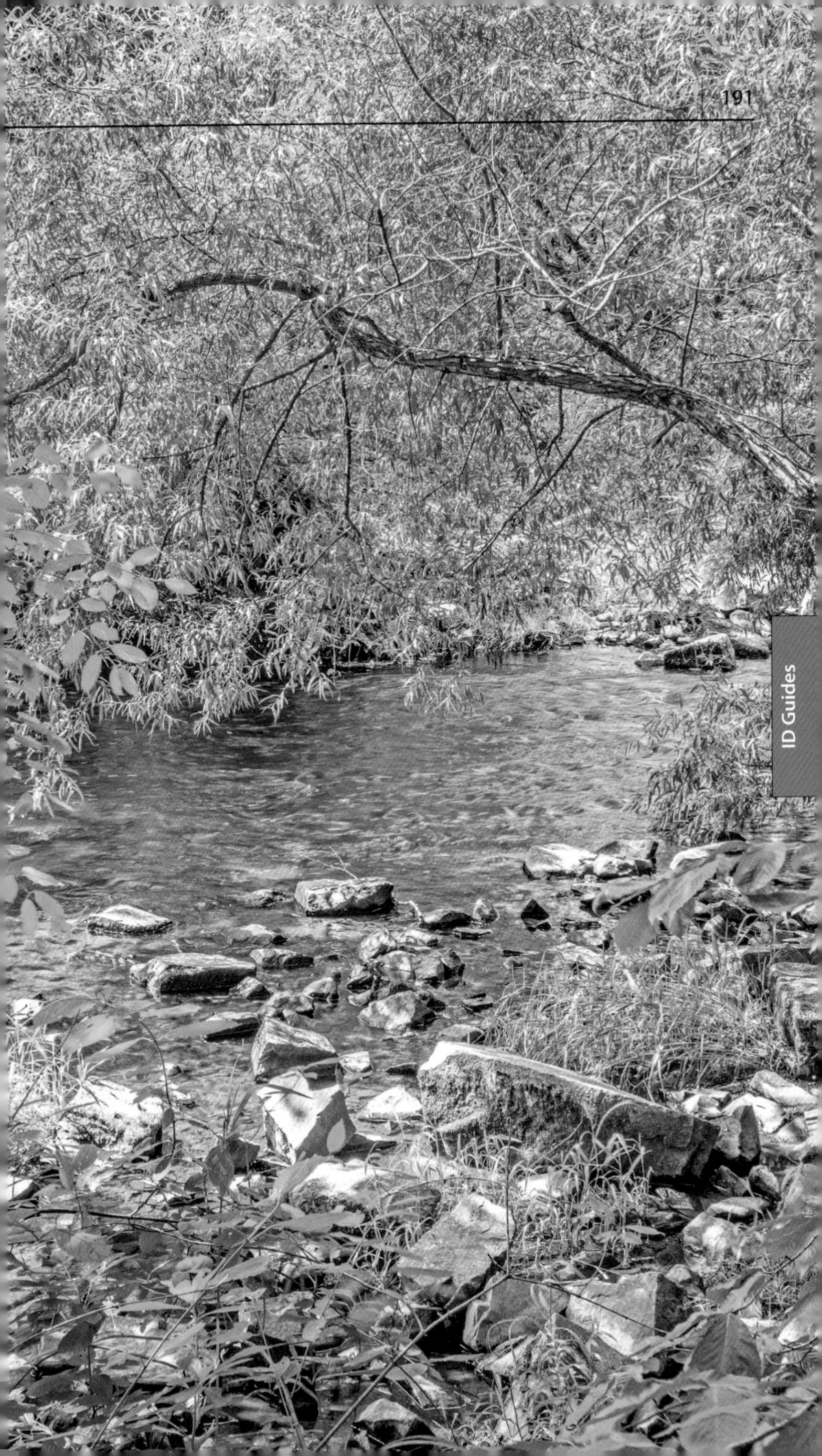

See p. 334 on the unique and unusual flora of bogs.

SKUNK CABBAGE *Symplocarpus foetidus*

PICKERELWEED *Pontederia cordata*

ARROWHEAD *Sagittaria latifolia*

ARROW ARUM *Peltandra virginica*

COMMON CATTAIL *Typha latifolia*

NARROW-LEAVED CATTAIL *Typha angustifol*

See p. 304 on the freshwater marshes. See p. 394 for information on brackish marsh species.

SOCK SEDGE *Carex stricta*

nickkurzenko

AMERICAN BUR-REED *Sparganium americanum*

OLGRASS *Scirpus cyperinus*

UMBRELLA SEDGE *Cyperus alternifolius*

MMON REED *Phragmites australis*

NORTHERN WILD RICE *Zizania palustris*

Wetland Plants

Many of these species are not strictly wetland plants but commonly occur near and on the edges of wetlands.

BLOODROOT *Sanguinaria canadensis*

OXEYE DAISY *Leucanthemum vulgare*

BONESET *Eupatorium perfoliatum*

JACK-IN-THE-PULPIT *Arisaema triphyllum*

TROUT LILY *Erythronium americanum*

BLUET *Houstonia caerulea*

MON BLUE VIOLET *Viola sororia*

RED TRILLIUM *Trillium erectum*

Hamiza Bakirci

NTED TRILLIUM *Trillium undulatum*

EASTERN RED COLUMBINE *Aquilegia canadensis*

RSH MARIGOLD *Caltha palustris*

BUTTERCUP *Ranunculus bulbosus*

Wildflowers

Many of these species are not strictly wetland plants but commonly occur near and on the edges of wetlands.

JOE-PYE WEED *Eutrochium purpureum*

nickkurzenko
CARDINAL FLOWER *Lobelia cardinalis*

PURPLE LOOSESTRIFE *Lythrum salicaria*

HARLEQUIN BLUE FLAG IRIS *Iris versicolor*

YELLOW IRIS *Iris pseudacorus*

BUR-MARIGOLD *Bidens cernua*

KERELWEED (flower) *Pontederia cordata*

ARROWHEAD (flower) *Sagittaria latifolia*

DENROD *Solidago spp.*

JEWELWEED *Impatiens capensis*

OW WATER-LILY *Nuphar lutea*

WHITE WATER-LILY *Nymphaea alba*

Wildflowers

Many of these species are not strictly wetland plants but commonly occur near and on the edges of wetlands.

SWAMP MILKWEED *Asclepias incarnata*

COMMON MILKWEED *Asclepias syriaca*

BUTTERFLY WEED *Asclepias tuberosa*

ORANGE HAWKWEED *Hieracium aurantiacu*

skymoon13

RAGGED ROBIN *Silene flos-cuculi*

lmladus

FIREWEED *Chamaenerion angustifolium*

andreusK

GERANIUM *Geranium maculatum*

DAME'S ROCKET *Hesperis matronalis*

MP ROSE *Rosa palustris*

DEPTFORD PINK *Dianthus armeria*

OHN'S WORT *Hypericum perforatum*

NEW ENGLAND ASTER *Symphyotrichum novae-angliae*

Wildflowers

COONTAIL *Ceratophyllum demersum*

WATERWEED (ELODEA) *Elodea sp.*

WATERMILFOIL *Myriophyllum sp.*

SURFACE MAT OF SPIROGYRA *Spirogyra sp.*

COMMON DUCKWEED *Lemna minor*

WATER CLOVER *Marsilea quadrifolia*

Many of these species are not strictly wetland plants but also occur near and on the edges of wetlands.

SITIVE FERN *Onoclea sensibilis*

OSTRICH FERN *Matteuccia struthiopteris*

NAMON FERN *Osmundastrum cinnamomeum*

ROYAL FERN *Osmunda regalis*

RSH FERN *Thelypteris palustris*

LADY FERN *Athyrium filix-femina*

Aquatic plants, ferns

See p. 318 for more on shrub swamps.

BUTTONBUSH *Cephalanthus occidentalis*

There are three very similar Alder species.
SMOOTH ALDER *Alnus serrulata*

HIGHBUSH BLUEBERRY *Vaccinium corymbosum*

BLACK WILLOW *Salix nigra*

POISON IVY *Toxicodendron radicans*

Note the red branches. Uncommon, but worth kno
POISON SUMAC *Toxicodendron vernix*

UNTAIN LAUREL *Kalmia latifolia*

NORTHERN SPICEBUSH *Lindera benzoin*

OOTH SUMAC *Rhus glabra*

STAGHORN SUMAC *Rhus typhina*

Hause

-OSIER DOGWOOD *Cornus sericea*

SWEET PEPPERBUSH *Clethra alnifolia*

Shrubs

See p. 320 for more on wooded swamps and vernal pools.

EASTERN COTTONWOOD *Populus deltoides*

RED MAPLE *Acer rubrum*

BLACK TUPELO *Nyssa sylvatica*

QUAKING ASPEN *Populus tremuloides*

PAPER BIRCH *Betula papyrifera*

YELLOW BIRCH *Betula alleghaniensis*

dictus

AMERICAN HORNBEAM *Carpinus caroliniana*

Diana Samson

BLACK ASH *Fraxinus nigra*

PUSSY WILLOW *Salix discolor*

Batya

AMERICAN SYCAMORE *Platanus occidentalis*

andı Kisel

SILVER MAPLE *Acer saccharinum*

Anghi

BOXELDER MAPLE *Acer negundo*

Trees

Note: Small invertebrates often require professional expertise to identify to the species level.

janmiko

WATER STRIDER *Gerridae family*

Olvita

WHIRLIGIG BEETLE *Gyrinidae family*

float

BACKSWIMMER *Notonectidae family*

GRFischer

WATER BOATMAN *Corixidae family*

evergenesis

GIANT WATER BUG *Lethocerus americanus*

phototrip

DIVING BEETLE *Dytiscidae family*

ND LEECH *Hirudinea family*

Michael

FISHING SPIDER *Dolomedes sp.*

AYFISH *Various families, about nine species*

Vitalii Hulai

DRAGONFLY LARVA *Order Odonata*

tography

JSSEL *Mytilidae family, about a dozen species*

gardzam

MAYFLY *Order Ephemeroptera, many species*

Small animals

WANDERING GLIDER
Pantala flavescens

COMMON WHITETAIL
Plathemis lydia

TWELVE-SPOTTED SKIMMER
Libellula pulchella

HALLOWEEN PENNANT
Celithemis eponina

RUBY MEADOWHAWK
Sympetrum rubicundulum

WIDOW SKIMMER
Libellula luctuosa

All species are shown to scale

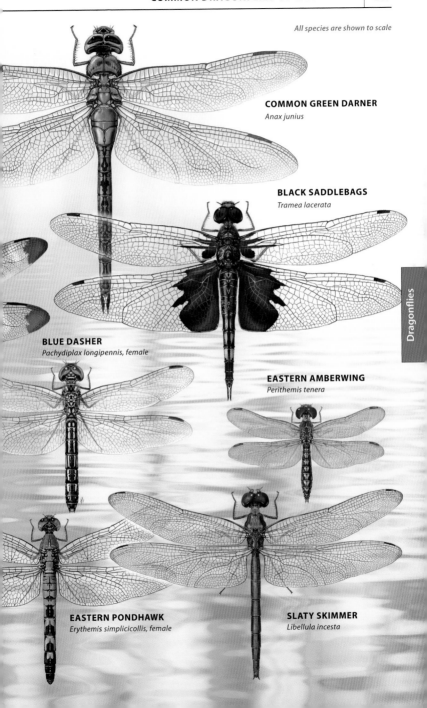

COMMON GREEN DARNER
Anax junius

BLACK SADDLEBAGS
Tramea lacerata

BLUE DASHER
Pachydiplax longipennis, female

EASTERN AMBERWING
Perithemis tenera

EASTERN PONDHAWK
Erythemis simplicicollis, female

SLATY SKIMMER
Libellula incesta

Dragonflies

J. Stone

EBONY JEWELWING *Calopteryx maculata*

Samuel

FAMILIAR BLUET *Enallagma civile*

phototrip

NORTHERN SPREADWING *Lestes disjunctus*

Ray Akey

EASTERN FORKTAIL *Ischnura verticalis*

fabiosa_93

EASTERN RED DAMSEL *Amphiagrion saucium*

rbkelle

RIVER JEWELWING *Calopteryx aequabilis*

ER-SPOTTED SKIPPER *Epargyreus clarus*

PECK'S SKIPPER *Polites peckius*

G DASH SKIPPER *Polites mystic*

TAWNY-EDGED SKIPPER *Polites themistocles*

AD-WINGED SKIPPER *Poanes viator*

V A moth that immitates skippers and bumblebees
SNOWBERRY CLEARWING *Hemaris diffinis*

Damsels, skippers

All species are shown to scale

MOURNING CLOAK
Nymphalis antiopa

RED ADMIRAL
Vanessa atalanta

QUESTION MARK
Polygonia interrogationis

RED-SPOTTED PURPLE
Limenitis arthemis

**EASTERN
TIGER SWALLOWTAIL**
Papilio glaucus

**SPICEBUSH
SWALLOWTAIL**
Papilio troilus

**BLACK
SWALLOWTAIL**
Papilio polyxenes

Butterflies

All species are shown to scale

COMMON WOOD NYMPH
Cercyonis pegala

PAINTED LADY
Vanessa cardui

COMMON BUCKEYE
Junonia coenia

NORTHERN PEARLY-EYE
Enodia anthedon

CLOUDED SULPHUR
Colias philodice

Butterflies

GREAT SPANGLED FRITILLARY
Speyeria cybele

VICEROY
Limenitis archippus

MONARCH
Danaus plexippus

Beth Baisch

ACADIAN HAIRSTREAK *Satyrium acadica*

Mark

BANDED HAIRSTREAK *Satyrium calanus*

Brian Lasenby

CORAL HAIRSTREAK *Satyrium titus*

Annette Shaff

GRAY HAIRSTREAK *Strymon melinus*

Paul Sparks

JUNIPER HAIRSTREAK *Callophrys gryneus*

Randy Anderson

EASTERN TAILED-BLUE *Cupido comyntas*

LE WOOD-SATYR *Megisto cymela*

CABBAGE WHITE *Pieris rapae*

RL CRESCENT *Phyciodes tharos*

COMMON RINGLET *Coenonympha tullia*

RICAN COPPER *Lycaena phlaeas*

CLOUDED SULPHUR *Colias philodice*

Butterflies

"Insects are the little things that run the world."— E. O. Wilson

COMMON EASTERN BUMBLE BEE *Bombus impatiens*

EASTERN CARPENTER BEE *Xylocopa virgin*

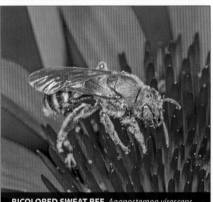

BICOLORED SWEAT BEE *Agapostemon virescens*

HONEY BEE *Apis mellifera*

COMMON LONG-HORNED BEE *Melisodes communis*

FURROW BEE *Halictus sp.*

...er flies imitate the look and behavior of bees.

...GINED CALLIGRAPHER FLY *Toxomerus marginatus*

Want more butterflies in your garden? Plant Joe-Pye Weed.

TIGER SWALLOWTAIL ON JOE-PYE WEED

...NGHORN BEETLE *Leptura quadrifasciata*

Spiders are Arachnids, not insects.

BRILLIANT JUMPING SPIDER *Phidippus sp.*

Insects

...AT GOLDEN SAND DIGGER *Sphex ichneumoneus*

TWELVE-SPOTTED SKIMMER *Libellula pulchella*

FLIES AND MOSQUITOS THAT BITE AROUND PONDS AND STREAMS

Flies shown 3x life size for clarity

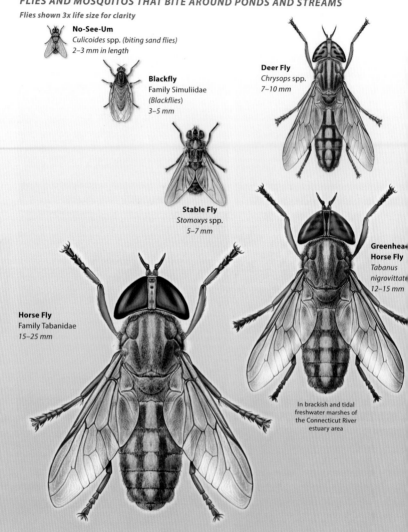

No-See-Um
Culicoides spp. *(biting sand flies)*
2–3 mm in length

Blackfly
Family Simuliidae
(Blackflies)
3–5 mm

Deer Fly
Chrysops spp.
7–10 mm

Stable Fly
Stomoxys spp.
5–7 mm

Greenhead Horse Fly
Tabanus nigrovittate
12–15 mm

Horse Fly
Family Tabanidae
15–25 mm

In brackish and tidal
freshwater marshes of
the Connecticut River
estuary area

COMMON MOSQUITOS *Shown 4x life size for clarity*

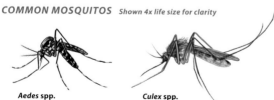

Aedes spp.   *Culex* spp.   *Anopheles* spp.

hie Photo

CKLEGGED TICK *Ixodes scapularis*

Melinda Fawver

AMERICAN DOG TICK *Dermacentor variabilis*

OWN DOG TICK *Rhipicephalus sanguineus*

ondreicka

LONE STAR TICK *Amblyomma americanum*

Hazards

ISON IVY *Toxicodendron radicans*

Usually deep within wetlands. Note the red leaf stems and branches

POISON SUMAC *Toxicodendron vernix*

PUMPKINSEED
Lepomis gibbosus
3–6 in.

BLUEGILL
Lepomis macrochirus
4–8 in.

REDBREAST SUNFISH
Lepomis auritus
4–6 in.

BLACK CRAPPIE
Pomoxis nigromaculatus
6–11 in.

ROCK BASS
Ambloplites rupestris
5–7 in.

WHITE CRAPPIE
Pomoxis annularis
6–11 in.

YELLOW PERCH
Perca flavescens
6–11 in.

SMALLMOUTH BASS
Micropterus dolomieu
6–16 in.

Pond fish

WALLEYE
Sander vitreus
10–20 in.

NORTHERN PIKE
Esox lucius
18–30 in.

WHITE SUCKER
Catostomus commersonii
6–18 in.

REDFIN PICKEREL
Esox americanus americanus
5–9 in.

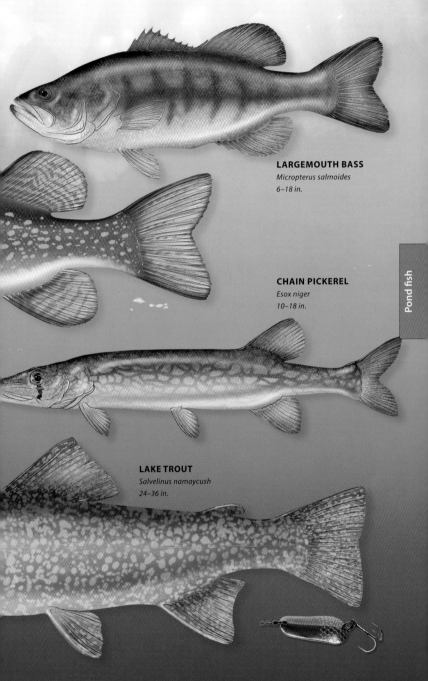

LARGEMOUTH BASS
Micropterus salmoides
6–18 in.

CHAIN PICKEREL
Esox niger
10–18 in.

LAKE TROUT
Salvelinus namaycush
24–36 in.

Pond fish

COMMON FISH OF STREAMS AND SMALLER RIVERS

TESSELLATED DARTER
Etheostoma olmstedi
1–3 in.

ALEWIFE
Alosa pseudoharengus
9–11 in., migratory

Landlocked
Alewives
3–6 in.

BLACKNOSE DACE
Rhinichthys atratulus
1–3 in.

RAINBOW TROUT
Oncorhynchus mykiss
8–16 in.

SMALLMOUTH BASS
Micropterus dolomieu
6–16 in.

COMMON SHINER
Luxilus cornutus
2–5 in.

GOLDEN SHINER
Notemigonus crysoleucas
3–9 in.

BROOK TROUT
Salvelinus fontinalis
6–10 in.

BROWN TROUT
Salmo trutta
6–10 in.

AMERICAN SHAD
Alosa sapidissima
15–24 in.

Stream fish

Frogs and Toads of New England
Species photos courtesy of Twan Leenders

American Toad
Anaxyrus americanus

Fowler's Toad
Anaxyrus fowleri

American Toad mating cluster
Two mating toads in amplexus are surrounded by other males competing to mate. Note the speckled linear toad egg masses below the group.

Male

Male

Male

Female

Linear egg masses below the toads

Toad photo by Pat L

Wood Frog egg mass close-up

Wood Frog tadpole
Rana sylvatica (Not to scale with the adult frogs.)

COMMON FROG SPECIES

Spring Peeper
Pseudacris crucifer

Pickerel Frog
Lithobates palustris

Gray Treefrog
Hyla versicolor

Northern Leopard Frog
Lithobates pipiens

Wood Frog
Lithobates sylvaticus

Species are shown approximately to scale

Bullfrog
Lithobates catesbeianus
Female–Note the white throat; males usually have bright yellow throats

Green Frog
Lithobates clamitans

Frogs

Species photos courtesy of Twan Leenders.

COMMON SALAMANDER SPECIES

Salamanders of New England
Species photos courtesy of Twan Leenders

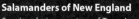

Northern Two-Lined Salamander
Eurycea bislineata 3–4.5 inches long

Female   Male

Red-Spotted Newt, adult forms
Notophthalmus viridescens 3–5 in. lc

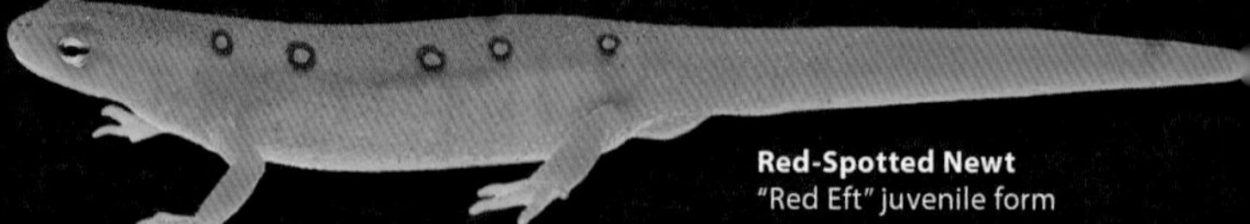

Red-Spotted Newt
"Red Eft" juvenile form

Mudpuppy
Necturus maculosus
8–17 in. long

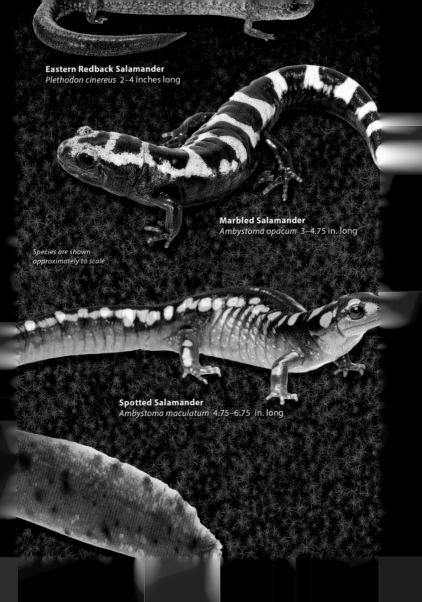

Eastern Redback Salamander
Plethodon cinereus 2–4 inches long

Marbled Salamander
Ambystoma opacum 3–4.75 in. long

*Species are shown
approximately to scale*

Spotted Salamander
Ambystoma maculatum 4.75–6.75 in. long

Common Mask Turtle
Sternotherus odoratus 3–5 inches long

*Species are shown
approximately to s*

Spotted Turtle
Clemmys guttata 4–5 in. long

Eastern Box Turtle
Terrapene carolina 4.5–6.5 in. l

Turtle photos are from the forthcoming book by Twan Leenders,
Title of the Book Goes Right Here, Publisher Info.

Northern Diamondback Terrapin
Malaclemys terrapin
6–9 in. long (females)

Northern Diamondba
Terrapins live in the s
and brackish marshes
the southern-most ar
of the Connecticut Ri
near Long Island Sour

Eastern Painted Turtle
Chrysemys picta
4.5–6 inches long

Red-eared Slider
Trachemys scripta
6–8 in. long

The Red-eared Slider is an invasive, non-native species. Sliders that escaped from the pet trade now breed in Connecticut and Massachusetts.

Wood Turtle
Glyptemys insculpta
6–9 in. long

Common Snapping Turtle
Chelydra serpentina 10–16 in. long

See pp. 374–376 for more on herons and pp. 380–382 for more on the Osprey.

BELTED KINGFISHER *Megaceryle alcyon*

BLACK-CROWNED NIGHT-HERON *Nycticorax ny*

AMERICAN BITTERN *Botaurus lentiginosus*

GREAT BLUE HERON *Ardea herodias*

GREEN HERON *Butorides virescens*

GREAT EGRET *Ardea alba*

MON LOON *Gavia immer*

PIED-BILLED GREBE *Podilymbus podiceps*

BLE-CRESTED CORMORANT *Phalacrocorax auritus*

OSPREY *Pandion haliaetus*

Birds

-TAILED HAWK *Buteo jamaicensis*

RED-SHOULDERED HAWK *Buteo lineatus*

OSPREY *Pandion haliaetus*

BALD EAGLE *Haliaeetus leucocephalus*

TURKEY VULTURE *Cathartes aura*

South of Massachusetts; range extends north every

BLACK VULTURE *Coragyps atratus*

Jeffrey

GREAT BLUE HERON *Ardea herodias*

Fritz

NORTHERN HARRIER *Circus hudsonius*

D TURKEY *Meleagris gallopavo*

BARRED OWL *Strix varia*

DEER *Charadrius vociferus*

GREATER YELLOWLEGS *Tringa melanoleuca*

Birds

SON'S SNIPE *Gallinago delicata*

WOODCOCK *Scolopax minor*

CANADA GOOSE *Branta canadensis*

MALLARD *Anas platyrhynchos*

NORTHERN PINTAIL *Anas acuta*

BLUE-WINGED TEAL *Anas discors*

GREEN-WINGED TEAL *Anas carolinensis*

WOOD DUCK *Aix sponsa*

FLEHEAD *Bucephala albeola*

SORA *Porzana carolina*

INIA RAIL *Rallus limicola*

AMERICAN COOT *Fulica americana*

DED MERGANSER *Lophodytes cucullatus*

COMMON MERGANSER *Mergus merganser*

Birds

BGSmith

RED-WINGED BLACKBIRD *Agelaius phoeniceus*

Dollar Photo Club

YELLOW WARBLER *Setophaga petechia*

Robin Ladouceur

COMMON YELLOWTHROAT *Geothlypis trichas*

Dollar Photo Club

SONG SPARROW *Melospiza melodia*

Alex Papp

NORTHERN WATERTHRUSH *Parkesia noveboracensis*

Chase D'Animulis

SWAMP SPARROW *Melospiza georgiana*

SH WREN *Cistothorus palustris*

CAROLINA WREN *Thryothorus ludovicianus*

E-THROATED SPARROW *Zonotrichia albicollis*

COMMON GRACKLE *Quiscalus quiscula*

RICAN GOLDFINCH *Spinus tristis*

AMERICAN TREE SPARROW *Spizelloides arborea*

Birds

Dollar Photo Club

EASTERN COTTONTAIL *Sylvilagus floridanus*

serhio272

AMERICAN MINK *Neovison vison*

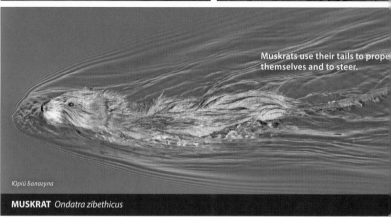

Muskrats use their tails to propel themselves and to steer.

Юрій Балагула

MUSKRAT *Ondatra zibethicus*

Beavers use their tails to steer and their webbed hind paws to propel themselves.

Christian Musat

NORTH AMERICAN BEAVER *Castor canadensis*

Connecticut and north.

TH AMERICAN PORCUPINE *Erethizon dorsatum*

Increasingly common in all areas.

AMERICAN BLACK BEAR *Ursus americanus*

Mammals

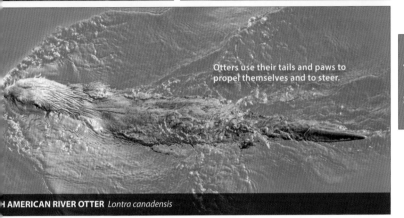

Otters use their tails and paws to propel themselves and to steer.

H AMERICAN RIVER OTTER *Lontra canadensis*

Raccoons use their paws to propel themselves and to steer. Raccoons do not use their tails to swim or steer.

graphy

ON *Procyon lotor*

The Mill River, in Sleeping Giant State Park, Hamden, Connecticut.

RIVERS AND STREAMS

The physical dynamism of streams and rivers makes them some of our most complex and interesting environments. Streams can change from a trickle across the landscape into a broad flood in mere hours, a unique transformation in freshwater environments.

*Riparian refers to plants or environments near or directly on the banks of a stream or river.

Rivers are the product of their local landscapes but also profoundly influence the lands around them. Geology determines the supply of sediments and nutrient chemicals, and the nearby topography governs the stream's gradient. Climate and soils determine the surrounding riparian* vegetation, and thus the amount of light that hits the stream and the character and amounts of plant matter that enter the stream. Although ecologists see broad characteristics that most New England streams have in common, each stream you visit will also be a unique expression of the local topography, geology, and surrounding riparian communities.

Diversity in the physical character of streams and rivers supports biological diversity. Although rivers cover less than 1 percent of the earth's surface, rivers and streams across the globe are home to more than 13,000 species of fish. By comparison, oceans cover 70 percent of the earth's surface and contain 16,000 marine fish species. Streams are narrow, winding ribbons of

Rivers & Streams

Photo courtesy of Robin Ladouceur

habitat. Though two streams may be only a mile apart, each could harbor a unique mix of species, particularly when separated by the hilly landscapes familiar across central New England. That very diversity can also make life in rivers and streams vulnerable: rivers contain more varieties of threatened or endangered wildlife than any other environment.

Healthy rivers consume and process vast amounts of minerals and plant remains from the ecosystems surrounding them and help sustain healthy estuaries and coastal waters. Unhealthy and polluted rivers do the opposite and distribute the destructive effects of excess nutrients and chemical pollution throughout the surrounding landscape.

Defining flowing waterways
There are no complex technical differences among rivers, streams, brooks, and creeks. The term "river" tends to be reserved for the largest bodies of flowing water, such as the Connecticut, Farmington, Deerfield, and White Rivers. Definitions are roughly guided by size, with creeks and brooks being the smallest flowing waters; many of these are seasonal and often disappear into dry washes in late summer. A stream is an intermediate-sized flowing body of water. The standing assumption in New England is that a stream flows all year and doesn't disappear seasonally. Ephemeral or intermittent brooks and creeks run only after larger rain events or during wet seasons such as spring and fall. Perennial streams run year-round. An underground source such as a spring or artesian flow from a hillside often supplies perennial streams.

Hydrology
A river's watershed comprises all the surrounding upland environments that contribute water to a particular river. Rivers and streams in the Northeast average one cubic foot per second of flow for every square mile of watershed area, so the amount of area a river draws from is directly related to its size and flow rate.

The primary factor in determining the character of a stream is the gradient or change in elevation along its course. Steep slopes in rocky or mountainous areas form small, active streams that are often cool, with

The east bank of the Connecticut River at Hadley, Massachusetts, near Mitch's Island.
The river here is high on its banks after recent autumn rains.

highly oxygenated water. Such streams are usually cool not just because of elevation but also because they typically flow through forests that allow little light to reach the streambed. Streams often meander in flatter landscapes, with sunwarmed waters containing less dissolved oxygen because of the higher temperatures. Streams usually start along steep gradients in rocky highland areas but eventually join larger streams and rivers in flatter valley areas. Water movement in streams can be deceptive: the overall flow speed in smaller, rocky upland streams is often just a fraction of the flow speed in streams that run over flatter ground. All the bubbling and splashing of mountain streams slow down the stream's overall speed and flow volume, even though the water surface can look very active.

The cool, highly oxygenated waters of headwater streams are ideal for many kinds of stream fish, including Rainbow Trout (*Oncorhynchus mykiss*).

The headwaters of streams form a distinct microclimate, with trees on the steep valley walls that shade the river forming a cool, moist tunnel where little sunlight reaches the riverbed. Oxygen levels in upland streams are typically high, as the many riffles and small rapids churn the flowing water. Vegetation in these steep, cool stream cuts and shaded watery ravines often has a more northern character than the local forests, featuring such species as Striped Maple, Eastern Hemlock, and Yellow Birch that are more characteristic of northern forests. Many fern species thrive in the low light and high humidity of hillside stream banks.

In general, fast-flowing stream banks have less acidic soil because the highly oxygenated water prevents the buildup of acidic plant debris by encouraging rapid decomposition. Slower streams moving through wet floodplains or shrub swamps typically have more acidic waters. On sandy or fine gravel stream banks, you may see acid-loving plants such as sundews or azaleas, indicating a moist, acidic soil.

Older streams have had time to widen and deepen their valleys. The pitch becomes less steep, the valley floor and stream banks grow wider, and the rate of stream bank erosion lessens to at least a temporary equilibrium with the flowing water. No balance in nature lasts, and erosion in stream banks is often worst in storms that flood the stream valley with large volumes of fast-flowing water. Dry weather slows the stream and lowers the water level. Larger rainstorms may bring the stream over its regular banks, eroding the banks but also depositing new sand and sediment on the floodplains of the stream area. Most people visit streams in mild weather, so the winter source of much stream bank erosion may be invisible to you. River ice and the movement of large ice chunks in the spring thaw can leave deep gouges in riverbanks.

Flowing water is powerful: a mere doubling of the stream flow velocity can create a 64-fold increase in

When is a river not a river?
The famous Oxbow Lake of Northhampton, Massachusetts, began life as a near-circular bend in the main stem of the Connecticut River. In 1840, during a flood, the river broke through the narrow neck of the bend and isolated The Oxbow as a lake. Today, The Oxbow retains a narrow connection to the river.

Rivers & Streams

The young, shallow, rapid-filled Connecticut River at Pittsburg, New Hampshire.

the kinetic power of a stream. A stream flowing one mile per hour can move small sand and silt particles. The same stream flowing at 11 miles per hour can roll over boulders weighing thousands of pounds. Thus even small, placid-looking streams can sometimes rage with flash floods that destroy bridges and houses and move three-foot glacial boulders hundreds of feet downstream.

The Connecticut River has many characters in its 406-mile journey to Long Island Sound. From its origin in the Fourth Connecticut Lake in northern New Hampshire, the young Connecticut River drops almost 400 feet in its first few miles. In its northern reaches, the Connecticut looks like a geologically young river, running over shallow rapids through steep and rocky valleys. In the stretch between central Vermont and New Hampshire, the river has a mixed character, with stretches of young-looking rocky river rapids alternating with more expansive valleys that show the terraces formed by various depths of the ancient Glacial Lake Hitchcock. As the Connecticut flows south of New Hampshire, it enters New England's broad, flat Central Valley. The river flows across the flat and broad ancient lake bed of Glacial Lake Hitchcock, giving the river the aged, meandering look of southern rivers that never saw the disruption of glaciation and the ice ages. As the Connecticut River exits the Central Valley near Middletown, Connecticut, it reacquires the look of a much younger river as it flows through narrow bedrock straits. High rock walls line the Connecticut River estuary between Middletown and Deep River, but then the Connecticut River finally enters Long Island Sound as a broad estuary lined with rich brackish marshes.

Stream substrates

Streams that run over granite or other tough rocks have cold, clear, highly oxygenated waters that derive few nutrients from the rocky substrate. Streams that run over softer limestone or sandstone have less clear water but pick up many kinds of nutrients from the rocks and sand of the streambed. Streams that run through the broad river meadows of New England's Central Valley pick up a lot of sediment and nutrients from the soils around them. These bottomland streams often have warmer, murkier waters than rocky high-land streams, but the cloudier water often supports a more extensive and diverse community of plants and animals.

The size and nature of the rocks, gravel, and sand on the stream bottom determine the kinds of animals that can live in flowing water. Streams with many boulders and stone cobbles are often rich with invertebrate animal life because smaller creatures find shelter and food in the many spaces among the bottom rocks. As water flows around and through rocky obstacles in upland streams, the water becomes more oxygenated and able to support all forms of aquatic life. In shallow streams, larger rocks and cobbles become important substrates for algae, diatoms, and plants on the sunny tops of the rocks and protective shelter for many kinds of insect larvae in the dark spaces near the bottom. Riffle areas usually have the most exposed large rocks because the active water sweeps away smaller sand and silt particles.

Riffles and rocks play a vital role in oxygenating stream waters. As the shallow water churns over riffles, it mixes with oxygen in the air, and this increases the level of dissolved oxygen in the water.

Groundwater is a major reservoir for regional water and helps feed both streams and ponds. Once rainwater and meltwater enter the cracks and crevices of bedrock below ground, it may take decades for the water to reemerge on the surface.

Groundwater movement

Soils and rock rubble first absorb the meltwater and rainwater that falls within a river watershed. Under gravity, this groundwater eventually flows downward in the landscape until it encounters a river or pond, where it becomes visible on the surface. Sediments and soils can be quite absorbent, even when they look solid. For example, about 40 percent of the space in a jar of sand is air, and there is plenty of room in most soils for significant amounts of water to be absorbed and flow under the influence of gravity. The point where all available space within local soils is full of water is called the water table. Seasonal changes in precipitation and meltwater will cause variations in the depth of the water table, and the water table generally follows the contours of the local landscape. Water tables tend to be deeper in upland hill areas but much closer to the surface in valleys or near surface ponds or streams. You can estimate the level of the local water table just by looking at the edge of a pond or stream nearby. By definition, the water table level is where a stream is visible on the ground surface or where the pond's edge meets the higher ground surrounding the pond.

Gaining and losing streams

The water table level near a stream can profoundly affect the flow volume and seasonality of the stream (see the opposite illustration). Where the water table is typically above or at the stream's level, these "gaining streams" will flow all year, even in very hot, dry conditions. Streams that depend primarily on surface drainage often flow above the average annual water table. These "losing streams" are typically seasonal, with dry streambeds in late summer and early fall.

Nearby plant communities can significantly affect how much groundwater moves into streams and rivers, especially in ecosystems dense with plant life, such as healthy forests and swamps. Plant roots pull groundwater from the soil and into plant tissues, particularly during the spring and summer growing seasons. As the plants photosynthesize, they release moisture from their leaves, and this transpired water vapor is lost to the local atmosphere (see The Freshwater Cycle, p. 152). Ecologists estimate that 60 percent of the rainwater that falls on upland forests transpires to the atmosphere within hours and never reaches local streams and rivers.

Seasonal cycles in streams

River systems are intimately linked to the surrounding climate. In the typical forest environments of New England, the thick leaf litter and soils act like a sponge, buffering the effects of typical storms by absorbing most precipitation before it flows into streams and rivers. The postglacial soils and glacial till are particularly good at rapidly absorbing rainfall. Water quickly percolates into the postglacial soils and tills. Depending on how porous the soil and bedrock are, it can take tens or even hundreds of years for groundwater to reemerge on the surface and flow into streams and rivers.

The recent local weather is the primary determinant of stream flows and water levels. Heavy precipitation from storms or sudden warming periods that rapidly melt the local snowpack can cause huge increases in

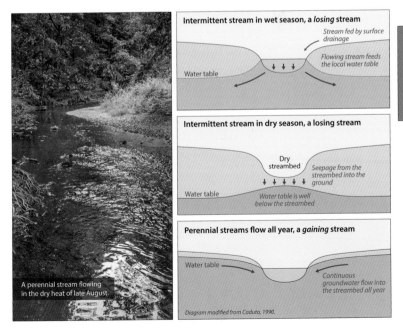

A perennial stream flowing in the dry heat of late August.

Intermittent stream in wet season, a *losing* stream

Stream fed by surface drainage

Flowing stream feeds the local water table

Water table

Intermittent stream in dry season, a losing stream

Dry streambed

Seepage from the streambed into the ground

Water table

Water table is well below the streambed

Perennial streams flow all year, a *gaining* stream

Water table

Continuous groundwater flow into the streambed all year

Diagram modified from Caduto, 1990.

Rivers & Streams

Volodymyr

Hard, impervious, nonabsorbent street drainage systems are a constant threat, increasing the chance that large flows of stormwater will overwhelm municipal water treatment facilities and cause flood damage to homes and businesses.

stream flow in just a few hours. Once the local soils near a stream become saturated with water, further rain or meltwater flows directly across the ground surface and into streams and rivers. This is the most common cause of significant river flood events. For example, the severe New England floods of 1936 were caused when several back-to-back March rainstorms suddenly melted much of the snowpack in northern New Hampshire and Vermont. The still-frozen soils under the snow quickly shed torrents of rain and meltwater into local streams and rivers and ultimately into the Connecticut River, causing multiple catastrophic flood events.

The postglacial landscape also determines the typical flow patterns of New England rivers. Because the landscape is relatively young (15,000 to 20,000 years old since the retreat of the glaciers), smaller rivers and streams typically flow into and out of the many ponds that fill depressions left behind by the glacial ice.

Unfortunately, the developed environment comprises impervious surfaces such as streets, parking lots, sidewalks, and building roofs that quickly shed rainwater into sewers and drainage channels. The fast stormwater flows often overwhelm these artificial drainage systems, leading to destructive flooding. Impervious surfaces also prevent rainwater and meltwater from percolating into the local groundwater, and this lack of groundwater recharge can exacerbate the effects of late summer and early fall droughts.

Effects of winter ice

In winter, ice sheets expand and contract, pushing against riverbanks with a force large enough to kill tree roots and uproot shrubs. In spring, the moving ice chunks tear away at riverbanks, leaving just bare earth for several feet above water level and ripe for erosion in the spring freshet. Few woody trees, shrub species, or perennial herbs can survive direct contact with river ice. Even rivers with healthy riparian forests on their banks often show a band of annual pioneer grasses and herbs, which quickly take advantage of the barren soil in spring. Tough, shrubby Black Willows are common on stream and riverbanks because they are one of the

Seasonal River Flows and Precipitation

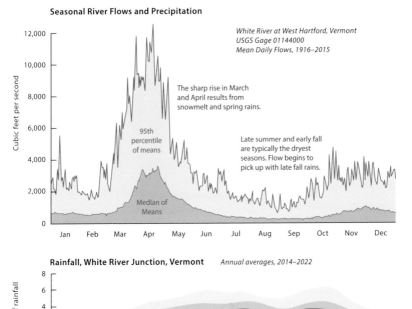

White River at West Hartford, Vermont
USGS Gage 01144000
Mean Daily Flows, 1916–2015

The sharp rise in March and April results from snowmelt and spring rains.

95th percentile of means

Late summer and early fall are typically the driest seasons. Flow begins to pick up with late fall rains.

Median of Means

Cubic feet per second

12,000 — 10,000 — 8,000 — 6,000 — 4,000 — 2,000 — 0

Jan Feb Mar Apr May Jun Jul Aug Sep Oct Nov Dec

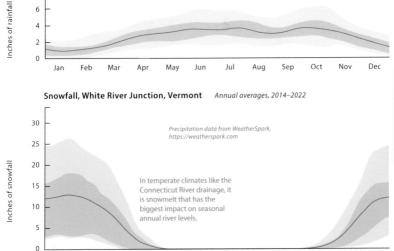

Rainfall, White River Junction, Vermont   *Annual averages, 2014–2022*

Inches of rainfall

8 — 6 — 4 — 2 — 0

Jan Feb Mar Apr May Jun Jul Aug Sep Oct Nov Dec

Snowfall, White River Junction, Vermont   *Annual averages, 2014–2022*

Precipitation data from WeatherSpark, https://weatherspark.com

In temperate climates like the Connecticut River drainage, it is snowmelt that has the biggest impact on seasonal annual river levels.

Inches of snowfall

30 — 25 — 20 — 15 — 10 — 5 — 0

Jan Feb Mar Apr May Jun Jul Aug Sep Oct Nov Dec

Rivers & Streams

Precipitation patterns, evaporation, and temperature drive annual flow cycles in rivers and streams. There is a significant increase in water flow during the spring and early summer months as the snow melts and rainfall increases, followed by a reduction in flow during the fall and winter months as rainfall decreases. The lower volume of flow in the late summer months also affects salinity levels in the estuary portion of the Connecticut River (see p. 349). In recent years, late summer droughts have also become a significant factor influencing flow volume in the regional rivers and streams (see p. 96). These annual flow cycles are essential for many aspects of river and stream ecology, including the migration patterns of fish and other aquatic organisms and water availability for human use.

few species that can survive the year-round erosion and winter ice along stream banks.

Flood pulses in streams

The primary long-term way that streams and rivers interact with and shape their local riparian environments is through erosion, removal, and deposit of sediments over time. A river in flood is an extraordinary geologic force. Over time, water saturated with grit and sand can wear down the hardest rocks. In shorter periods, rivers shape the riparian landscape through annual flooding events. As rivers inundate the landscape in the spring meltwater freshet or after rainstorms, the flowing water reshapes landforms, bringing new sediments onto the local floodplain and drawing sediments and nutrients from the land as waters recede.

In flood, rivers become wide temporary lakes. These broad temporary lakes across the floodplain help buffer the effects of swiftly running water. The silt layers left behind as the river recedes produce excellent farmland, as in the Central Valley areas of Massachusetts and the riparian floodplains south of Hartford.

As the river water level comes over the top of the existing banks, the current suddenly slows, leaving loads of sediment along the riverbanks and extending out to add sediment to the floodplains beyond the banks. As

On January 15, 2018, a combination of unusual factors led to the formation of a spectacular 12-mile ice jam at the Swing Bridge between Haddam and East Haddam, Connecticut. A long cold spell in the previous weeks and a sudden increase in river flow volume created the jam. The rising river broke the ice on the river surface into massive plates, which then moved downriver to jam against the supports of the Haddam bridge. The ice acted as a dam and pushed the river well above the seven-foot flood stage, causing flooding as far north as Bloomfield and East Granby, Connecticut. The huge ice blocks also caused damage to docks and marinas at and north of the Haddam bridge. Two US Coast Guard icebreakers arrived on January 18 to break up the jam, which lasted until late January 2018.

Matthew Male

sediments pile up along the riverbanks, repeated floods produce low natural levees along the riverbanks, which become thick bands of riparian shrubs and woodland in unmodified rivers. As a stream gets larger and runs permanently (as opposed to seasonally), more wetland the floodplain environments form, and the riparian areas become more extensive and diverse in structure and inhabitants (see pp. 290–91, river cross-section).

Young Bald Eagles on river ice (grudgingly) share the remains of a carp near Haddam, Connecticut. Bald Eagles are now a major wildlife spectacle all along the Connecticut River, particularly in winter on the estuary portion of the river from Middletown south to the river mouth in Old Saybrook. *Photo courtesy of Matthew Male.*

Rivers & Streams

The ice jam at the Haddam–East Haddam Swing Bridge, January 20, 2018.

Common Mergansers (*Mergus merganser*)

Common Mergansers are a quintessential waterbird species of the Connecticut River. They are found all along the river from the Connecticut Lakes of New Hampshire down to Long Island Sound. Common Mergansers breed on the far northern lakes, reservoirs, and deeper river areas of the Connecticut River drainage and winter in large numbers near the Atlantic coastline and wherever the river waters remain open in winter. Large rafts of Common Mergansers mix with other diving duck species in the brackish areas of the Connecticut River, mainly south of Middletown, Connecticut. Along with Bald Eagles, Double-Crested Cormorants, and Great Cormorants, Common Mergansers define winter birding on the lower Connecticut River.

Common Merganser
Female

Common Merganser
Male

damedias

Stream structure

The basic physical dimensions of a river are the local topography, the channel width and depth, the flow gradient, and the flow volume. Any of these parameters can substantially change the river, temporarily or permanently.

There is constant evolution in flowing waters, particularly in larger rivers and streams. The bubbling and splashing of headwater streams can easily disguise that water in such streams moves more slowly and at small volumes compared to larger, more mature streams and rivers. In headwater areas, the typically rocky bottom and sides of the stream slow the overall flow of water. In upslope headwater streams, the water runs clear for two reasons: small streams aren't capable of moving large volumes of sediment, and small, forested streams don't typically receive enough sunlight to support photosynthesis. As flow volume and speed increase in larger streams and rivers, the volume of suspended sediments also increases.

Even in average weather and flow conditions, rivers are constantly changing shape and evolving through the forces of erosion and sediment deposition. As a river moves across a landscape as hilly and variable as central New England, river channels typically bend around the higher ground of hills and bedrock outcrops. As a river moves around a bend, water will flow the fastest at the outer curve of the bend. This faster water flow has a greater erosive force, creating exposed and eroded river sides called cutbanks. The slower current speed on the inner side of the river bend cannot hold as much sediment in suspension, and as the river slows, deposits drop to the bottom and inner side of the bend. These deposition areas on the inner sides of river bends are called point bars, and the areas of sediment are often visible as exposed sandbars and gravel beds at river bends.

The river curves can become so pronounced on flat river floodplains that the river forms wide loops. On older rivers, these rounded loops can become separated from the river's main channel, forming oxbow lakes. One of the world's most famous oxbow lakes

Continued on p. 266

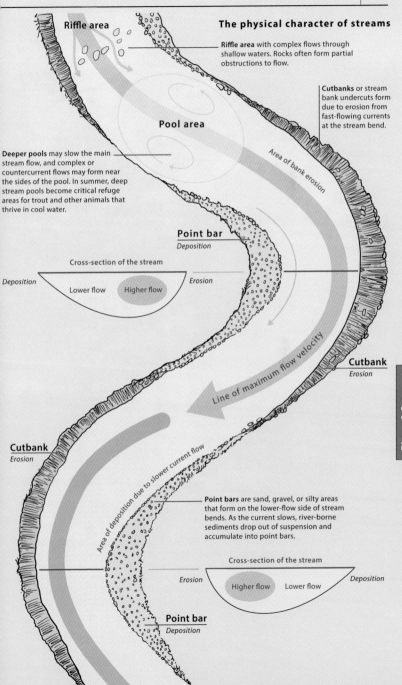

The physical character of streams

Riffle area

Riffle area with complex flows through shallow waters. Rocks often form partial obstructions to flow.

Cutbanks or stream bank undercuts form due to erosion from fast-flowing currents at the stream bend.

Pool area

Area of bank erosion

Deeper pools may slow the main stream flow, and complex or countercurrent flows may form near the sides of the pool. In summer, deep stream pools become critical refuge areas for trout and other animals that thrive in cool water.

Point bar
Deposition

Cross-section of the stream

Deposition   Lower flow   Higher flow   *Erosion*

Line of maximum flow velocity

Cutbank
Erosion

Cutbank
Erosion

Area of deposition due to slower current flow

Point bars are sand, gravel, or silty areas that form on the lower-flow side of stream bends. As the current slows, river-borne sediments drop out of suspension and accumulate into point bars.

Cross-section of the stream

Erosion   Higher flow   Lower flow   *Deposition*

Point bar
Deposition

Rivers & Streams

The Pomperaug River flows through National Audubon's Bent of the River Sanctuary in South-bury, Connecticut. Here a wide bend in the Pomperaug nicely illustrates several common features of stream structure. On the bend's outer, faster-flowing (right) side, the river has cut into the bank—a cutbank formation— and undercut the bank at several points. On the slower, inner side of the curve (left), the current has deposited a gravel and sand point bar (see p. 261).

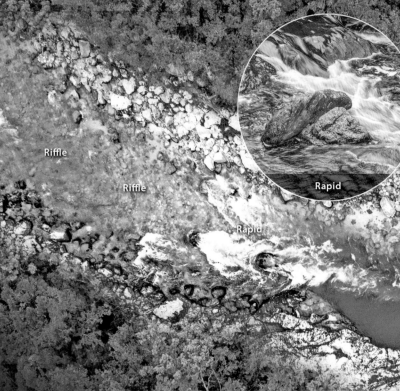

Riffle

Riffle

Rapid

Rapid

A distant run
downstream

Shallow riffle area

Side pools around
a central run

Pools are deep, still areas of a river or stream that provide a calm and protected habitat for a variety of aquatic species, including fish, amphibians, and invertebrates. Pools are important habitats for many species, as they provide refuge from the heat of summer, from predators, and a stable environment for reproduction and growth.

Rapids, Riffles, Runs, and Pools
The structure of running streams

Rapids, riffles, and pools are basic elements of stream structure, and are also essential habitats for aquatic species. The movement of water, sediments, nutrients, and animals through rapids, riffles, and pools helps to create a dynamic and diverse river or stream system. Human activities, such as dam construction, pollution, and habitat destruction, can alter the structure of rapids, riffles, and pools and harm the health of a river or stream system.

Riffle

fle

Pool

Run

Run

Side pool

Rivers & Streams

Run (or glide)

Rapids are sections of a river or stream where the water flows rapidly over rocks and other obstructions. These areas are characterized by turbulence, fast-moving water, and white water.

Riffles are shallow areas of a river or stream where water flows over a series of rocks and boulders, creating turbulence and oxygen-rich water. Riffles are essential habitats for various aquatic insects, such as mayflies and caddisflies, and are also used by fish as feeding areas.

formed on the Connecticut River in Northampton, Massachusetts, in 1840, when floodwaters cut through a near-circular meander loop of the Connecticut and isolated the bend from the main river channel. In 1836 the landscape artist Thomas Cole famously captured the newly forming oxbow lake in his painting *The Oxbow* (see pp. 120–21).

Pool-riffle-pool patterns

Most streams and smaller rivers exhibit an alternating pattern of a riffle, an intervening stretch of deeper or smooth-running water called a pool, and then another riffle area. Riffles are topographic high points

TYPICAL POOL–RIFFLE–POOL STRUCTURE OF STREAMS AND SMALL RIVERS

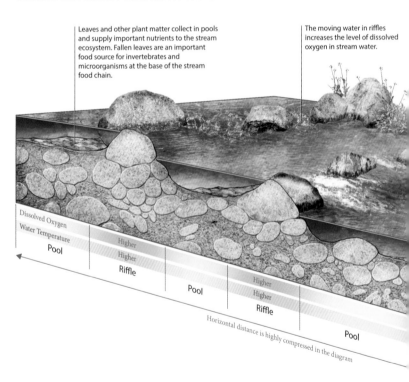

Leaves and other plant matter collect in pools and supply important nutrients to the stream ecosystem. Fallen leaves are an important food source for invertebrates and microorganisms at the base of the stream food chain.

The moving water in riffles increases the level of dissolved oxygen in stream water.

Dissolved Oxygen
Water Temperature

Pool

Higher
Higher

Riffle

Pool

Higher
Higher

Riffle

Pool

Horizontal distance is highly compressed in the diagram

in the stream channel bottom. In stony New England, riffles are composed of rocks, boulders, or bedrock outcrops. Water depth over ripples is relatively shallow, and as the water moves around and over rocks, it often appears fast, rough, and active. In fact, however, the many obstacles in riffles slow the overall flow of the stream. The complex flow patterns in riffle areas often trap leaves and other plant debris in the autumn and after storms, further slowing water movement. By contrast, pools are deeper areas of the stream channel where the water flows more smoothly and quickly (even if it appears placid), particularly near the surface. In the deeper areas of pools, friction from the streambed causes finer sand and silt particles to settle out of the water column. Pool-riffle sequences repeat with some regularity in New England streams because of the complex underlying rocky topography. Even so, pool-riffle patterns also often appear in very

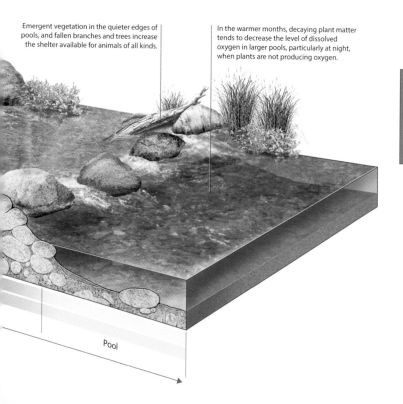

Emergent vegetation in the quieter edges of pools, and fallen branches and trees increase the shelter available for animals of all kinds.

In the warmer months, decaying plant matter tends to decrease the level of dissolved oxygen in larger pools, particularly at night, when plants are not producing oxygen.

Pool

Rivers & Streams

damedias

As the weather warms in spring and summer, deeper pools in rivers and streams become critical thermal refuges for cool-water fish such as trout. The colder water near the bottom of pools can retain more dissolved oxygen as long as the water is clean and clear. In polluted streams, cold water may not be able to counteract the oxygen-robbing effects of excess algae from nitrogen and phosphorus runoff from developed areas near streams and rivers.

shallow stretches of rivers without rocky reefs. Riffles typically form at predictable intervals of about five to seven times the overall width of the stream, perhaps as banks of sediments deposited during flood periods that alternate with areas scoured of sediments by the same floods.

The pool-riffle pattern increases the complexity and diversity of stream environments, and each area supports a slightly different population of stream invertebrates. Riffles are areas of higher dissolved oxygen thanks to all the splashing and complex water movements. This higher dissolved oxygen level attracts many kinds of invertebrates both as living areas and as places to deposit eggs. Aquatic larvae are typically more abundant in riffle areas. Trout, salmon, and other stream fish favor laying their eggs in riffle areas. By contrast, some invertebrates specialize in the lower oxygen levels found in pool areas. Experienced anglers know that mature trout and other fish use the deeper, calmer water of pools both to rest and to wait in ambush to capture insects that float by on the surface waters above. Trout fishers often refer to more extended pool areas in a stream as runs or glides—smooth-moving areas with few obstructions and deeper water.

In small upslope streams that move over a steep gradient, pool-riffle patterns are more like a series of steplike alternating pools and small waterfalls. In large streams and rivers, pool-riffle patterns are usually absent, as the deeper waters and smooth sediment river bottoms are simply too deep for noticeable riffles to form.

Fallen trees in streams

Fallen trees and heavy branches are very important to the overall ecology of streams and small rivers. Tree trunks in and just above the river surface create complex sheltered areas that attract all kinds of river life. The sheltered areas under and around fallen trees create microenvironments that slow water flows and help aquatic animals avoid predators. In larger, more mature streams and rivers with smooth, featureless sediment bottoms, these reefs of woody debris may be the only areas of shelter within the channel.

Tree roots along river channels also help stabilize the riverbanks against erosion, particularly in flood conditions. In floods that overtop the normal riverbanks, riverside shrubs such as the ubiquitous Black Willow slow down the floodwaters, causing sediments to fall out of solution and build up along riverbanks and floodplains. Thus not only do riparian trees and shrubs moderate the effects of floodwaters but the sediment deposits around plants and roots also enrich and build the depth of floodplain soils (see river cross-section diagram, pp. 290–91).

Ecology of streams

River ecology begins on land, particularly in smaller headwater streams, where most food production is from the breakdown of leaves and other plant materials derived from the surrounding riparian forest. Streams and rivers can form the "circulatory system" of natural areas, allowing wildlife to move among blocks of wild habitat, even in developed areas. Streams also distribute the organic matter and sediment-based nutrients they collect, particularly in floods and their normal day-to-day flows. In the increasingly developed New England landscape, riparian areas along streams are often the only connection among natural areas and function as important wildlife corridors and shelters.

Sources of energy

At the base of the aquatic food chain in streams are fungal and microbial decomposers that break down plant material that falls into the stream. Microinvertebrates (collectively termed the meiofauna) feed on algae, bacteria, and fungal cells. As their name suggests, microinvertebrates are mostly too small to see with the naked eye. The larger (but still tiny) insects and other invertebrates that are easy to see are called macroinvertebrates; they feed on microinvertebrates and algae and help break down fallen leaves by physically shredding plant material. All the usual functions of an animal's life—moving, eating, mating, laying eggs to reproduce—require special adaptations to life in a moving stream of water.

In fall and winter, streams receive vast amounts of organic matter in the form of leaves, branches, fallen

Thick, natural areas of riparian (streamside) woodland are critical to keeping our rivers and streams healthy. Riparian trees, shrubs, and herbs help filter runoff pollutants and excess siltation, keeping river water clean and clear. Fallen branches in the stream can literally comb and filter the water, trapping leaves, branches, and human trash.

Riparian shrub branches that extend out over streams offer excellent refuges for aquatic life on the stream surface. Here a Mallard duckling uses the umbrella of a streamside shrub to avoid predators. *Photo and advice courtesy of Sue Sweeney.*

Fallen trees in streams and rivers aren't just accidents of fate from storms and natural attrition—they form a critical natural habitat resource. Fallen trees and branches help create structural complexity in streams, providing hiding places from predators and shady places to rest in the summer heat.

Rivers & Streams

jonnysek

For small aquatic animals like this Predaceous Diving Beetle (*Cybister fimbriolatus*), life in water is like living and moving in clear glycerine or honey.

limbs, or trunks of trees, as well as the bodies of invertebrates and larger animals that perish with the onset of cold weather. Physical processes, mechanical shredding by invertebrates, and decomposition by bacteria break down this organic material. Aquatic animals then transfer the energy to the surrounding riparian environment in the form of amphibians, such as frogs, toads, and salamanders, as well as reptiles, birds, and mammals that eat aquatic and streamside animals.

Life in moving water

Moving water is heavy and dense and has tremendous kinetic force. For tiny animals, water isn't water as we humans commonly experience it. To a mayfly or dragonfly larva, water is as thick and heavy as honey, the flow of which can vary in minutes between the calm quiet of a summer pool and a hurricane of rushing water, silt, and sand after heavy rain. The stream's flow automatically brings fresh oxygenated water with potential food and nutrients and carries away wastes and local pollutants. The most basic nutrients derive primarily from leaves and plant matter that enter the stream in the fall and winter and are then processed and used again and again by many life-forms before finally washing into larger rivers.

In smaller streams and rivers, especially those with shallow riffle areas, dissolved oxygen is generally near the maximum amount physically possible for the current temperature (see graphs, pp. 158–59). Dissolved oxygen levels can change with the seasons, even in very clean streams. In summer's heat and reduced flows, dissolved oxygen is lower but sufficient for animal activity. Smaller forest streams benefit from surrounding tree shade, and the cooler water can hold more dissolved oxygen. In the fall, most streams are again flowing actively. Still, forest streams receive most of their load of fallen leaves in autumn, and the decomposition of leaves absorbs oxygen from chemical interaction with rotting leaves and in the respiration of stream animals that feed directly on plant materials.

Larger, slow-moving rivers usually have a daily rhythm of oxygen saturation, much as in other freshwater environments (see p. 158). In the daylight hours, plants, algae, and photosynthetic bacteria produce oxygen during photosynthesis, and dissolved oxygen rises. At night photosynthesis ceases, but plants still require oxygen, so the dissolved oxygen falls. This daily cycle is especially pronounced in summer when the water's heat also limits the amount of dissolved oxygen. In New England, almost all rivers of any size also carry a load of organic pollutants from sewage leakage and stormwater runoff. The organic pollutants stimulate excess algae activity and directly absorb oxygen. The lower flow volumes in the relative droughts of late summer also act to concentrate excess nutrients and pollution. This combination of warm, shallow, more slow-moving polluted water can seriously limit dissolved oxygen levels. This is why fish kills from hypoxia (critically low oxygen levels) usually occur in summer and early fall.

The effects of pollution on a river or stream

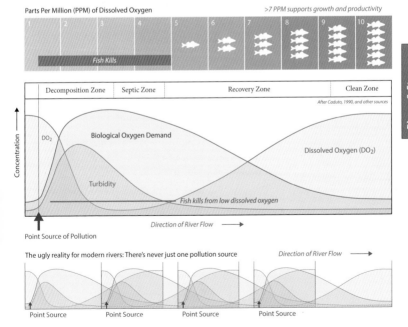

After Caduto, 1990, and other sources

Rivers & Streams

Small River Habitat
Mill River, Arcadia Wildlife Sanctuary, Northampton, MA

Red
Maple trees

LARGEMOUTH
BASS, 6–18 in.

SMALLMOUTH
BASS, 6–16 in.

YELLOW PERCH
6–18 in.

CHAIN PICKEREL
10–18 in.

NORTHERN PIKE
18–30 in.

For component photography credits, please see pp. 415–17.

Shagbark Hickory tree

Osprey

Wild Rice

Belted Kingfisher

Great Horned Owl

Painted Turtles on log

Eastern Coyote

Black Bear

Rivers & Streams

WHITE PERCH
6–9 in.

American Beaver

TESSELLATED DARTER
1–3 in.

Eastern Painted Turtle

BLACKNOSE DACE
1–3 in.

Biofilms

In healthy aquatic environments, anything immersed in water for a few hours becomes covered with a biofilm composed of microscopic algae, bacteria, and fungal cells. These biofilms form a critical base component of the food chain, particularly in the relatively simple ecosystems of headwater streams. Thus leaves, tree branches, and even rocks and boulders within the stream are coated with biofilms, which are rich in nutrients and form both a microhabitat and a rich food source for larger grazers such as insect larvae, snails, and other macroinvertebrates. As leaves fall into stream water, they immediately acquire a biofilm coating and begin to leach nutrients directly into the water. The leaf typically loses about 75 percent of its biomass in about a week as bacteria and fungi break down its tissues. The lighter leaf framework now falls prey to insect larvae that shred the leaf structure as they feed. The insects feed primarily on the nutrient soup of the biofilm coating. By the sixth week, most leaves are skeletons, slowly decaying as bacteria and fungi consume them.

River Continuum Concept

The River Continuum Concept (see pp. 278–79) describes and explains how the mix of nutrients, physical conditions, microscopic communities, plant communities, and large and small animals changes in regular and predictable ways over the total length of river systems. The physical size of mountain headwater streams differs in obvious ways from medium-sized streams and larger rivers. Still, the changing physical and geological conditions of flowing waters also determine how microorganisms, plants, and animals interact to form unique ecological communities in each type of flowing water. The River Continuum Concept is not universally accepted among freshwater biologists. The concept best describes pristine streams in wild habitats, a situation that is all too rare today. Still, the concept helps describe the way rivers evolve "from source to sea" and highlights the less visible but hugely important role of stream invertebrates in freshwater ecology.

Shady forest streams produce very little photosynthesis—it's just too dark under the trees. The primary production at the base of the stream food chain is in biofilms on fallen leaves. Invertebrates feed directly on the bacteria and fungi in biofilms and also break down the leaf tissues to return their nutrients to the stream.

Daniel Vincek

Small streams

Small headwater streams run clear and relatively cold because they are usually under heavy shade from the surrounding riparian forest. The lack of photosynthesis can make small streams poor in dissolved oxygen. Still, headwater streams and brooks generally run over the rough terrain of mountainsides and hillsides, and all the splashing, riffling, and small waterfalls oxygenate the water. The heavy forest shade over headwater streams also keeps the water cool, and cool water can hold more dissolved oxygen. Because of the lack of sunlight, the base of the stream food chain is not aquatic plants and algae but the leaves and plant materials from the surrounding forest that fall into the water and become covered with biofilms of bacteria and fungi. Ecologists call these leaves and other plant materials coarse particulate organic matter (CPOM). Stream invertebrates such as stonefly larvae, amphipods, and juvenile crayfish further shred apart leaves covered with biofilm, deriving their nutrients as they consume the biofilm. These shredder invertebrates also help physically break down old leaves into smaller

Fallen leaves and other plant materials in streams and ponds quickly become covered with a thin biofilm of bacteria, cyanobacteria, and fungi. The components of the biofilm quickly begin to break down the plant tissues. In the chill of winter the process of decomposition may take months, but in summer most leaves disintegrate with a few weeks.

Rivers & Streams

Continued on p. 282

THE RIVER CONTINUUM CONCEPT

The River Continuum Concept focuses primarily on the activities and feeding of stream invertebrates and characteristic fish species: **Shredders** are organisms that feed off of coarse particulate organic material (CPOM) such as small sections of leaves. The shredding reduces coarse organic matter like bits of leaves into fine organic particles. **Collectors** use of traps or other adaptive features to filter and catch coarse and fine organic matter, and their feeding further reduces vegetal matter to fine particles. **Grazers** or scrapers feed on the film of organic matter and fine particles of vegetation carried downstream. **Predators** are animals that specialize in eating the small shredding, collecting, and grazing animals of streams and rivers.

HEADWATER STREAMS

The headwaters of a river system are usually very narrow and lined by thick shore vegetation. This prevents the penetration of sunlight, in turn decreasing the production of organic material through photosynthesis in the water. The majority of the organic matter that does make its way into the system is in the form of leaves and other plant material that falls into the stream.

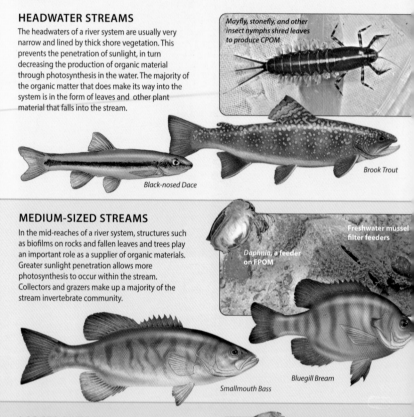

Mayfly, stonefly, and other insect nymphs shred leaves to produce CPOM

Brook Trout

Black-nosed Dace

MEDIUM-SIZED STREAMS

In the mid-reaches of a river system, structures such as biofilms on rocks and fallen leaves and trees play an important role as a supplier of organic materials. Greater sunlight penetration allows more photosynthesis to occur within the stream. Collectors and grazers make up a majority of the stream invertebrate community.

Freshwater mussel filter feeders

Daphnia, a feeder on FPOM

Bluegill Bream

Smallmouth Bass

LARGER RIVERS

In the lower and larger sections of the river system, the large flux in particulate material from upstream feeds collector invertebrates and fish. There is less photosynthesis here because the water is often cloudy with particulate organic matter and silt from upstream. Respiration outpaces photosynthesis in both aquatic algae and submerged aquatic vegetation, and this decreases the level of dissolved oxygen in the water. In summer the temperature of the water in large rivers often exceeds the tolerance of many fish species, sometimes resulting in fish kills.

Collectors like filter feeders dominate larger rivers

Common

Brown Bullhead

st trees near streams are
ortionate dominant in
water streams. Trees
uce large amounts of coarse
culate organic matter
M) as leaves and branches
ato the river.

ctor and grazer
tebrates break down the
es. CPOM flows downstream
ood source for all river
nisms.

ater is typically cool and
oxygenated.

The shade of trees around headwater streams prevents much photosynthesis in within the stream, but the shade helps cool the water and raise dissolved oxygen levels.

Flow of coarse particulate organic matter, CPOM

INVERTEBRATE COMMUNITIES

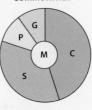

- Collectors
- Shredders
- Predators
- Grazers
- Microbes

edium-sized streams the
unding riparian forest is
ortionately less dominant.

se organic matter from
eam breaks down to fine
culate organic matter
M).

dominant food source in
um-sized streams is
tic algae and submerged
emergent vascular aquatic
s, along with FPOM.

er temperatures and lower
en levels are typical.

Fine particulate organic matter, FPOM

INVERTEBRATE COMMUNITIES

ian forests are a
vely small source of
nic matter in large rivers.

e rivers typically have
ficant plankton
lations, feeding on the
M and other plant matter
upstream.

umerically dominant
large rivers are often
es like carp and catfish
eed on plankton and
m organic matter.

lved oxygen levels are
ally much lower than in
ms, with very warm
in summer.

Very fine particulate organic matter, FPOM

INVERTEBRATE COMMUNITIES

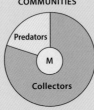

The riparian forests around large rivers provide little shade to cool the waters, and proportionately little of the organic matter that feeds aquatic life here.

There isn't enough sunlight in heavily shaded streams to sustain much submerged aquatic plant life. In such streams, the base of the food chain is formed by autumn fallen leaves. The leaves are broken down by biofilms of bacteria and fungi and are further processed by shredding and grazing aquatic insect larvae.

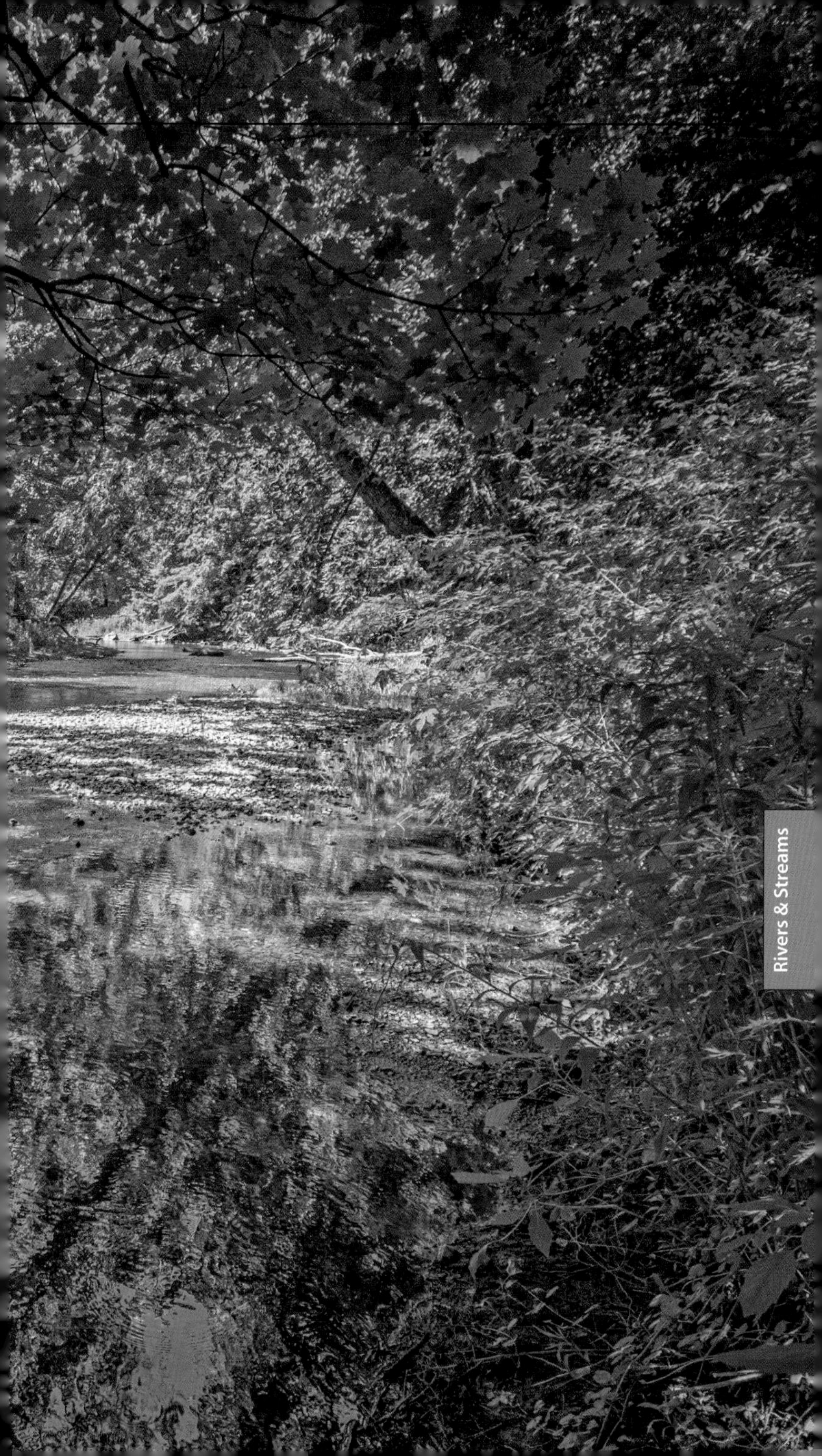

Headwater stream invertebrates
(Shredders)

Mayfly Larva
Hexagenia sp.

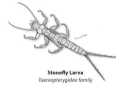

Stonefly Larva
Taeniopterygidae family

Blackfly Larva
Prosimulium mixtum

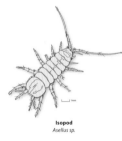

Isopod
Asellus sp.

particles. Over months of immersion in the stream, these tiny bits of leaves become fine particulate organic matter (FPOM). The small leaf particles, now coated with yet more biofilm, are filtered from the water stream by collector organisms such as mayfly, blackfly, stonefly, and caddisfly larvae. In small headwater streams' relatively simple food chains, dragonfly larvae, water beetle larvae, frogs, crayfish, salamanders, shiners, sculpins, and trout are the top predators that feed on the collector and shredder insect larvae. Wetland birds such as the Northern and Louisiana Waterthrushes, flycatchers, vireos, and other songbirds take significant amounts of invertebrate prey in riparian forests.

Stream alteration and channeling

In developed areas, smaller streams are often straightened into channels, usually to support the quick drainage of land after rainstorms. The banks of natural streams are often hardened with gravel or boulders to prevent bank erosion. These channelized streams are dramatically less productive environments for aquatic life: most of the structural complexity of the natural stream is lost when streams are effectively turned into ditches. Ironically, the channelizing of natural watercourses often promotes flash flooding. Stormwater quickly drains from impervious surfaces including streets, parking lots, and building roofs and flows directly into stream channels, which quickly fill with fast-moving water. In developed areas, the buffering and absorbent effects of natural stream wetlands and floodplains are lost under pavement and hard stream channels. Most stormwater flows into stream and river channels rather than being absorbed into groundwater.

Medium streams

As streams grow broader and deeper, new feeding opportunities and new plant and animal inhabitants are available. Wider streams receive more sunlight, and the greater light level enables more complex submerged and emergent aquatic plants to produce dissolved oxygen through photosynthesis during daylight. The sunlight increases the complexity of biofilms, as green algae, blue-green bacteria, and diatoms become a component of the coating on rocks, streambeds, and plant stems and leaves within the stream. Animals that graze on algae mats and biofilms become more common. These grazer organisms include aquatic snails, insect larvae, and specialized grazing fish such as suckers and some minnows. The sunlight also heats the water, so dissolved oxygen levels are lower in larger streams but still at levels high enough to support sunfish, minnows, dace, shiners, and Brook and Brown Trout. The large amount of FPOM suspended in the stream water supports larger populations of collector and grazer animals, and those animals, in turn, support the top fish predators. Medium-sized streams also support bird predators including the Belted Kingfisher, herons, Eastern Screech Owls, and Osprey.

Rivers

In large rivers, the water is often clouded with sediment and green algae. Submerged aquatic plants thrive only in shallow areas around sandbanks or along the river margins. Stretches of rivers with silty or sandy bottoms are the least diverse river environment

Flooded riparian forest in Rocky Hill, Connecticut, after the heavy rains from Hurricane Ida created 7 to 10-foot floods along the Connecticut River in September, 2021. The loads of silt that the river brings into the riparian forests help build up the natural levees along the banks and add rich nutrients to the forest soils.

Continued on p. 290

Cold Rocky Stream Habitat
Cool, well-oxygenated water supports a basic food chain

In smaller woodland streams the surrounding riparian forest shades the water and prevents lush plant and algae growth. Fallen leaves and other plant matter provide the main source of food and nutrients to stream animals.

SMALLMOUTH BASS, 6–16 in.

BROOK TROUT 6–10 in.

BROWN TROUT 8–20 in.

RAINBOW TROUT 8–16 in.

For component photography credits, please see pp. 415–17.

FALL LEAVES

Fall leaf drop forms the base of the stream food chain

BELTED KINGFISHER

Raccoon

Eastern Screech Owl

Eastern Coyote

Black Flies

SELLATED DARTER
in.

ACKNOSE DACE
in.

BIOFILMS
Fungi, bacteria

River Otter

MICRO CONSUMERS OF CPOM

Culex Mosquito

Nutrient-rich biofilms of fungi and bacteria coat all surfaces in the stream, and help break down complex organics like leaves into coarse particulate organic matter, **CPOM**.

Trout Stream
The Mill River at Sleeping Giant State Park, Hamden, CT

GOLDEN SHINER
3–9 in.

COMMON SHINER
2–5 in.

BROOK TROUT
6–10 in.

BROWN TROUT
8–20 in.

RAINBOW TROUT
8–16 in.

For component photography credits, please see pp. 415–17.

Belted Kingfisher

Black-Crowned Night-Heron

Great Blue Heron

Common Yellowthroat

American Goldfinch

Rivers & Streams

Largemouth Bass

Brown Trout

TESSELLATED DARTER
1–3 in.

BLACK-NOSED DACE
1–3 in.

Raccoon

Fish Species of Large Rivers
The Connecticut River at Rocky Hill, Connecticut

COMMON CARP
16–28 in.

YELLOW PERCH
6–11 in.

CHAIN PICKEREL
10–18 in.

BROWN BULLHEAD
8–14 in.

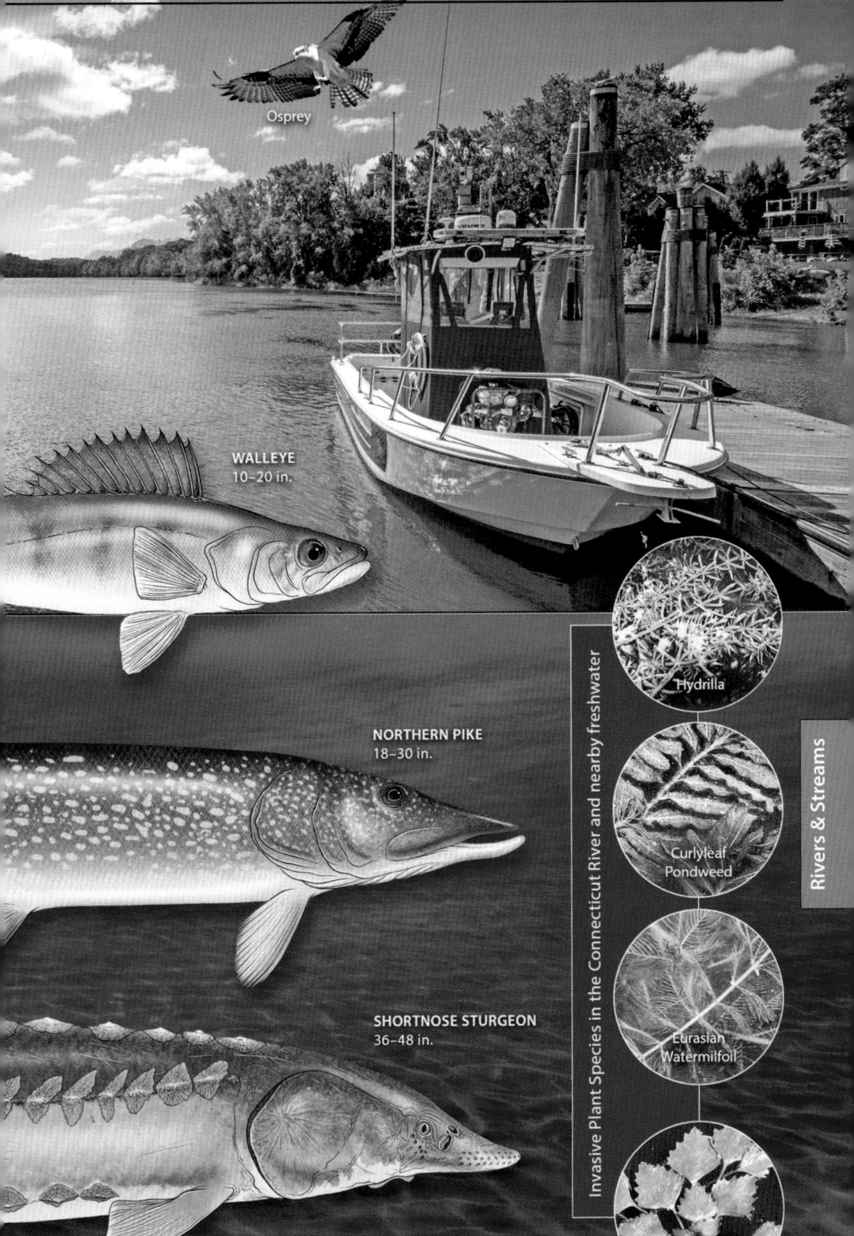

Osprey

WALLEYE
10–20 in.

NORTHERN PIKE
18–30 in.

SHORTNOSE STURGEON
36–48 in.

Rivers & Streams

Invasive Plant Species in the Connecticut River and nearby freshwater

Hydrilla

Curlyleaf Pondweed

Eurasian Watermilfoil

Water Chestnut

For component photography credits, please see pp. 415–17.

because both the water column and the river bottom are in constant motion and offer little shelter to smaller aquatic animals. What physical shelter and structural complexity rivers offer is usually along the banks, where grasses, sedges, and Arrowhead may thrive in more sheltered areas. The low flows of late summer expose point bars and sandbars, where quick-growing annuals such as sedges, grasses, ragweed, goldenrods, Coltsfoot, River St. Johnswort, and other herbs may move in temporarily.

Most primary production in larger rivers is suspended green algae (phytoplankton). With its many dams, long stretches of the Connecticut River north of central Massachusetts are more like a connected series of long, linear lakes than a flowing river. The open water in these lakelike stretches is dominated by phytoplankton

Cross-section of a river corridor and flood plain forests

Mixed Riparian and Upland Woodland

Riparian Woodland—Floodplain For

River Floodplain

Periodic flooding is a natural means to improve the richness and productivity of riverside soils. The floods also help build and maintain the natural riverside levees. Maintaining riparian woodlands and marshes is critical to preventing catastrophic flooding in storms.

Flood level

Natural Levee

Upland and Bluff

Floodplain Pond and Marsh

River Bank

Floodplain Trees	Woody Shrubs	Herbs	Ferns
American Sycamore	Arrowwood Viburnum	Arrow Arum	Cinnamon Fern
Black Cherry	Buttonbush	Arrowhead	Ostrich Fern
Black Willow	Highbush Blueberry	Cardinal Flower	Royal Fern
Blue Beech	Silky Dogwood	Jewelweed	Sensitive Fern
Eastern Cottonwood	Smooth Alder	Joe-Pye Weed	
Red Maple	Spicebush	Pickerelweed	
Silver Maple	Witch Hazel	Poison Ivy	
White Oak		Virginia Creeper	
Yellow Birch		Japanese Knotweed	
		Multiflora Rose	

and filter-feeding fish such as carp and catfish. Collector filter feeders predominate among invertebrates, and although larger rivers often lack the species diversity of smaller rivers and streams, large rivers are full of nutrients and plankton from upstream and can support huge individual fish. Sturgeon, Common Carp, catfish, and other bottom and filter feeders can grow to huge sizes in mature rivers. Large river systems are quite dependent on the health and productivity of the many smaller tributaries far upstream that feed water, nutrients, and aquatic life into the downstream river ecosystem.

Large rivers change the landscapes and plant communities that surround them. Through repeated flood cycles over centuries, large rivers create a surrounding local ecology of floodplains, riparian forests, forested or marshy islands, and associated wetland marshes and swamps. As floods overwhelm the banks of the river, the surging waters carry a rich soup of nutrients,

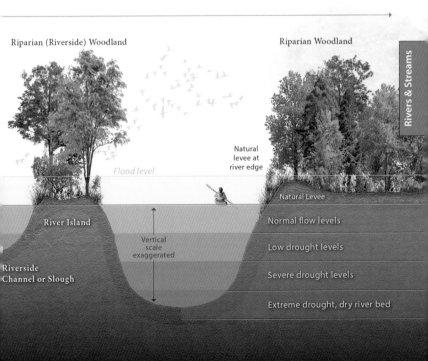

Riparian (Riverside) Woodland

Riparian Woodland

Rivers & Streams

Flood level

Natural levee at river edge

Natural Levee

River Island

Normal flow levels

Vertical scale exaggerated

Low drought levels

Riverside Channel or Slough

Severe drought levels

Extreme drought, dry river bed

sand and silt sediments, and aquatic species far out of the normal river channel. Though a river flood may seem disastrous in the short term, floods are vital to maintaining the health of riparian environments. When people insisted on building along riverbanks and floodplains, these regular flooding events became "natural disasters."

Rivers as wildlife corridors

Most wild animals require some degree of movement to complete their life cycles. Urban and suburban parks, wildlife refuges, undeveloped wetlands, and forested lands are vital for wildlife. Even fragmented habitat patches are islands in a sea of concrete, roads, and lawns. Without corridors among habitats, wild

COYOTE
Canis latrans
Eastern form

BOBCAT
Lynx rufus

Rivers & Streams

GRAY FOX
Urocyon cinereoargenteus

RED FOX
Vulpes vulpes

animal populations can become isolated, inbred, and without enough of a home range to reliably obtain food and shelter. In our increasingly developed urban and suburban landscapes, streams and rivers are crucial habitat corridors. As the animals travel, these corridors provide shelter, protection from predators, and food sources.

Stream and river habitats also have many benefits for the people who live around them. Streams are natural greenbelts for recreation and generally improve the value of the property around them. Well-maintained riparian habitat corridors can also help reduce flooding damage, acting as a physical barrier to flowing water and a sponge to absorb stormwater.

Beavers

Humans are not the only species to create dams on rivers and streams. North American Beavers are expert water managers and generally build their dams at the narrowest point along a stream, where the shortest dam can hold back the maximum amount of water. Beavers build dams to impound water into broad, shallow lakes that protect their lodge homes from raids by predators. But in building dams and ponds, beavers often create aquatic ecosystems that benefit many wildlife species. Beaver dams have the same water-regulating effect as human dams. Beaver dams leak and overflow in times of flood but also hold water during summer and early fall droughts when many other shallow wetlands have gone dry. In this way, Beavers regulate the year-round water economy of their local environments (see pp. 322–28 for more on Beavers).

Beaver lodge

Rivers & Streams

NORTH AMERICAN BEAVER
Castor canadensis

Jordan Feeg

Daniel Vincek

The wide variety of aquatic habitats along rivers and streams provide food, shelter, and movement routes for wildlife. Riverine forests, marshes, shrub swamps, and the subsurface environment of the river itself are rich in wildlife of all kinds. Protecting rivers and streams entails far more than just protecting rivers and their banks. Rivers sustain the riparian environment around them, but the reverse is also true. Without the plant and animal communities of the river floodplains, healthy, safe, and productive rivers can't exist.

The Johns River that feeds into Cherry Pond at the Pondicherry Wildlife Refuge in Whitefield, New Hampshire. As it enters the Cherry Pond, the Johns is essentially a boggy creek that emerges from a larger marsh area to the west of the Pond. Ecologists class the marshes at Pondicherry as an interesting mix of poor bog-fen vegetation, mixed into mostly a classic wet meadow that surrounds both the Johns River and Cherry Pond (see p. 182). Along with the common Tussock Sedges, Cinnamon and Royal Ferns, and Highbush Blueberries, you may spot boglike patches of sphagnum moss, Purple Pitcher Plants, and (in June) the bright flowers of Grass Pinks.

Marshes, Swamps, Vernal Pools, and Bogs

Green Frog (*Rana clamitans*). Tread carefully in wet meadows and the verges of ponds. You may get better looks at frogs out in the grass than in the water.

When we speak confidently about streams, rivers, and marshes, we draw imaginary lines over a natural landscape that doesn't recognize our boundaries. Artificial creations such as reservoirs and dammed sections of rivers sometimes have hard, precise, steep-sided edges. But natural wetlands are almost always some blend of lake edge and marsh, streams that flow through shrub swamps, or wet meadows that blur the boundaries of ponds so thoroughly that the concept of a shoreline becomes meaningless. Consider that the scene at left is simultaneously a stream, a marsh, and bits of wet meadow, edged by a spruce-fir-maple swamp.

State and federal laws protect wetlands from filling and development in the United States. As such, the strict legal definitions of what is or is not a wetland are complex and often controversial because the laws limit commercial development. This book concentrates on the basic and easily recognizable ecological types of wetlands seen by birders, hikers, fishers, and amateur naturalists. The US Geological Survey defines wetlands as "transitional areas, sandwiched between permanently flooded deep water environments and well-drained uplands, where the water table is usually at or near the surface or the land is covered by shallow water." In general terms, wetlands are lands where saturation with water is the dominant factor determining the nature

of soil development and the types of plant and animal communities living in the soil and on its surface.

For all their importance to flood control, water management, or environmental preservation, wetlands are unusual in most places. Only 5.5 percent of the land in the 48 contiguous states of the United States is defined as wetlands. The relative rarity of freshwater wetlands today is primarily due to human activities and the extirpation of beavers. In the 1600s, there were about 220 million acres of inland wetlands in the Lower 48 States. About half that total is gone today (110 million acres in 2009). Today, wetlands protection is widely recognized as critical to flood control and water management. About 10,000–12,000 acres of freshwater wetlands are lost each year due to various kinds of development. Despite better legal protection, wetlands and the wildlife they contain are still in grave jeopardy.

Wetland environments

Wetlands may be permanently flooded, but most shallow wetlands vary significantly in extent and depth over the seasons. Thus the boundaries of wetlands can change month by month and respond to longer-term climate changes such as the increasingly frequent late summer droughts throughout New England (see p. 96).

All plants that live in wetlands must overcome similar challenges. In a wetland, the local water table is at or above the soil level for long periods. Most plants are adapted to live in soils that naturally contain air spaces that allow roots to interact with soil microbes and fungi. When soils are saturated with water, the normal soil microbiome around plant roots cannot survive, and the plant roots can't exchange oxygen and other gasses. Only plants adapted to low-oxygen, water-saturated soils can survive long immersion in water.

Ecologists define wetland types mainly by the mix of plant species in each community. Marshes are the wettest wetland community, with shallow standing water all year, although the water depth may vary widely with the seasons. Slightly drier marshes are dominated by grasses, sedges, and rushes and are called wet meadows. A swamp is a wetland dominated by woody shrubs or larger trees. Swamps have water-saturated soils for most of the year but may not show standing water in the driest parts of late summer and early fall. Most older streams and rivers have various kinds of marshes and swamps on their floodplains, where the soil is wet for only part of the year. These floodplain or riparian wetland communities (see pp. 290–91, river cross-section) are dominated by plants that can withstand both immersion in water and long periods of relatively dry soil. Bog wetlands are rare in most of south and central New England and unusual even in the northern Connecticut River region. However, the unique combination of mosses and specialized plants that comprise a bog community can also be found along northern lakeshore edges, mixed in with other more common wetland plants (see pp. 182–83, Pondicherry).

A Slaty Skimmer dragonfly (*Libellula incesta*) and a Common Eastern Bumble Bee (*Bombus impatiens*) on a Pickerelweed flower (*Pontederia cordata*).

Succession in wetlands

All marshes are associated with a sustained water supply, usually from a stream or river that both supplies and drains the marsh. In hillier terrain, groundwater flows may also contribute water to a marsh. In both geological and ecological terms, most wetlands are short-lived communities that eventually fill with a combination of peat from plant roots and sediments carried in by the streams that feed the wetland. Open grassy marshes become dominated by shrubs and evolve into swamps. Shrub swamps become hardwood tree swamps as the ground becomes drier (see pp. 164–65, pond succession). Finally, old wetlands fill to become bottomland or riparian hardwood forests. However, some New England wetlands have persisted for thousands of years, where the combination of dependable water supplies and local geology allows wetlands to resist filling and drying. The more extensive surviving marshes and hardwood swamps along the Connecticut River probably developed after the retreat of the Wisconsinan ice sheet 20,000–13,000 years ago. Many of today's riverine wetlands (see pp. 274–75) persist on the ancient lake bed sediments left behind by the drainage of Glacial Lake Hitchcock 15,500 years ago.

Marshes

Freshwater marshes are rarely just one type of marsh, and they always combine various vegetation patterns determined mostly by water depth. Here what is primarily a shrub swamp around the edges also has large patches of grass and sedge wet meadow marsh in the middle. The small Red Maples aren't necessarily small because they are young. They are probably older but dwarfed by the less-than-ideal growing conditions for their soaked roots.
Bantam River–Little Pond marshes along Whites Wood Road, Litchfield, Connecticut.

Marshes

A marsh is a wetland dominated by emergent vegetation, usually grasses, sedges, rushes, and herbaceous species, whose roots can withstand constant immersion in water. Ecologists often distinguish between marshes with deep water (averaging four to 15 inches of standing water) versus shallow-water marshes or wet meadows.

The wide variety of plants and animals living in or near marshes makes freshwater marshes one of the most diverse and productive natural environments. Marshes are incredibly rich ecosystems because the dominant grassy and herbaceous plant leaves wither and die back each winter. A large proportion of the plant nutrients are recycled back into the marsh environment each year. Most marsh grasses, sedges, and rushes are perennial plants that overwinter and spread through rhizomes or underground stems. The plants lose their leaves but then sprout again from rhizomes in the spring.

Marsh waters are typically well oxygenated because shallow waters have a high surface-to-volume ratio for gas exchange, preventing stagnation. Dense marsh plant leaves, stems, and surface root systems act as a

Ghosts of the marsh

CLAPPER RAIL
Rallus crepitans

VIRGINIA RAIL
Rallus limicola

SORA
Porzana carolina

giant sponge and filter for waterborne silt and nutrients. The typically clear and well-oxygenated marsh water supports a wide range of animal life. However, the water-logged soils and peat under the marsh are poor in oxygen content, and this low-oxygen soil environment prevents most forest and field plants from colonizing marshlands. Only plants with adaptations to bring oxygen to their root systems can survive in wet, marshy soils.

Zonation in marshes

Freshwater marshes are rarely a uniform mix of one plant community from edge to edge. Most marshes show three distinct but sometimes intermixed zones of plants based on average water depth. Emergent plants such as cattails, Northern Wild Rice, Common Reeds, and other taller grass species dominate in the deepest marsh waters. The second deeper zone is the wet meadow or shallow marsh, dominated by grasslike plants (true grasses, rushes, and sedges). The third shrub-dominated marsh zone has the shallowest water; through succession, this shrub zone eventually evolves into a shrub swamp (see below). Wet-tolerant shrubs including Smooth Alder, Buttonbush, Red-Osier Dog-

I highly recommend two superb books if you are interested in a deep dive into the details of New England wetlands. Although nominally about Vermont and New Hampshire, both titles are helpful throughout the Connecticut River region, from its source to Long Island Sound:

The Nature of New Hampshire: *Natural Communities of the Granite State*, by Dan Sperduto and Ben Kimball (Hanover, NH: University Press of New England, 2011).

Wetland, Woodland, Wildland: *A Guide to the Natural Communities of Vermont*, 2nd ed., by Elizabeth H. Thompson, Eric R. Sorenson, and Robert J. Zaino (White River Junction, VT: Chelsea Green, 2019).

Clapper Rails are secretive birds found in the far southern estuary areas of the Connecticut River region. **King Rails** are uncommon freshwater marsh birds that may be found as far north as central Massachusetts. The **Virginia Rail** and **Sora** are common (though stealthy) throughout the wetlands of the Connecticut River drainage.

KING RAIL
Rallus elegans

Marshes

Freshwater Marsh Habitat
Little Pond, White Memorial Foundation, Litchfield, CT

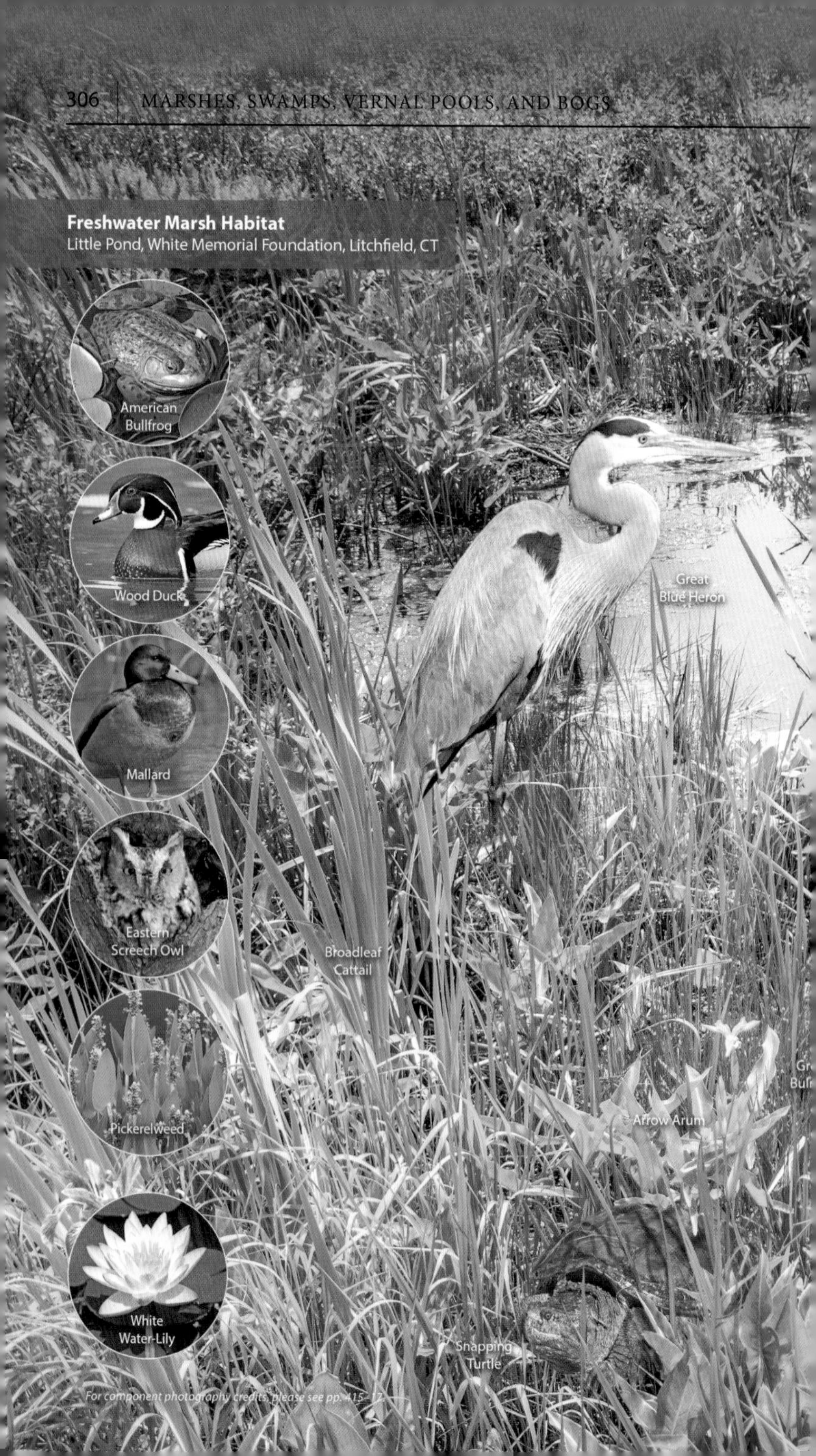

American
Bullfrog

Wood Duck

Mallard

Eastern
Screech Owl

PickerelWeed

White
Water-Lily

Great
Blue Heron

Broadleaf
Cattail

Arrow Arum

Gre
Bull

Snapping
Turtle

Royal Fern

Red-Winged Blackbirds, male and female

Tussock Sedge

Northern Blue Flag Iris

Arrow Arum

Common Muskrat

Virginia Rail

Arrow Arum

Yellow Water-Lily

Blue Dasher

Common Whitetail

American Kestrel

Yellow Flag Iris
Invasive

Purple Loosestrife
Invasive

Marshes

An emergent marsh dominated by Northern Wild Rice (fore-ground center), with mixed Common and Narrow-Leaved Cattails and more Northern Wild Rice in the distance. Along the raised roadside at the bottom of the picture are Bur-Marigold (Beggar's Tick, yellow flowers) and Purple Loosestrife spikes with flowers that have gone to seed.

wood, Black Willow, and Highbush Blueberry ring the shallow marsh edges.

Emergent marshes

Taller grasses such as Broad-Leaved Cattails, Northern Wild Rice, and Common Reed (Phragmites) and larger sedges including Tussock Sedge, American Bur-Reed, and Giant Bur-Reed usually dominate deeper marshes. Mixed among these taller grasslike plants are wetland shrubs such as alders and Buttonbush. The Royal Fern is a common inhabitant of both shallow and deeper marshes. Pickerelweed and Arrow Arum are common in shallow emergent wetlands, and both plants seem to favor the edges of creeks and open water spots within emergent marshes.

Marshes often have scattered small Red Maples, but the maples are typically dwarfed by the constant immersion in standing water and seldom reach the mature sizes seen in drier maple swamps. Even marshes dominated by grasses and other grasslike plants will have scattered wetland shrubs, including Smooth and Speckled Alder, Silky Dogwood, and Buttonbush. The scattered woody shrub species may indicate the first stages of succession from a grass-dominated marsh to a shrub swamp. As woody wetland shrubs become more numerous, the shrubs shade and outcompete their lower grasslike neighbors, and over time what was marsh evolves into a shrub swamp. Larger marshes often contain a mix of communities in the same area: a grass-dominated marsh or wet meadow with patches of shrub swamp growing on the drier ground around the edges of the marsh.

Marshes dominated by grasses, sedges, and rushes are home to marsh specialists such as the American Bittern, Virginia Rail, and Sora (a small rail species). Many heron species also feed and sometimes breed in freshwater marshes. And, of course, wetlands are full of dragonflies, damselflies, and other flying and aquatic insects. Joe-Pye Weed is a widespread wildflower in marshes and wet meadows, where its light-violet flowers attract butterflies, dragonflies, and other insects.

Deeper marshes almost always have patches of open water, often near the center of the marsh. These open waters are ideal feeding grounds for dabbling ducks including Mallards, American Wigeons, Blue-Winged Teals, and Pintails. Dabbling duck species do not dive under the water surface to feed, and the shallow water of marshes offers rich feeding at just the right

American Bittern
Botaurus lentiginosus

Joe-Pye Weed (*Eutrochium purpureum*) is a very common wildflower in northeastern wetland edges and grassy fields. The light pink flowers are very attractive to all kinds of butterflies, here an Eastern Tiger Swallowtail (*Papilio glaucus*). Dragonflies also seem to like hanging around Joe-Pye Weed, probably to pick off smaller pollinating insects.

Marshes

We can thank the North American Beaver (Castor canadensis) for this beautiful cattail marsh along Webster Road in Litchfield, Connecticut. The beavers have long dammed up the Miry Brook, but because the brook is small, the low water flows of summer result more in marshes than in open water. The emergent marsh is mostly Common Cattail (Typha latifolia), with Tussock Sedges (Carex stricta) and a Red Maple (Acer rubrum), a classic wetland tree species, in the foreground.

Common (Broad-Leaved) Cattail
Typha latifolia

NLC shows a gap between male (top) and female flowers.

Narrow-Leaved Cattail
Typha angustifolia

depth. Open marshes also offer ducks and other birds protection from predators such as foxes and coyotes, which have difficulty moving in deeper marshes. The marshes, open wetlands, and farm fields along the Connecticut River and Central Valley of New England offer essential feeding and resting areas in the spring and fall migration seasons. Birders know the Central Valley flyway as one of the best areas to see migrants, especially in autumn.

Cattail marshes

Almost all deeper freshwater marshes have some cattail species present. Stands of cattail often form a scattered mosaic alongside patches of Tussock Sedge or other marsh grasses. But some emergent marshes are so dominated by cattail species that they form a distinct marsh ecosystem. The most common cattail in freshwater marshes is the Broad-Leaved or Common Cattail, which forms dense stands that typically exclude other native plants except for scattered Northern Wild Rice or Big Cordgrass. Unfortunately, the stands of cattail are often mixed with the invasive Common Reed (Phragmites). The salt-tolerant Narrow-Leaved Cattail forms dense reed marshes along the banks of the Connecticut River estuary near the mouth of the river in places such as Lyme, Connecticut (see pp. 364–65). Narrow-Leaved Cattails are more tolerant of brackish water and are often found along the edges of brackish marshes and salt marshes on the New England coast.

Narrow-Leaved Cattails are also much more tolerant of water polluted by sewage. Thus a stand of Narrow-Leaved Cattails in inland areas may indicate a problem with runoff waters polluted by sewage or excess nutrients from lawn fertilizers and household soaps. Narrow-Leaved Cattail stands in roadside ditches may also indicate salt pollution from wintertime salt washing off roads. The Narrow-Leaved Cattail and the invasive Common Reed (*Phragmites*) are tolerant of the alkaline waters created by excess salts and pollutants, so the two types of grass often grow in mixed stands along roadsides. However, some stands of Narrow-Leaved Cattails are perfectly natural and an indicator of neutral to basic soil types.

A mixed grassy and emergent marsh adjacent to a pond, with a rich combination of Tussock Sedge, Northern Wild Rice, Tall Cordgrass, Royal Fern, Cinnamon Fern, and Common Cattail (not yet in bloom). Duckweed spots the water surface, and skinny alder shrubs mix in on the slightly higher ground.

Ongley Pond, White Memorial Foundation, Litchfield, Connecticut.

Shallow marshes and wet meadows

Shallow marshes are dominated by grasslike plants (grass, sedges, rushes) mixed with many herbaceous species. The maximum water depth may only be a few inches to a foot, but that is often sufficient to limit the growth of trees and shrubs. Plants that dominate low marshes and wet meadows must tolerate a wide range of water depths, but the flooding fluctuations increase the marsh's nutrient richness. In low-water periods, old leaves and dead plant materials break down more quickly in the presence of oxygen from the air, and these nutrients are recycled promptly into the marsh environment. Streams usually feed marshes, but most marshes also receive groundwater and rainwater runoff from the uplands around the marsh, and the runoff water is often rich in mineral nutrients.

Wet meadows (also called sedge meadows) are freshwater marshes with very shallow standing water for part of the year. Still, they typically lose much of their standing water in the heat and dryness of late summer and early autumn. Many wet meadows are dominated by dense clumps of Tussock Sedges, which can function almost like little islands in the marsh, particularly in the wetter seasons. Red-Winged Blackbirds often use the center of large Tussock Sedges as dry platforms to build their nests well above the marsh water level.

Red-Winged Blackbirds (*Agelaius phoeniceus*)

The Red-Winged Blackbird is found throughout North and Central America and is very common in wetlands in the Connecticut River region. Red-Wings are named for the male's brilliant scarlet epaulets against a deep black body. The brown, mottled Red-Wing females look like stocky, oversized sparrows.

Red-Winged Blackbirds inhabit open areas such as marshes, meadows, fields, and wetlands. In summer, Red-Wings feed mainly on insects and eat grains, berries, and other small fruits. In winter, their primary diet shifts to seeds, stray corn kernels in farm fields, and berries and nuts. The Red-Wings' breeding season begins in early spring and continues through early summer. During this time, males establish and defend their territories and attract females with their unique "cong-ga-reeee!" calls, one of the most familiar sounds in all wetlands. Females typically build cup-shaped nests in low shrubs at the periphery of marshes or trees and lay two to five eggs per clutch. Within wetlands, Red-Wings also build nests in the centers of large Tussock Sedges. The young birds leave the nest after about two weeks and can fly after another two weeks.

The edges of wet meadows can be excellent places for watching birds, butterflies, and dragonflies. Wet meadow wildflowers such as Joe-Pye Weed, Ironweed, Blue Vervain, and Swamp Milkweed are particularly attractive to larger easily-spotted butterflies like the Monarch, the swallowtail species, fritillaries, and buckeyes.

With their abundant insect life, shallow marshes and wet meadows are a paradise for the common frog species: Bullfrogs, Green Frogs, Northern Leopard Frogs, Pickerel Frogs, Gray Treefrogs, and Spring Peepers. Marshes attract a wide range of bird species. Long-legged waterbirds, such as herons, rails, and the large but secretive American Bittern, are all characteristic marsh and wet meadow birds. Smaller birds such as Song Sparrows, Swamp Sparrows, and Marsh Wrens are common in freshwater marshes.

Marshes

Maple–Alder–Buttonbush-Dogwood Shrub Swamp
Bantam River marshes along Whites Wood Road, Litchfield, CT

Red Maple

Smooth Alder

Buttonbush

Silky Dogwood

Royal Fern

Tussock Sedge

Red-tailed Hawk

Red Maple

Black Gum (Tupelo)

Mixed: Smooth Alder Buttonbush Silky Dogwood Royal Fern

Mixed Tussock Sedges and Bulrushes

Wild Rice

Buttonbush

For component photography credits, please see pp. 415–17.

CAROLINA
WREN

MARSH
WREN

Red Maples

GRAY
CATBIRD

Black Willow

WOOD
DUCKS

Shrub Swamps

The abundant wildlife, wide open spaces of wet meadows, and shallow marshes attract predators. Nocturnal predators such as Eastern Screech Owls and Barred Owls happily take frogs, toads, Meadow Voles (wild mice), and other small animals. Northern Harriers are frequently seen over wet meadows in spring and fall migration seasons. But the most commonly seen predator over grassy marshes is the Red-Tailed Hawk. It's rare to spend time in wetland meadows and not see a Red-Tail flying in broad circles over the marsh.

Shrub swamps

In the northeastern United States, a shrub swamp is a wetland dominated by woody plants, including Smooth Alder, Speckled Alder, Buttonbush, Silky Dogwood, Red-Osier Dogwood, and Black Willow. The alder species are particularly tolerant of standing water, and alders have tough, flexible branches that can withstand the force of flowing water in flood periods.

Immature
plumage

Generally, a wetland is considered a shrub swamp when at least 50 percent of the area is covered with wetland shrub species. Water depth is variable with the seasons. The water table may drop below ground level in dry summers, although the soil remains saturated.

Shrub swamps are typically found in low-lying areas with poor drainage and are flooded by groundwater or surface water. Shrub swamps are often considered a transitional succession stage between wet meadows and true swamps dominated by larger trees such as Red Maple, Black Tupelo, Yellow Birch, Black Ash, Balsam Fir, and Black Spruce. These dense, tangled environments provide important refuge habitats for many kinds of wildlife. Shrub swamps are also important in regional water filtration and help to reduce erosion and flooding in the surrounding area.

The dense tangle of shrub swamps make them ideal refuge habitat for nesting birds and small aquatic animals.

Red-Tailed Hawks *(Buteo jamaicensis)*

This large hawk is one of North America's most common and most versatile avian predators. Red-Tails can be found in almost all New England habitats except deep forest woodlands and swamps with mature trees. As a daytime (diurnal) hunter, the Red-Tail is New England's most commonly seen bird of prey.

You'll see Red-Tailed Hawks soaring above every kind of freshwater or brackish wetland. Red-Tails are visual hunters, constantly scanning open environments such as marshes from the air as they soar or from high lookouts while perching on dead trees. Gray Squirrels are their most common prey, but these hawks will take almost any small animal, including many aquatic animals such as frogs and young turtles.

Adult plumage

Shrub Swamps

Swamps

A swamp is a wetland dominated by large trees. Swamps are often found next to woodland streams or on older river floodplains, near ponds and lake edges where the shoreline rises very gradually. They are found where the ground is level and the local water table is generally at or a few inches above ground level. Hardwood swamps are often a late successional stage of earlier shrub swamps, and in most hardwood swamps, woody shrubs form a dense understory layer above the wet soil. Swamps are often seasonally flooded; even a true mature hardwood swamp may be difficult to distinguish from a floodplain forest when the ground is dry in late summer. Even in drier seasons, true swamps often have a dense carpet of mosses and wetland ferns including Cinnamon Fern, Sensitive Fern, and Lady Fern. In contrast, drier floodplain forests show only occasional patches of moss and upland ferns such as Bracken Fern and Ostrich Fern.

You can recognize a mature swamp by the combination of shallow standing water under large wet-tolerant tree species including Red Maple, Black Tupelo, Yellow Birch, Red Spruce, Black Spruce, and American Larch. Most hardwood swamps have a well-developed shrub layer of wetland species such as Sweet Pepperbush, Highbush Blueberry, Sheep Laurel, Leatherleaf, and Northern Arrowwood. A dead giveaway for swamp habitat is dense patches of Skunk Cabbage under mature trees, as Skunk Cabbages favor areas where the soil is saturated for much of the year. The drier edges of swamps often have a mix of Eastern Hemlocks, Red Maples, and various birch species, often with a dense understory of Mountain Laurel.

Swamps are critical wildlife habitats because they are often hellishly difficult for people to move around in. The dense, tangled understory shrubs and mucky soils make swamps a natural refuge for many bird and mammal species. Swamps next to rivers also create natural wildlife corridors where wild animals can range over large areas while also having shelter from predators. Swamps make ideal nesting habitats for many warblers and other small songbirds, including the Northern Waterthrush, which only nests within

The Northern Waterthrush (*Parkesia noveboracensis*) is a classic bird of swamps, shrub swamps, and woodland creeks. Waterthrushes have unusually long legs for a warbler, and this allows them to wade into shallow water in search of food.

cratervalley

hardwood swamps. Wood Ducks are one of the few dabbling duck species that nest in tree cavities, and hardwood swamps next to ponds make perfect shelter and feeding habitats for Wood Duck parents and their ducklings. Wooded swamps are also home to vernal pools (described below, pp. 328–39), a critical wetland wildlife habitat dependent on wet soil sheltered under a canopy of trees that shed their leaves in autumn.

Beavers and wetlands

If we could travel back to the precontact New England of the 1500s, we might barely recognize many of the familiar rivers and streams in our landscape today. Streams and small rivers back then were more like chains of shallow lakes impounded behind tangled wooden dams. Extensive freshwater marshes and wet meadows broke up the forest cover of New England, and few streams flowed for more than a mile or two before entering a pond or deep marshland. The profusion of freshwater wetlands supported vast numbers of waterfowl and other wetland inhabitants, and countless migratory fish brought the nutrients of the sea to the farthest inland brooks and streams of Vermont and New Hampshire. This rich but very wet landscape was heavily engineered, but not by humans.

Wood Ducks *(Aix sponsa)*

Wood Ducks are among the few North American ducks that make their nests in trees, usually in swamps or at the edge of a pond or marsh with open water. The female will lay a clutch of six to 14 eggs, which she incubates for about 30 days. Once the eggs hatch, the ducklings leave the nest within 24 hours and jump to the ground. The mother guides them to the water, where they feed on aquatic insects, small fish, and other food sources.

In the winter, you'll find Wood Ducks in various habitats, including freshwater marshes, ponds, lakes, and rivers. They feed on aquatic vegetation, seeds, and small invertebrates. They also feed in harvested farm fields, looking for leftovers such as corn and rice grains.

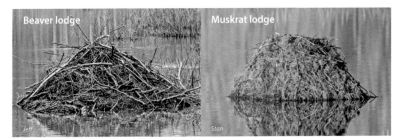

Beaver lodge

Muskrat lodge

Biologists call Beavers a keystone species, meaning that they profoundly impact their ecosystem by creating habitats for many other species. Beavers modify streams and wetlands by building dams, thereby creating new ponds, marshes, and swamps, increasing natural water storage, and improving water quality.

Beaver lodges are large structures six to eight feet wide and have many large branches on the exterior. **Muskrat lodges,** though similar, are smaller and made with the leaves of aquatic plants, with only a few smaller sticks showing.

Before 1620 and the arrival of European settlers, there were an estimated 400 million Beavers in North America. By 1900, the Beaver population in the Lower 48 States had dwindled to around 100,000, thanks to relentless hunting and trapping. North America has lost half its wetland acreage since 1620, but most of

Swamps

Beaver workings are pretty easy to spot. Favorite wetland or riparian trees include aspens, cottonwoods, birches, and willows.

those vanished marshes and swamps were not filled or bulldozed by people. When trappers and fur hunters extirpated the Beaver in New England, the Beaver's works were also lost. Within a few decades, the ponds and marshes behind Beaver dams disappeared as the barriers disintegrated and washed away.

By 1900, North America's largest rodent was absent from New England. In the early twentieth century, enlightened naturalists and foresters realized how much wetland habitat diversity had been lost with the disappearance of Beavers. From the 1910s to the 1930s, small numbers of Beavers were reintroduced to Connecticut, Massachusetts, Vermont, and New Hampshire, where they had been absent for decades. The reintroduced Beaver population increased rapidly across New England. In the early twentieth century, abandoned farmland throughout New England was returning to forest, and the new Beavers had no competition. Today there are no hard estimates for the Beaver population of central New England. Still, wildlife biologists estimate that the Beaver population has almost reached the carrying capacity of current wetlands. This is a far lower population than before 1620, but the much-reduced wetland acres now hold

Wetland mammals are often mistaken for one another when swimming. There are very substantial size and weight differences among the common mammals, so it pays to be skeptical when you hear stories of "giant swimming rats" in the local park. Muskrats, beavers, and even otters are more widespread than you think, even in urban park wetlands.

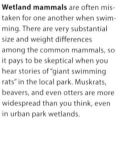

RACCOON
Procyon lotor
28 in. long, 10–20 lbs.

Muskrats have horizontally flattened tails, which they use to swim.

MUSKRAT
Ondatra zibethicus
20 in. long, 3–4 lbs.

BROWN RAT
Rattus norvegicus
15 in. long, .75 lbs.

Photos: Eric Isselée, Iri-sha, rabbit75, Cloudtail, jnjhuz

about as many Beavers today as the current streams, ponds, and riverine forests can support. Beavers can't repopulate the wetlands that have vanished since 1620, but steadily, today's Beavers are rebuilding what was lost.

Beavers dam streams to create ponds deep enough to not entirely freeze over in the winter. Swimming under the ice gives Beavers protection from predators, shelter from the elements, and a safe place to raise their young. Beavers build their lodges in water deep enough for them to enter and leave the lodge while underwater.

Beavers are sophisticated water engineers. In building their dams, Beavers generally choose locations where a natural narrowing of a stream occurs, such as between rock formations or where the stream enters a narrowing valley. This efficient siting allows the dam to be as short as possible and as high as needed to dam ponds to at least four to five feet deep.

Two recent books on beavers and their importance to both human and natural history:

Eager: The Surprising, Secret Life of Beavers and Why They Matter, by Ben Goldfarb (White River Junction, VT: Chelsea Green, 2018).

Beaverland: How One Weird Rodent Made America, by Leila Philip (New York: Twelve, Hachette, 2022).

NORTH AMERICAN BEAVER
Castor canadensis
40–42 in. long, 40–70 lbs.

NORTH AMERICAN RIVER OTTER
Lontra canadensis
30–42 in. long, 10–33 lbs.

Swamps

Beavers have vertically flattened tails and use their tails to steer, not to swim.

Marshes created by Beavers are easy to spot, since all but the oldest beaver marshes will have a large number of dead trees standing amid marsh vegetation. These woodland trees died after their roots were permanently soaked when water rose behind a beaver dam and created a new wetland. This marsh was later drained when people removed the beaver dam, and the area is now a wet meadow marsh, with no open water.

Swamps

Ronnie Howard

Mature beaver dams are massive structures that the animals constantly maintain to prevent leaks. Beavers are said to be extremely sensitive to the sounds of flowing water—a warning that their dam may be leaking.

The reintroduction of Beavers has had many ecological and direct benefits to human health and safety. Beaver ponds create more numerous and diverse wetlands than might otherwise exist, and these wetlands act as both a filter for pollutants and a sponge to regulate water flows. In droughts, beaver ponds provide a steady supply of water. In storms, beaver ponds and dams buffer the flow of destructive stormwater. Ecologists call these benefits ecosystem services and assign dollar values to habitat restoration, pollution control, water regulation, and stormwater management. Beavers provide many millions of dollars in ecosystem services, and the damage from the Beaver's nuisance flooding is a tiny fraction of the benefits they provide.

Vernal pools

Vernal pools are small depressions or low spots in swamp forests, in floodplain forests, or near more extensive wetlands that fill with rainwater or snow-melt for at least several months in spring. Most vernal pools have a second annual act when they fill again in autumn. Vernal pools may be located near streams but are not fed by streams or groundwater flows. Deeper or more extensive vernal pools may persist for much of the year, but generally, vernal pools have no standing water in dry, hot summer weather. Vernal pools depend on the forests around them, and most pools will quickly dry up if the tree cover is lost due to development or logging. Once most of the trees are gone, the ground is exposed to heat and sun, and the vernal pools lose the fallen autumn leaves that are the vital base of their food chains.

Unlike most wetland environments, vernal pools are defined by the animal communities the pools support and not by characteristic vegetation. Most vernal pools are unvegetated within the pool, and their bottoms are typically lined with a layer of leaves that fell the previous autumn. These months-old rotting leaves host a rich biofilm composed of bacteria and fungi. These biofilms form the base of the vernal pool food chain, and the films are consumed directly by fairy shrimp, amphipods, and insect larvae. Some vernal pools host a variety of wetland plants at or around their edges, including scattered Skunk Cabbages, Wood Violets,

Highbush Blueberry, Red Maple saplings, and Buttonbush shrubs. However, most vernal pools are found in forests, where they are in deep shade for much of the year, so plant life in and around vernal pools is not usually lush owing to the lack of sunlight.

Vernal pools are a critically important habitat for breeding amphibians. Seasonal dry periods prevent vernal pools from hosting resident fish species that might eat amphibian eggs. On warm spring nights, American Toads and many other frog and salamander species make their way from upland forest areas down to vernal pools to breed and lay eggs. Short-lived vernal pools can support frog and toad eggs and tadpoles that require about four months to mature, but most salamanders require pools that persist for at least five months, so only larger vernal pools usually have salamander eggs.

Out in the spring woods searching for vernal pools? Keep an eye—and ear—out for American Woodcocks (*Scolopax minor*). Spring is their mating season. At dusk, these normally secretive and camouflaged birds perform amazing display flights preceded by a loud "peeent" call. During these erratic display flights, special feathers on the male's wings also emit a whirling and twittering sound. The Woodcock uses its long, very sensitive bill to probe wetland and swamp mud for worms and other invertebrates.

Spring and Autumn Vernal Pools
Temporary but critical wildlife communities

American Toad

Eastern Comma Butterfly, an early spring species

Spring Peeper

Wood Frog

Gray Treefrog

Wood Frog Egg Mass

Diving Beetle larva preying on a tadpole

Wood Frog Tadpoles

Spotted Salamanders

Animals are not to scale

Hatchling Eastern Painted Turtle

Red-Spotted Newt

Common Snapping Turtle

Common Gartersnake

For component photography credits, please see pp. 415–17.

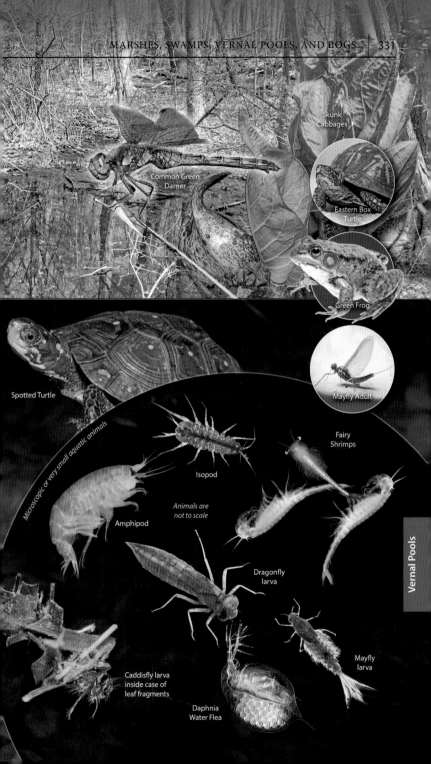

Common Green Darner

Skunk Cabbages

Eastern Box Turtle

Green Frog

Spotted Turtle

Mayfly Adult

Microscopic or very small aquatic animals

Isopod

Fairy Shrimps

Amphipod

Animals are not to scale

Dragonfly larva

Caddisfly larva inside case of leaf fragments

Daphnia Water Flea

Mayfly larva

Vernal Pools

A classic vernal pool in early spring. This pool sits in a swampy bottomland forest area watered mostly by artesian leakage from the steep hillsides nearby. American Toads, Wood Frogs, Pickerel Frogs, and Spotted Salamanders use this and nearby pools to mate and lay eggs. Pools here last until about midsummer, and by the normally dry period in early September, no standing water will remain under the trees, although the soil will stay moist.

Kevin

The Grass Pink (*Calopogon tuberosus*) is a common orchid found in bogs throughout the Northeast.

Bogs

Bogs are one of the rarest wetland environments in the Connecticut River region. In northern New England, bog environments can form along the shallow edges of ponds and lakes, but they mostly form in cool, moist microclimates such as isolated valleys and glacial kettle hole ponds. These "frost pocket" or bottomland bog ponds are fed usually by rainwater and sometimes by small, low-volume streams, and they may not have an outlet stream. Plant decay in bogs is extremely slow, and bog water is highly acidic and lacking in nutrients. The dominant sphagnum moss cover builds up over centuries, converting a formerly open pond into a basin filled with sphagnum peat, covered with a dense mat of living mosses.

Bogs are a remnant environment from the end of the Wisconsinan Glaciation 20,000–15,000 years ago, when the central New England environment was more like northern Canada is today. Arctic heaths and bog environments survived in isolated, cold, pocket valleys or on mountaintops. At the same time, everything around them evolved into the climax forests and typical temperate wetlands we see in today's Connecticut River region. With their highly acidic water, specialized flora, and poor nutrient supply, bogs attract few animal species besides insects. Still, their unique flora makes bogs a fascinating environment to visit.

Carnivorous plants are the most unusual species found in bogs. Bog plant roots tend to be shallow and stay within the sphagnum surface layer of the bog and thus don't reach down to the mineral soils on the bottom of the bog. Bog water is particularly poor in nitrogen and phosphorus, so plants such as pitcher plants and the Round-Leaved Sundew supplement their nutrient intake by trapping and digesting insects and other small animals. Pitcher plants have deep, slippery pitcher tubes filled with a sweet-smelling liquid. Insects fly or crawl into the pitcher seeking nectar, are trapped by the slick walls of the pitcher, and fall into the nectar. Once the insect is trapped, digestive enzymes secreted by the pitcher plant break down the insect, and the plant absorbs the resulting nutrients.

Sundews have leaves covered in sticky hairs that trap small flying insects.

The Hawley Bog in west-central Massachusetts is a spectacular and easily accessible example of a bog environment, with good trails to the bog and a long boardwalk that takes you from the upland edges well out onto the sphagnum surface of the bog. All the major bog plant species are well represented, and the boardwalk also passes by Potash Brook, which feeds the Hawley Bog. Potash Brook is a small but very interesting transitional area with characteristics of a conventional freshwater wetland mixed with more typical bog shrubs and trees as the brook passes into the actual bog area (see pp. 338–39).

The sticky leaves of the tiny but gorgeous Round-Leaved Sundew (*Drosera rotundifolia*) are deadly to small insects and may even trap insects as large as damsel-flies. Sundew plants are easy to overlook in bogs because they are so small, but in the Hawley Bog there are countless thousands embedded in the dense sphagnum surface of the bog.

Matauw

Bogs

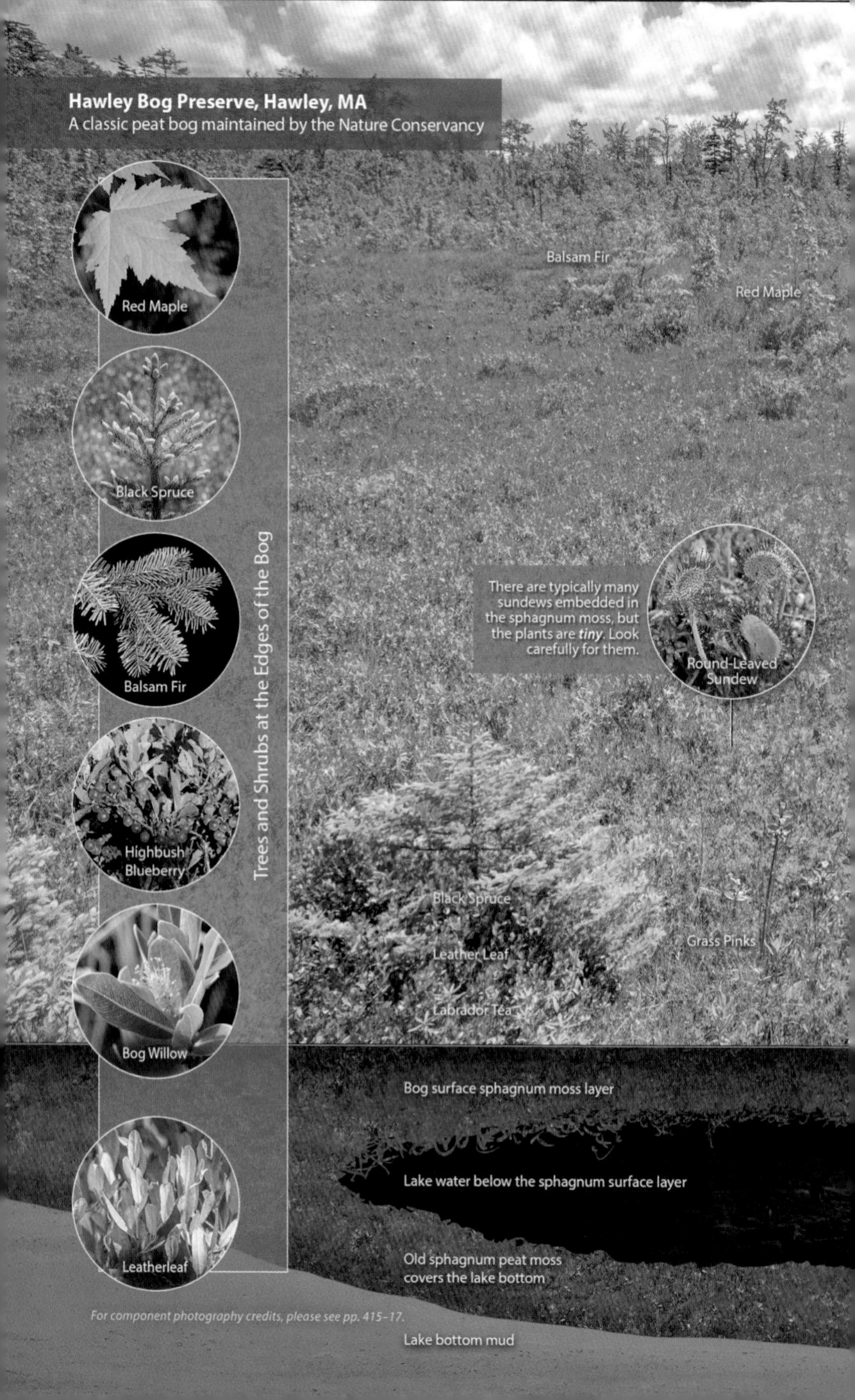

Hawley Bog Preserve, Hawley, MA
A classic peat bog maintained by the Nature Conservancy
Trees and Shrubs at the Edges of the Bog
Red Maple
Black Spruce
Balsam Fir
Highbush Blueberry
Bog Willow
Leatherleaf
Balsam Fir
Red Maple
There are typically many sundews embedded in the sphagnum moss, but the plants are *tiny*. Look carefully for them.
Round-Leaved Sundew
Black Spruce
Leather Leaf
Labrador Tea
Grass Pinks
Bog surface sphagnum moss layer
Lake water below the sphagnum surface layer
Old sphagnum peat moss covers the lake bottom
Lake bottom mud

For component photography credits, please see pp. 415–17.

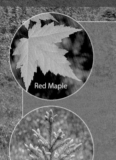

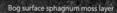

Black Spruce, Red Maple, Leatherleaf, and Highbush Blueberry along the bog edges

Black Spruce and Labrador Tea

Pitcher Plant Flowers

Purple Pitcher Plants

Plants at the Center of the Bog

Sphagnum Moss forms the bog surface

Purple Pitcher Plant

Grass Pink

Round-Leaved Sundew

Labrador Tea

Bog Laurel

Water depth below the sphagnum layer can vary from a few inches to many feet.

There is a small area of open water at Hawley Bog, but it is far to the right of this view.

Bogs

Potash Brook, at the edge of the Hawley Bog
A transition between the forest creek and bog environments

Black Spruce

Hawley Bog in the background

Red Maple

Tussock Sedge

Potash Brook

Yellow Water-Lily

Red Maple

Black Spruce

American Larch

Spicebush Swallowtail

Balsam Fir

Royal Fern

Leather

Highbush Blueberry

American Bullfrog (female)

Bog
A ve
spe
four
Haw

Red Maple

Red Maple

Arrowwood Viburnum
Bog Laurel
Black Chokeberry
Leatherleaf

Leatherleaf
Highbush Blueberry
Bog Laurel
Royal Fern

Common
Cattail

Tussock Sedge

Eastern Pondhawk
Dragonfly (female)

Green Darner
Dragonfly

Yellow
Water-Lily

Tussock
Sedge

Leatherleaf

Arrowwood
Viburnum

Cinnamon
Fern

Black
Chokeberry

Bogs

Best reference to bog plants: *Bogs and Fens,* by Ronald B. Davis (Lebanon, NH: University Press of New England, 2016).

RED MAPLE *Acer rubrum*

BLACK SPRUCE *Picea mariana*

BALSAM FIR *Abies balsamea*

AMERICAN LARCH *Larix laricina*

RED SPRUCE *Picea rubens*

NORTHERN WHITE CEDAR *Thuja occidentalis*

GHBUSH BLUEBERRY *Vaccinium corymbosum*

BOG WILLOW *Salix pedicellaris*

ATHERLEAF *Chamaedaphne calyculata*

LABRADOR TEA *Rhododendron groenlandicum*

G LAUREL *Kalmia polifolia*

SWEET GALE *Myrica gale*

Bogs

Best reference to bog plants: *Bogs and Fens,* by Ronald B. Davis (Lebanon, NH: University Press of New England, 2016).

SMALL CRANBERRY *Vaccinium oxycoccos*

BOG ROSEMARY *Andromeda polifolia*

CREEPING SNOWBERRY *Gaultheria hispidula*

ROYAL FERN *Osmunda regalis*

SPATULATE-LEAVED SUNDEW *Drosera intermedia*

ROUND-LEAVED SUNDEW *Drosera rotundifo*

AGON'S MOUTH ORCHID *Arethusa bulbosa*

SWAMP LOOSESTRIFE *Decodon verticillatus*

SE POGONIA *Pogonia ophioglossoides*

STARFLOWER *Trientalis borealis*

RPLE PITCHER PLANT *Sarracenia purpurea*

GRASS PINK *Calopogon tuberosus*

An overview of the brackish tidal reed marshes of the Lord Cove Wildlife Area, in Lyme, Connecticut. The channel in the foreground is a tidal creek in front of the Olivers Hole area of the marsh, with the main channel of the Connecticut River in the distance.

THE CONNECTICUT RIVER ESTUARY

The lower Connecticut River is the most pristine large-river tidal marsh system in the Northeast, thanks mainly to the lack of a major port at or near its mouth. Constantly shifting sandbars and sediment reefs have always made the lower Connecticut River a difficult place for larger ships. The lack of an urban, industrialized port has preserved the unspoiled rural character of the landscape around the river and protected its many brackish and freshwater environments. In addition to hosting large populations of migratory waterfowl, the rich tidal marshes of the Connecticut are home to several rare, threatened, or endangered species, including the Bald Eagle, Shortnose Sturgeon, Puritan Tiger Beetle, and the tiny, beach-nesting Piping Plover and Least Tern.

Old Lyme's Lieutenant River. The Lieutenant is a brackish tidal river, with extensive salt, brackish, and freshwater marshes along its length. The Florence Griswold Museum in Old Lyme offers a gorgeous walking trail along the river, as well as a world-class collection of American Impressionist paintings. The art museum is also next to the Connecticut Audubon Society's Roger Tory Peterson Estuary Center, which also offers excellent views of the river. Both institutions are open to the public.

The lower Connecticut River is generally defined as the southernmost 36 miles of the river, from Portland and Cromwell, Connecticut, south to the river's mouth at Old Lyme and Old Saybrook. This lower section of the river is about 9 percent of the total length of the river, and the lower Connecticut drains about 115,260 acres of the Connecticut landscape, or about 2 percent of the river's total drainage area.

The Connecticut River estuary and tidal wetlands complex has long been recognized as a global ecological treasure. In 1995, the international Ramsar Conven-

Hamburg Cove, Lyme, Connecticut, is one of the distinctive coves that line the lower Connecticut River. Hamburg Cove was formed as a river valley that was flooded by the rising seas after the end of the Wisconsinan Glaciation (the Ice Age).

tion on Wetlands, which works to ensure that wetlands of all kinds are properly protected and managed, designated the lower Connecticut River as a Wetland of International Importance. More recently, the State of Connecticut and the National Oceanic and Atmospheric Administration have jointly created a National Estuarine Research Reserve (NERR) for Long Island Sound, bounded by the Sound's two largest estuarine rivers, the Connecticut and the Thames. The Long Island Sound NERR effort seeks to preserve and manage these valuable coastal and riverine wetlands against pollution, habitat degradation, and invasive species. In addition to the Connecticut River and Thames River estuaries, the NERR encompasses the Lord Cove Wildlife Area, the Great Island Wildlife Management Area, and nearby Connecticut coastal parks such as Bluff Point and Haley Farm State Parks.

The Connecticut River estuary

The Connecticut River's lower reaches are an estuary, where freshwater flowing from inland meets the ocean's salt water or extensions such as Long Island Sound. Estuaries are some of the earth's most productive natural environments and serve as a breeding ground and home for many important seafood species and sport fish. Through its direct connection to Long Island Sound, the lower Connecticut is also a tidal estuary. The twice-daily pulse of tides influences the flow rate and height of the river. The tidal range between high and low tides is about three feet at the river's mouth in Old Saybrook, directly reflecting the adjacent Eastern Basin of Long Island Sound's average tidal range.

A tidal river

The term "tidal" is often associated with salty ocean waters, but most tidal rivers run entirely fresh until they near the sea. On an average day, the surface waters of the Connecticut River under the I-95 Baldwin Bridge are fresh. However, heavier saltwater can intrude under the fresh surface waters as far north as Essex and Nott Island. Long Island Sound's salinity three miles south of the I-95 Baldwin Bridge near the Connecticut River's mouth is typically about 28–30

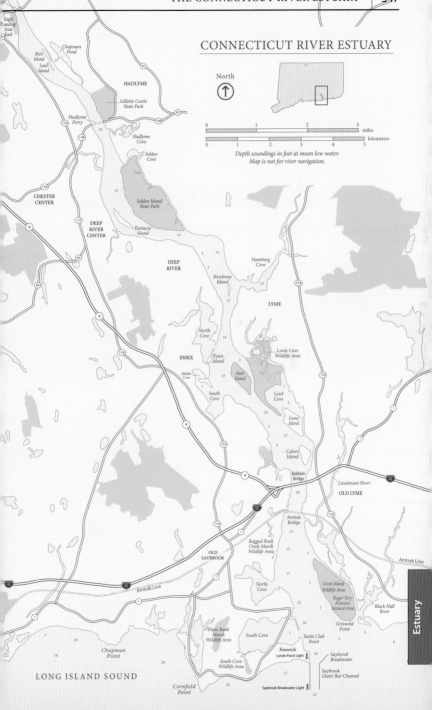

CONNECTICUT RIVER ESTUARY

North

↑

0   1   2   3 miles

0   1   2   3   4   5 kilometers

*Depth soundings in feet at mean low water.
Map is not for river navigation.*

Eagle
Landing
State
Park

Rich
Island
Lord
Island

Chapman
Pond

HADLYME

Gillette Castle
State Park

Hadlyme
Ferry

Hadlyme
Cove

Selden
Cove

CHESTER
CENTER

Selden Island
State Park

DEEP
RIVER
CENTER

Eustacia
Island

DEEP
RIVER

Brockway
Island

Hamburg
Cove

LYME

North
Cove

Essex
Island

Lords Cove
Wildlife Area

ESSEX

Middle
Cove

Nott
Island

South
Cove

Lord
Cove

Goose
Island

Calves
Island

Baldwin
Bridge

Lieutenant River

OLD LYME

Amtrak
Bridge

Ragged Rock
Creek Marsh
Wildlife Area

OLD
SAYBROOK

Amtrak Line

Amtrak Line

North
Cove

Great Island
Wildlife Area

Roger Tory
Peterson
Natural Area

Black Hall
River

Plum Bank
Marsh
Wildlife Area

South Cove

Griswold
Point

Chapman
Point

Yacht Club
Point

South Cove
Wildlife Area

Fenwick
Lynde Point Light

Saybrook
Breakwater

LONG ISLAND SOUND

Cornfield
Point

Saybrook
Outer Bar Channel

Saybrook Breakwater Light

Estuary

Salinity, productivity, and biological filtering in the estuary

Salinity in parts per thousand (ppt)   0   5   10   15   20   25   30

Physical and chemical filtration *Connecticut River flow speed lessens in deeper water*

Sediment particles lose their negative charge in brackish water

Gravity helps settle particles

Coated sediment particles clump together on bottom

River flow into estuaries
Sediment particles in freshwater have negative charges and repel each other. As sediment enters salty water, the particles lose their charge, acquire a coating of algae and bacteria, and clump together in muddy organic sediments.

Vegetation and biological filtration before the river was developed and polluted

Connecticut River flow into Long Island Sound

The historical collapse of oyster beds over the past century throughout the East Coast has sharply decreased filtering in estuaries.

Low brackish marsh
Marshes and submerged vegetation physically filter estuary water with their leaves and absorb sediments and pollutants. Natural oyster beds once filtered biological materials from the Connecticut River.

Submerged aquatic vegetation

Eelgrass beds

Oyster beds

Freshwater, brackish, and marine species

Number of species

Freshwater species

Brackish water salinities 5 ppt – 18 ppt

Marine species

Brackish water species

0   5   10   30

Although relatively few species can thrive in brackish areas, they often exist there in great numbers. Menhaden, shad, and oysters are examples.

Abundance of brackish water organisms

Number of animals

Healthy estuaries can support large numbers of individual animals

Brackish water salinities

0 ppt   5   10   15   20   25   30

The key to the extraordinary productivity and ecological importance of the estuary is the confluence of the Connecticut River's freshwater and the salt water of Long Island Sound. Freshwater is lighter than salt water, and this creates a wedge-shaped profile in the river's depths, with salt water sliding northward upriver underneath the freshwater at the river's surface (diagram at right). The maps below show the extent of the brackish areas of the river, which are dependent on the volume of river flows in various seasons. Estuary plants and organisms are also important in filtering and cleaning the water, and this increases the overall productivity of the river estuary.

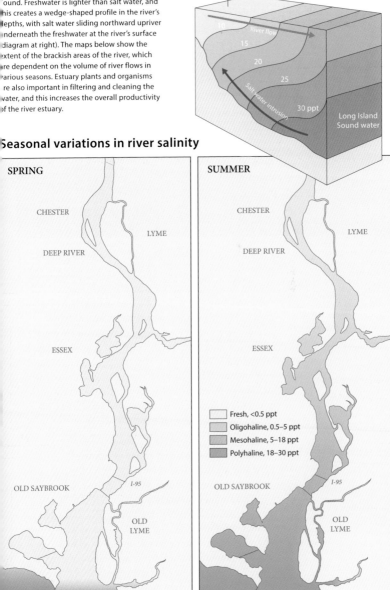

Connecticut River water outflow into Long Island Sound

Profile of a salt wedge estuary

River flow
10
15
20
25
30 ppt
Salt water intrusion

Long Island Sound water

Seasonal variations in river salinity

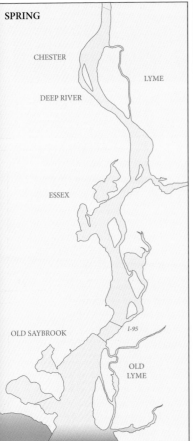

SPRING

CHESTER
LYME
DEEP RIVER
ESSEX
OLD SAYBROOK   I-95
OLD LYME

SUMMER

CHESTER
LYME
DEEP RIVER
ESSEX

☐ Fresh, <0.5 ppt
▨ Oligohaline, 0.5–5 ppt
▨ Mesohaline, 5–18 ppt
▨ Polyhaline, 18–30 ppt

OLD SAYBROOK   I-95
OLD LYME

Estuary

In a river rich with sandy postglacial sediments, many of the features of the lower Connecticut River are analogous to the barrier islands and peninsulas seen on ocean coasts. As sediments accumulate above the high tide level, plants quickly move in to colonize the new area and stabilize the sediments. Lord Island, Rich Island, and the northern tip of Chapman Pond, along the river in East Haddam, Connecticut.

ppt (parts per thousand), slightly less saline than the Atlantic Ocean's 34–37 ppt salinity.

When flowing against a rising tide, the river water slows slightly and is partially impounded by Long Island Sound's rising water. This backup of higher water travels northward along the river as a wave pulse of rising tides. As the level of Long Island Sound decreases in low tide, the river flows more easily, and the river surface falls to reflect the easier flow, creating a low tide in the river. The river is tidal as far north as the Enfield Rapids in Windsor Locks, Connecticut, 80 miles north of the mouth of the river, where the tide range at Enfield is about two feet.

Estuary salt wedges and zones of salinity

The Connecticut River flow rates are highly seasonal, from an average low of 968 cubic feet per second in the dry months of late summer to a high of 282,000 cubic feet per second in the spring flood. This wide variation in flow volume affects the profile of the salinity of the river. Average salinities range from 10 ppt to 30 ppt near the mouth of the Connecticut off Old Saybrook. The river may be entirely freshwater (<5 ppt) even at high tide near the river mouth in the spring flood. In the low flows of late summer, the Connecticut's surface waters may be brackish as far north as Eustasia Island off Deep River (see maps, p. 349).

The Connecticut River estuary is what ecologists call a salt wedge estuary. Salt wedges occur when heavier salt water from Long Island Sound intrudes upriver, creeping northward under the south-flowing fresh river water at the surface. In large water bodies, salt water and freshwater don't readily mix, and they maintain separate layers in the river's water column. There is so much fresh meltwater flowing in the Connecticut River in the spring flood that the deep salt wedge may be absent, even near the river mouth.

The geology of the estuary

The extensive marshes and river islands of the lower Connecticut River are a legacy of the most recent ice age, the Wisconsinan Glacial Episode that peaked about 25,000 years ago and effectively ended in the region about 15,000 years ago. The larger geologic story of the Connecticut River is covered in "The River Landscape" chapter; the focus here is on how the glacial melting and subsequent sea level rise helped form the lower Connecticut River estuary of today.

Great Island, Marvin Island, and the marshes at the mouth of the Lieutenant River in Old Lyme, Connecticut, near the mouth of the Connecticut River. The marsh islands here are built on a combination of glacial ice–contact outwash deltas and sediments carried downriver and trapped by marsh vegetation.

Estuary

As the Wisconsinan glacial ice sheet melted over Connecticut, the vast volumes of meltwater and sediments trapped within the decaying ice sheet formed ice-margin deltas of sand and silt all along the lower Connecticut River Valley. Thick layers of glacial deposits also filled the riverbed itself. The sediment beds of the lower Connecticut River are deep. Bedrock lies about 150 feet below the river at Portland, Connecticut, and 250 feet below the I-95 Baldwin Bridge in Old Saybrook.

Ice-margin delta deposits underlie all of the major marshes along the lower Connecticut River (see map of river marshes, facing page), as well as all the significant salt marshes along Connecticut's Long Island Sound coastline. Another prominent feature of the lower Connecticut River reflects the volume of glacial sediment still remaining in the river complex: the many river islands and sandy peninsulas in the river's final 10 miles.

In the warm months many boats moor in the lee of Calves Island, just north of the I-95 Baldwin Bridge in Old Lyme. The small channels that run between river islands and the shoreline provide boats, fish, waterbirds, and other river animals with shelter. The channels can also be rich with submerged aquatic vegetation, which is critical for a healthy river ecosystem.

These river islands are composed mostly of sand and silt, although some of the larger islands initially formed over and around exposed bedrock outcrops. In a sense, these river islands and peninsulas are analogous to barrier islands and peninsulas along ocean coasts. The river's strength and power in flood can move huge volumes of sediments over time, and once shallow sand structures form, they are quickly colonized by riverbank vegetation, which holds the sand in place to resist erosion. Selden, Eustacia, Brockway, Nott, Goose, Calves, and Great Islands were all formed from river sediments derived from both ice-margin delta deposits along the lower river and the general load of eroded sand and silt that the Connecticut River carries from its larger drainage area.

Ironically, the relatively pristine wetland and upland forest environments we see today along the Connecticut River banks owe their survival to the huge volumes of postglacial sediment still in the river channel. The lower Connecticut River is notorious for its shallows and constantly changing sand shoals. These navigation hazards prevented the development of a major port at the river's mouth where it meets Long Island Sound.

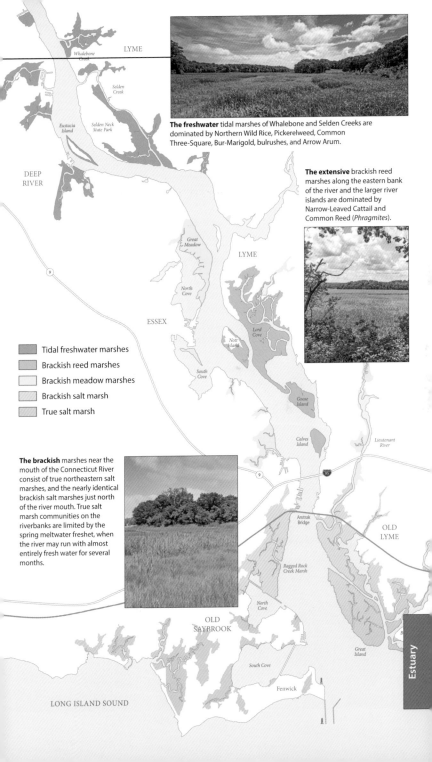

The **freshwater** tidal marshes of Whalebone and Selden Creeks are dominated by Northern Wild Rice, Pickerelweed, Common Three-Square, Bur-Marigold, bulrushes, and Arrow Arum.

The extensive brackish reed marshes along the eastern bank of the river and the larger river islands are dominated by Narrow-Leaved Cattail and Common Reed (*Phragmites*).

- Tidal freshwater marshes
- Brackish reed marshes
- Brackish meadow marshes
- Brackish salt marsh
- True salt marsh

The brackish marshes near the mouth of the Connecticut River consist of true northeastern salt marshes, and the nearly identical brackish salt marshes just north of the river mouth. True salt marsh communities on the riverbanks are limited by the spring meltwater freshet, when the river may run with almost entirely fresh water for several months.

LYME

Whalebone Creek

Selden Creek

Eustacia Island

Selden Neck State Park

DEEP RIVER

Great Meadow

LYME

North Cove

ESSEX

Nott Island

Lord Cove

South Cove

Goose Island

Calves Island

Lieutenant River

OLD LYME

Amtrak Bridge

Ragged Rock Creek Marsh

North Cove

Great Island

OLD SAYBROOK

South Cove

Fenwick

LONG ISLAND SOUND

Estuary

With no industrialized port city at its mouth, the lower Connecticut River area has retained much of its rural charm and natural beauty.

The river islands and peninsulas help shield the waters between the islands and the riverbanks. These sheltered habitats are rich with submerged aquatic vegetation. That makes these quiet-water areas important for aquatic animals and the large numbers of birds that crowd the river during spring and fall migration.

The sizable Great Meadow marsh in Essex sits behind the lower Connecticut's largest sand peninsula, and small sand peninsulas shelter cove and marsh areas in Essex's Middle Cove, Lyme's Lord Cove, and Old Saybrook's South Cove. The sand beaches and small barrier islands around Old Lyme's Griswold Point area are also formed from river sediments and other sediments carried by longshore drift along the Connecticut coastline. Although relatively small, the sand beach areas around the Connecticut River's mouth are important breeding areas for the endangered Piping Plover and Least Tern.

The brackish marshes near the mouth of the Connecticut River are barely distinguishable from the nearby salt marshes that line the shores of Long Island Sound.

A drowned coastline and river valleys

At the peak of the Wisconsinan Glacial Episode, so much of the earth's water was bound up in the continent-sized ice sheets that the global sea level 25,000 years ago was as much as 400 feet lower than it is today. As the earth warmed at the end of the glacial episode, the meltwater created rising sea levels. The rising sea eventually flooded Long Island Sound's basin and reached and entered the lower Connecticut River valley about 4,000–5,000 years ago. Along Connecticut's Long Island Sound coastline, all of the larger rivers are tidal estuaries, because all of their southernmost river valleys were "drowned" by the rising salty waters of Long Island Sound. Today the Housatonic, Quinnipiac, Connecticut, and Thames Rivers are all brackish tidal estuarine rivers ending in shallow drowned valleys that meet the Sound. The lower Connecticut River's unique coves are also mostly features created by this postglacial sea level rise when smaller tributary river valleys were drowned and became brackish as the sea level rose. Hamburg Cove, the Falls River pond and marsh complex in Essex, and the Hadlyme-Whalebone Cove are drowned tributary river valleys. At the Connecticut River's eastern mouth, the Black Hall and Lieutenant Rivers are also shallow drowned river valleys. On the

A few miles upriver from the I-95 Baldwin Bridge, the riverside wetlands are mostly brackish and tidal reed marshes, dominated by the native Narrow-Leaved Cattail and the invasive Common Reed (Phragmites). Here the marshes of Lord Cove in Lyme are almost completely Narrow-Leaved Cattail.

Estuary

Picturesque Hamburg Cove on the east bank of the Connecticut River estuary in Lyme was once a tributary river valley formed by the ancient ancestor of today's Eightmile River. As the sea level rose after the Ice Age, the old river valley flooded to become today's cove.

The slightly brackish tidal reed marshes of the upper Lord Cove area might be indistinguishable from other similar inland marshes if you visited at only one point in the tide cycle (top photo). The lower photo shows the same marsh at almost low tide. Even in marshes well upriver, the daily tide range is almost three feet. This Narrow-Leaved Cattail marsh is on Deep Creek, near where the creek meets Lord Cove. *Upper photo courtesy of Robin Ladouceur.*

river's western bank, the North and South Coves of Old Saybrook and Essex are mostly not drowned river valleys but coves formed as low spots between glacial moraines or sheltered areas behind sand peninsulas that were later flooded by sea level rise.

Brackish estuarine tidal wetlands

Tidal estuary freshwater environments differ from inland wetland environments in that the water level in tidal areas changes continuously every day. Estuary wetlands are also defined by the saltiness of the water, which forms a gradient both in the river's main stem and in the many coves and tributary rivers along the course of the last 15 miles of the Connecticut River.

Robin Ladouceur

Three general types of ecosystems are present in the lower Connecticut River: brackish estuarine, riverine, and palustrine wetlands. Brackish and salt marshes form where the river water and tidal water from Long Island Sound range in salinity between 0.5–30 ppt and there is a sufficient bed of shallow sediments to support the marsh.

Plants are most actively growing in the spring and early summer, so salinity conditions during the spring are most influential in determining the character of Connecticut River estuarine marshes. Salinities in the lower Connecticut River are relatively low in spring and early summer, limiting the range of highly salt-adapted salt marsh species. Estuarine habitats in the lower Connecticut River extend from the mouth of the river north about eight miles to Brockway Island, the marshes of Great Meadows in Essex, and the mouth of Hamburg Cove.

Ten miles upriver from the mouth of the Connecticut River, the marshes of Hadlyme Cove are entirely fresh but still have at least a two-foot daily tide cycle.

A true Connecticut River salt marsh exists only at the very southern tip of Great Island in Old Lyme. Still, as usual in natural habitats, there are no hard and fast boundaries between environments. To all but professional ecologists, the brackish marshes that line both banks of the Connecticut River mouth look like salt marshes. They are dominated by the same species of grasses and sedges found in true salt marshes: Saltwater Cordgrass, Saltmeadow Cordgrass, Spike Grass, and Blackgrass. Ecologists call most of the marshes south of the I-95 Baldwin Bridge brackish marshes primarily because some true salt marsh plant species are absent or uncommon in these river marshes. For example, highly salt-tolerant plants such as Sea Lavender and Glassworts are seen less frequently in river mouth marshes. Other less salt-tolerant plants such as Seaside Goldenrod and Marsh Arrowgrass are often more common in brackish river marshes. The different marsh plant distributions are caused primarily by the spring and early summer freshet. The river may flow with almost pure freshwater for several months due to the flood of meltwater from storm rains and thawing winter snows. Brackish marshes also line the banks of the Lieutenant River and the Black Hall River in Old Lyme and some areas along the shores of the North

General habitats of the Connecticut River estuary

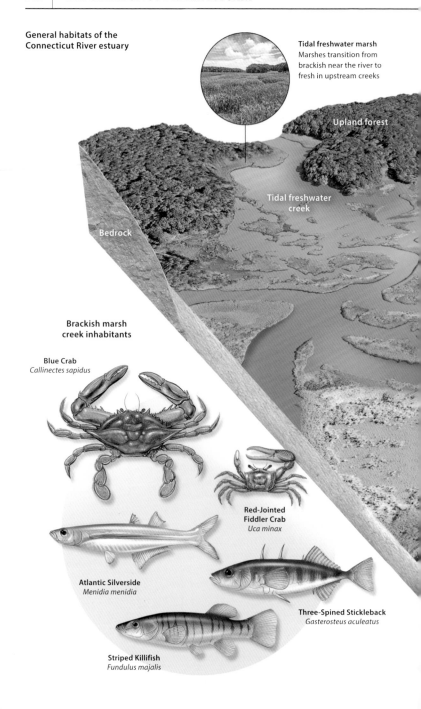

Tidal freshwater marsh
Marshes transition from brackish near the river to fresh in upstream creeks

Upland forest

Tidal freshwater creek

Bedrock

Brackish marsh creek inhabitants

Blue Crab
Callinectes sapidus

Red-Jointed Fiddler Crab
Uca minax

Atlantic Silverside
Menidia menidia

Three-Spined Stickleback
Gasterosteus aculeatus

Striped Killifish
Fundulus majalis

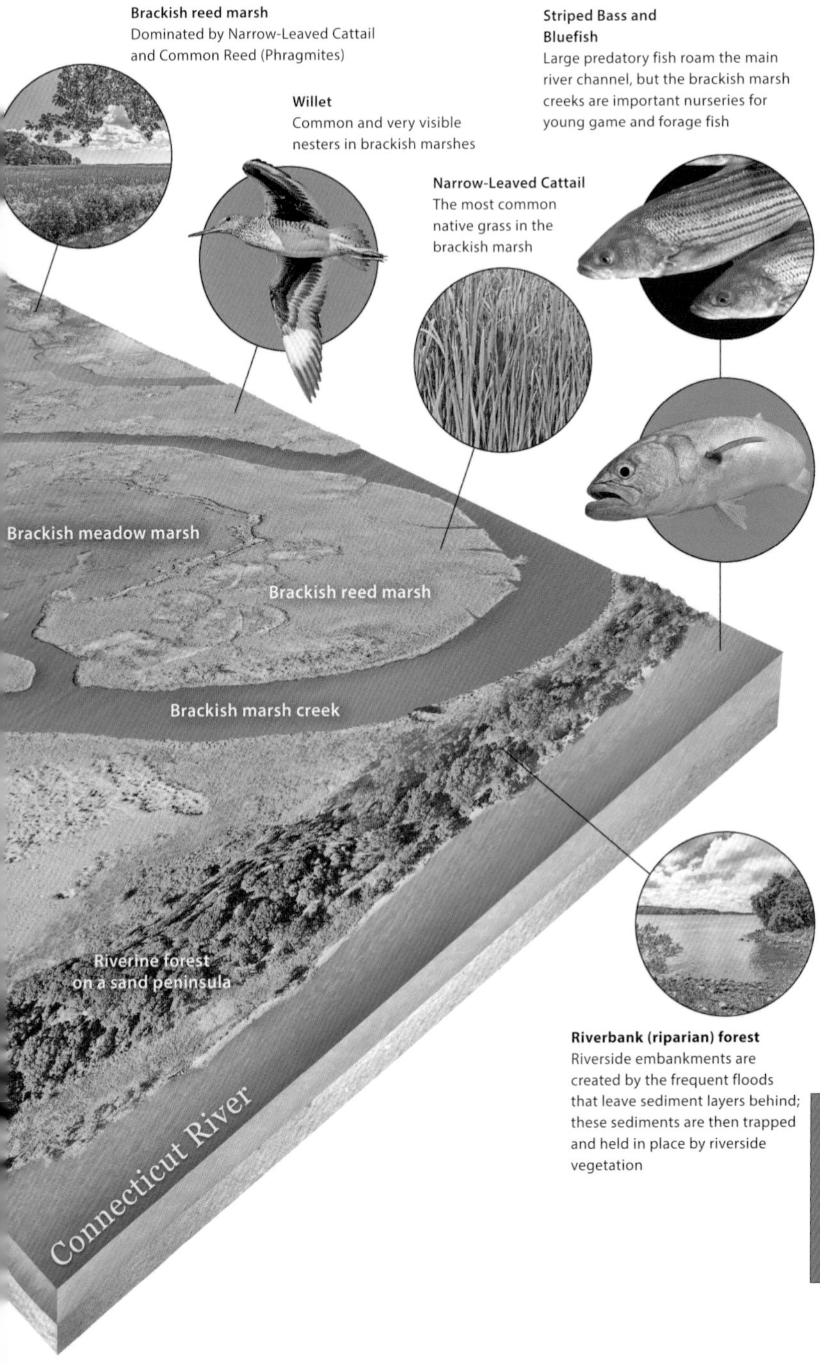

Brackish reed marsh
Dominated by Narrow-Leaved Cattail and Common Reed (Phragmites)

Striped Bass and Bluefish
Large predatory fish roam the main river channel, but the brackish marsh creeks are important nurseries for young game and forage fish

Willet
Common and very visible nesters in brackish marshes

Narrow-Leaved Cattail
The most common native grass in the brackish marsh

Brackish meadow marsh

Brackish reed marsh

Brackish marsh creek

Riverine forest on a sand peninsula

Connecticut River

Riverbank (riparian) forest
Riverside embankments are created by the frequent floods that leave sediment layers behind; these sediments are then trapped and held in place by riverside vegetation

Estuary

and South Coves of Old Saybrook (see vegetation map, p. 353).

The gradient of the river water's saltiness is reflected in brackish wetland types, from salt marsh look-alikes at the river mouth to tidal freshwater marshes eight miles upriver. The brackish marshes progress from salt meadows near the river mouth to brackish meadows for several miles north of the I-95 Baldwin Bridge, to the reed-dominated cattail and Phragmites marshes of Lord Cove, Nott Island, and southern Selden Island. From Selden Island north to Hadlyme Cove and Whalebone Creek, the marshes are tidal freshwater wetlands, dominated by freshwater plant species such as Northern Wild Rice, Pickerelweed, and Arrow Arum. Unfortunately, all the river marshes near and north of the Amtrak bridge also have heavy infestations of Common Reed (Phragmites), an invasive species of Eurasian origin that displaces native plants that are much more valuable to wildlife. Phragmites thrives in brackish conditions just above the high tide line and on riverbanks disturbed by human activity.

Brackish meadows

These open marsh meadows are transitional between salt and fresh environments. As in true salt marshes, the dominant grass here is Saltmeadow Cordgrass,

A cross-section through a tidal brackish marsh, showing the way various common plant species sort themselves by exposure to both the salt of brackish water and the overall height of the daily tides. As in true salt marshes, some plants are both salt-tolerant and can grow in soaked ground. But most plants, such as Saltmeadow Cordgrass, can only survive occasional wet soil during twice-monthly spring tides.

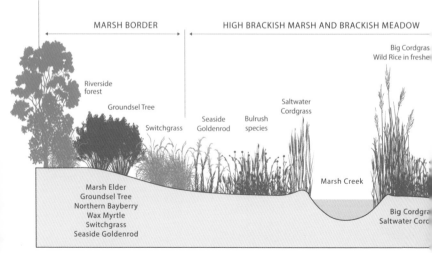

MARSH BORDER

HIGH BRACKISH MARSH AND BRACKISH MEADOW

Big Cordgrass
Wild Rice in freshe[r]

Riverside forest

Groundsel Tree

Switchgrass

Seaside Goldenrod

Bulrush species

Saltwater Cordgrass

Marsh Creek

Marsh Elder
Groundsel Tree
Northern Bayberry
Wax Myrtle
Switchgrass
Seaside Goldenrod

Big Cordgra[ss]
Saltwater Cord[grass]

but bulrushes and sedges become common. Common Three-Square, Olney Bulrush (also called Olney Three-Square or Chairmaker's Rush), and Sea-Coast Tuber-Bulrush join the marsh mix in brackish meadows. As the salinity falls upriver, the sedges begin to predominate. Less salt-tolerant but familiar coastal species, including Seaside Goldenrod, Marsh Elder, Groundsel Tree, Northern Bayberry, and Switchgrass, line the edges of brackish meadows.

Seaside Goldenrod
Solidago sempervirens

Brackish reed marshes

As the average river salinity continues to fall upstream, the riverbank marshes begin to be dominated by taller grass and reed species. The dominant native species in these marshes is Narrow-Leaved Cattail, but the cattails are joined by—and in some places supplanted by—Common Reed (*Phragmites*). The vast marshes around Nott Island and Lord Cove (see map, p. 347) are typical brackish reed marshes, as are sections of the Great Meadows marshes in Essex and the banks of Essex's North Cove. Near freshwater sources such as the smaller tributary rivers, these slightly brackish reed marshes quickly transition into typical freshwater reed marshes, as seen in the Lord Creek and Deep Creek areas of Lyme and along the banks of Hamburg Cove. Brackish reed marshes also predominate on the upper

Common Reed (Phragmites)
Phragmites australis

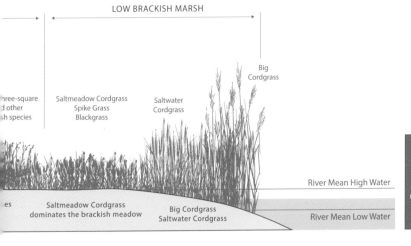

LOW BRACKISH MARSH

hree-square
d other
sh species

Saltmeadow Cordgrass
Spike Grass
Blackgrass

Saltwater
Cordgrass

Big
Cordgrass

River Mean High Water

es

Saltmeadow Cordgrass
dominates the brackish meadow

Big Cordgrass
Saltwater Cordgrass

River Mean Low Water

Estuary

The tidal reed marshes of Lord Cove, about six miles upriver from the mouth of the Connecticut Rive. The marshes here are dominated by the salt-tolerant Narrow-Leaved Cattail. The plants lining the marsh here are Rose Mallows (Hibiscus moscheutos) and various sedges and bulrushes. The I-95 Ba win Bridge is visible at the center horizon.

The tidal freshwater marsh at Hadlyme Cove, here dominated by Northern Wild Rice (*Zizania palustris*).

A flower head of Northern Wild Rice (*Zizania palustris*).

Lieutenant River near the Florence Griswold Museum, which offers an excellent walking path along the river.

Tidal freshwater marshes

The island of Selden Neck State Park and the complex of freshwater creeks around the Hadlyme Cove–Whalebone Creek complex just south of the Hadlyme Ferry are typical riverine freshwater marshes. The details of these freshwater marshes are all covered in previous chapters.

Wildlife of the estuary

Most fish, bird, and mammal species seen north of the brackish river areas are the same species found in freshwater environments farther upriver in freshwater marsh and riverine habitats covered in previous chapters. This section covers some of the more unusual animal species that define the Connecticut River estuary's character and its environments.

Fish

The lower Connecticut River estuary's rich fish life is mainly due to the diversity of salty, brackish, and freshwater habitats along the river. The many coves are a unique legacy of the dramatic sea level rise after the Wisconsinan Glaciation and the drowning of the river mouth, main channel, and major tributaries by the rising seas. The glaciers also left behind enough sediment to form the many large river islands and peninsulas that create quiet shallow-water areas that make perfect breeding grounds and nurseries for fish. Thus in the 15-mile segment from the East Haddam Swing Bridge south to the river mouth, you find such classic freshwater species as Largemouth Bass, classic pond and creek fish including Bluegills and Yellow Perch, and then large, swift ocean predators such as Bluefish, Striped Bass, and even Crevalle Jacks down near the river mouth.

Anadromous fish

Anadromous fish are born in freshwater streams, migrate to the ocean to live most of their lives, and then return to their birth streams to mate and lay eggs. Anadromous fish such as Alewives, American Shad, Hickory Shad, Rainbow Smelt, Blueback Herring, Shortnose Sturgeon, and Atlantic Salmon were once abundant in the Connecticut River and its tributaries. Dam building in the 1700s and 1800s closed off most substantial tributary streams to the fish, and their populations withered. In colonial and early American times, dams were built to power mill wheels in smaller workshops and grain mills. Steam power and later electric motors made the water mills obsolete more than a century ago, but dams are costly to remove, and most have remained in place. There are more than 4,000 stream dams in Connecticut alone, and about 85 percent of them are on private property, where their impact on stream wildlife can be challenging to assess.

Atlantic Salmon were once a major Connecticut River migratory species, but in 1794 the original Connecticut River dam built at Turners Falls, Massachusetts, largely destroyed the river's salmon population. Today in the Connecticut River estuary, there are small remnant breeding populations of Atlantic Salmon, Blueback Herring, and Alewives in the Eightmile and Salmon Rivers, both of which have fishways over the major dams.

The huge Connecticut River shad runs in colonial and early American times were an important dietary protein source for both the Indigenous and European

Anadromous fish species. The small mill dams on tributaries of the Connecticut River were valuable for processing local grain and to support early manufacturing. But the dams were often lethal for fish species that spawn in rivers, live their adult lives in the ocean, and then return to their ancestral rivers to breed. In recent decades New England towns have been removing old dams in an effort to revive anadromous fish migration into freshwater rivers and streams.

American Shad

Hickory Shad

Alewife

Blueback Herring

Estuary

Smaller tributary streams such as Lyme's Beaver Creek once had substantial Alewife and shad runs, but small abandoned mill dams still pose a major challenge to restoring access to the streams. A small fishway built on the creek to allow access to Moulson Pond has had some success with spring Blueback Herring runs.

immigrant populations. Those shad runs are now just a shadow of former days, but a small, artisan-scale commercial shad fishery still exists on the Connecticut River. The yields in this gill-net fishery have been declining in recent years. The Connecticut is the sole river in the state where recreational shad fishing is allowed during the spring run, only with hook and line tackle.

There are significant spring runs of Alewives in the Lieutenant River and its upstream tributary, Mill Brook, in Hamburg Cove and the Eightmile River, in Chester Creek, and in the smaller creeks that feed Chapman Pond in East Haddam. Alewives in local rivers and streams along the Connecticut River estuary are important food sources for many forms of river wildlife, including gulls, herons, cormorants, Belted Kingfishers, Ospreys, mammals such as Raccoons and Mink, and aquatic predators such as Striped Bass and Bluefish. Most fish migrations in the estuary area pass by unnoticed, but the Alewife runs are a migration you can see. During warm nights in April, streams and creeks will be running with Alewives moving upstream. Watch for gulls in the area—if the gulls are swarming, the Alewives are running.

The common but mysterious eel

American Eels are nearly ubiquitous in the estuary mainstream, tributaries, and coves, but unlike the species mentioned above, eels have a somewhat mystifying breeding cycle. These eels are catadromous fish that spend most of their lives in the Connecticut River drainage region in larger streams and coves but leave freshwater and migrate to the central Atlantic Ocean's deep waters to breed. Until the twentieth century, nobody knew where eels went to breed, and

American Eel
Anguilla rostrata

even today, many aspects of this strange breeding cycle are poorly understood. Some biologists speculate that since eels are an extremely ancient fish species, their mating behavior may predate the Atlantic Ocean itself. Today's Atlantic Ocean began to form about 200 million years ago, when the supercontinent of Pangaea broke apart, separating the ancestral North American Plate from what later became northwest Africa and Europe. As the plates drifted apart, the early Atlantic Ocean formed in the growing gap. Ancient eel populations were already established then on both sides of the Atlantic, and for millions of years, both east and west populations of eels met to breed in what was then a narrow sea between continents. As the Atlantic Ocean slowly kept getting wider over millions more years, the eels kept breeding in the central ocean, even as the distances and water depths grew. The American Eel is an odd-looking fish that many find hard to appreciate, but have some respect for this amazing and ancient resident whose mating behavior was probably established during the Age of Dinosaurs.

American Eel
Anguilla rostrata

Popular gamefish

Striped Bass are an anadromous river-breeding species, but as of 2021, there are no known breeding areas in New England rivers northeast of the Hudson River, where there is a Striped Bass breeding population. However, the presence in spring of large numbers of young "stripers" in the Connecticut River estuary has led some experts to speculate that with the warming environment, Striped Bass may begin to breed in the Connecticut River in the future. Though nominally a saltwater and brackish water species, Striped Bass range far up the Connecticut River—as far north as Hartford—particularly in the spring. Large Striped Bass feed on smaller anadromous fish species and follow shad, Blueback Herring, and Alewives as they move upriver to breed.

Bluefish, Summer Flounder (fluke), and Tautog (blackfish) are all saltwater species that readily enter estuary waters throughout the Northeast, and particularly in the lower Connecticut River. The coves and shallow backwater areas of the lower Connecticut River provide both food and shelter for large numbers of young

Atlantic Menhaden (bunker)
Brevoortia tyrannus

Bluefish
Pomatomus saltatrix

Atlantic Salmon
Salmo salar

Shortnose Sturgeon
Acipenser brevirostrum

Tautog (blackfish)
Tautoga onitis

Striped Bass
Morone saxatilis

The myriad tiny fish that you see in marsh creeks form a vital link in the estuary food chain between primary producers such as algae and larger predators, including crabs, gamefish, and marsh birds such as terns and herons. Some of the small fish you see are juvenile versions of larger fish, including Striped Bass, Bluefish, and Summer Flounder (fluke).

gamefish species. As adults, most Bluefish, Tautog, and Summer Flounder migrate out into Long Island Sound but also readily return to the estuary to follow schools of forage fish or migrating anadromous fish.

Forage fish

In recent decades marine biologists have become increasingly aware of the critical role forage fish species play in the ecosystem of coastal waters and estuaries. Often dismissed by anglers as "baitfish," these millions of mostly tiny fish form the critical base of the food chain in coastal waters, supporting game fish, seabirds, seals, and farther offshore, even large ocean predators such as dolphins and Humpback Whales. The Connecticut River estuary and the more extensive estuary of Long Island Sound are rich breeding and feeding grounds for the myriad but seldom-noticed small fish upon which many of the most iconic coastal and river species depend for their lives.

Many forage fish spend most of their lives in salt and brackish marsh creeks and backwaters. Striped Killifish, Three-Spined Sticklebacks, Sheepshead Minnows, and Mummichogs are classic marsh and river fish that seldom enter deeper waters. These are the fish that draw Belted Kingfishers, Least Terns, and herons into marsh creeks and shallow river coves. The Atlantic Silverside and American Sand Lance are tiny coastal species that exist in the millions in both sheltered estuary waters and deeper offshore waters. These more wide-ranging inshore forage fish are the primary food source for coastal and river birds including terns, cormorants, mergansers, and herons that hunt the broad

Atlantic Menhaden
Brevoortia tyrannus

American Sand Lance
Ammodytes americanus

Atlantic Silverside
Menidia menidia

Striped Killifish
Fundulus majalis

Three-Spined Stickleback
Gasterosteus aculeatus

Sheepshead Minnow
Cyprinodon variegatus

Mummichog
Fundulus heteroclitus

Estuary

Herons (opposite) are the emblematic birds of marshes. These waterbirds are graceful yet fierce predators of virtually all small animals: fish, turtles, voles, crabs, large insects, and the young of other birds are all fair game. Herons are solitary feeders. You will seldom see large flocks of herons, although Cattle Egrets are more gregarious than most other herons. More typical are small mixed-species clusters of herons feeding along marsh creeks. Great Blue Herons are particularly territorial toward other herons, especially toward fellow Great Blue Herons.

brackish river mouth area around and south of Essex and Old Lyme.

The most important forage fish, Atlantic Menhaden (bunker), are abundant in the brackish waters of the estuary from May through November. Although they can reach lengths of 15 inches or more as adults, menhaden are not sport fish that take lures. Most individuals found in and around the Connecticut River estuary are smaller juvenile or young fish, particularly in spring. Menhaden feed on plant and animal plankton in the water and thus form a critical link in the marine and estuary food chain between primary plant producers (green algae) and larger predators such as Bluefish and Striped Bass, seals, Ospreys, Bald Eagles, and even fish-eating land mammals such as American Mink and Raccoons.

Birds

The Connecticut River estuary is particularly rich in bird life for several reasons. First, the many subhabitats—the main river channel, the various marshes, coves, and shallow areas rich in submerged aquatic vegetation, and the extensive riverine forests around the river—provide food and shelter to a wide variety of birds. Second, the lower Connecticut River sits at the intersection of two of the East Coast's major bird migration corridors. The Connecticut River Valley itself is an important north-south migration corridor to and from interior New England and southern Canada. The coastline of southeastern New England and Connecticut is also a major migration corridor in spring and fall. The Connecticut River estuary and the surrounding region are thus doubly enriched in spring and fall. The marshes and tidal flats of the river estuary and the larger Long Island Sound estuary are bird habitats of regional and national importance.

Double-Crested Cormorants (*Phalacrocorax auritus*) stand on rocks in North Cove, Essex. Cormorants are one of the most commonly seen birds in the Connecticut estuary, particularly in the six or seven miles north of the river mouth.

Herons are present in the estuary all year, although most species wander south in the winter months. Great Blue Herons linger along unfrozen riverbanks and marshes through the winter but may be absent during unusually cold spells. Most heron species favor marshes, tidal flats, and shallow-water areas along river islands and coves. The Connecticut River estuary

Snowy Egret
Egretta thula

Great Egret
Ardea alba

Great Blue Heron
Ardea herodias

Little Blue Heron
Egretta caerulea

Green Heron
Butorides virescens

Estuary

Pied-Billed Grebe
Podilymbus podiceps

Common Loon
Gavia immer

Piping Plover
Charadrius melodus

Least Tern
Sternula antillarum

bird life benefits from its proximity to other extensive coastal salt marsh areas, including Hammonasset Beach State Park, Rocky Neck State Park, and Bluff Point State Park. In the river estuary marshes Great Egrets, Snowy Egrets, Green Herons, and Little Blue Herons are common, and on the brackish marshes the herons are sometimes joined by small groups of Glossy Ibises.

Some of the most obvious bird life are the large rafts of ducks seen in spring and fall migration. Large concentrations of ducks are also present in winter, and the river and its shallows and coves provide largely ice-free foraging habitat in all but the coldest winters. The deeper sections of the river and cove offer excellent feeding grounds for diving ducks such as Buffleheads, three species of mergansers, Common Goldeneyes, and, particularly near the river mouth, Greater and Lesser Scaups. In the deeper sections of the river channel and river mouth, there are smaller numbers of Double-Crested Cormorants and Common Loons. The shallow coves and tidal flats also provide rich food for dabbling ducks (ducks that duck down but do not fully dive), including Mallards, American Black Ducks, American Wigeons, Gadwalls, and both Green-Winged and Blue-Winged Teals.

The estuary's verdant fresh and brackish marshes are home to dozens of songbird and waterbird species. Black Ducks are important resident nesting birds in the many brackish marshes that line the main riverbanks and smaller tributary marshes along the Lieutenant and Black Hall Rivers. Over the past two decades, Willets have become common once again over estuary marshes, where these large shorebirds are noisy and noticeable nesters. In the twentieth century, Willets were once almost extirpated locally through a combination of market hunting, the feather trade, and habitat loss. Today, birders are heartened by this conservation success story. The river estuary brackish marshes are also critical habitat for the endangered Saltmarsh Sparrow, which is presently threatened by a combination of habitat loss and sea level rise. The nearly ubiquitous Belted Kingfisher is common throughout the fresh and brackish river habitats. Although barely larger than a Blue Jay, Belted Kingfishers' noisy rattling call, hovering flight, and spectacular dives into the water make them one of the most noticeable residents of the estuary riverbanks.

Two seriously threatened local nesters use the small but important sandy beach areas near the river mouth. Least Terns and Piping Plovers both nest in the sandy beach areas on the west and especially the east sides of the river mouth, particularly on the southern end of Great Island and the small sand island of Griswold Point. Although the nesting birds are never numerous and absent in some years, undeveloped sand beach habitat is so rare along the Connecticut coastline that even tiny patches of sand and small numbers of nesting pairs are important contributions to the survival of these two beach species.

Saltmarsh Sparrow
Ammodramus caudacutus
Photo courtesy of Patrick Comins

American Black Duck
Anas rubripes

Estuary

American Oystercatchers
(*Haematopus palliatus*) were once common nesters on sand beaches near the mouth of the Connecticut River, but market gunning and the feather trade destroyed the local population in the early twentieth century. In the past two decades the Oystercatcher has made a slow, sometimes halting recovery as a nesting species along the Connecticut coastline and river mouth. In late summer, adult birds can be spotted on beaches and shallow sandbanks along the river near Long Island Sound.

Bald Eagles

Today the Bald Eagle is almost as widely known as a symbol of the Connecticut River estuary as the Osprey. A combination of general habitat loss, river pollution, persecution by hunters and farmers, and finally the introduction of DDT in the late 1940s combined to wipe out Connecticut's historical population of Bald Eagles. DDT was a powerful organic pesticide that is fat-soluble. Thus, it traveled easily through the food chain and became concentrated in top predators such as Ospreys, Bald Eagles, Peregrine Falcons, and other large birds of prey. The DDT in the bird's bodies interfered with proper eggshell formation, and nesting success in contaminated birds dropped sharply. By the 1970s, the only eagles seen in the southern Connecticut River region were migrant birds and a few overwintering birds. DDT was banned in the United States in 1972, but it took decades for the poison and its chemical derivatives to fully degrade in the ecosystem.

The Connecticut River estuary is such excellent eagle habitat that even in the darkest days of the 1970s and 1980s, there were always a few Bald Eagles wintering in the region, but those birds were from isolated areas far to the north that were less affected by DDT. In 1992, a pair of Bald Eagles nested in Litchfield County, Connecticut, and successfully raised two chicks, the beginning of the modern nesting population of eagles near the Connecticut River estuary. Since the early 1990s, nesting eagles have slowly but steadily returned to the southern Connecticut River region. In 2019, there were several dozen Bald Eagle pairs maintaining nesting territories along the Connecticut River's length, and in the river estuary, there are typically active nests in Haddam, Deep River, Essex, and tributaries of the Connecticut River such as the Scantic River.

Today the Connecticut River estuary's wintering Bald Eagle population has become a major wildlife spectacle in Connecticut, with regular eagle-watching boat tours launching from Haddam, Deep River, and Essex. The river and estuary islands from Haddam south to the I-95 bridge in Old Saybrook are the best areas for eagle sightings. The tours generally run from February through April, with the later tours also watching for

Bald Eagle
Haliaeetus leucocephalus

Estuary

the spring return of Ospreys along the river. As many as 40 Bald Eagles have been spotted in a single winter cruise. About 100 Bald Eagles now winter in Connecticut, with the majority found along the lower Connecticut River and its major tributaries. In cold winters, river icing can concentrate the eagle populations in the brackish Connecticut River estuary, where there is less ice, and around larger freshwater reservoirs and lakes that don't completely freeze over.

Ospreys

In the early 1950s, the famed ornithologist Roger Tory Peterson came to live in Old Lyme, Connecticut, near the Connecticut River. Peterson said he chose the estuary region because of the rich birdlife and the large number of nesting Ospreys along the river. When Peterson arrived in Old Lyme, there were about 150 local Osprey nests and a wide variety of waterbirds in all seasons. But only 10 years later, in 1964, there were just 15 active Osprey nests on the lower Connecticut River, and chick survival in the few surviving nests was low.

Roger Tory Peterson was a friend of famed nature writer Rachel Carson, whose book *Silent Spring*, published in 1962, is recognized as one of the early landmarks of the environmental movement. Carson was one of the first to link the widespread use of organochlorine pes-

Osprey
Pandion haliaetus

Tree Swallows (*Tachycineta bicolor*) flock over Calves Island in Old Lyme, Connecticut.

ticides such as DDT to mass die-offs of birds and other wildlife. Peterson suspected that the sudden decline of Ospreys in the Connecticut River estuary was also linked to DDT spraying to control mosquitos. Peterson actively supported research by Old Lyme ornithologist Paul Spitzer, one of the first scientists to discover the link between DDT and eggshell thinning. After Rachel Carson's untimely death from cancer in 1964, Roger Peterson became one of the most prominent voices in advocating the banning of DDT because of its devastating effects on wildlife. The ban on DDT finally took place in 1972. Thus Old Lyme's Great Island and the Roger Tory Peterson Natural Preserve on the island are recognized as landmarks of the American environmental movement. Today there are 25 active Osprey nests on Great Island and more than 125 Osprey nests along the Connecticut River estuary between East Haddam and the mouth of the river. The revival of Osprey, Bald Eagle, and Peregrine Falcon populations are some of the most significant environmental success stories and a reminder of the good that thoughtful, science-based advocacy can accomplish.

Tree Swallows

Over the past decade, another Connecticut River estuary wildlife viewing spectacle has grown in popularity: observing the massive flocks of Tree Swallows that use the river islands and reed marshes as night roosting sites in the fall migration months of August, September, and early October. On estuary islands off the eastern riverbank, such as Nott Island, Goose Island, Calves Island, and Great Island (see map, p. 347), hundreds of thousands of Tree Swallows, along with other swallow species, some Common Grackles, Red-Winged Blackbirds, and Common Starlings, gather in huge swirling flocks at dusk over the islands. At sunset, massive, almost tornadolike flocks of swallows called murmurations form swirling patterns in the sky over the river islands before suddenly plunging into the reeds to roost for the night.

Studies have shown that the swallows in fall migration move in a relatively leisurely path down the East Coast, often stopping for weeks at a time in areas rich with flying insect life. The Connecticut River swallows are thought to forage over the Connecticut landscape as far as 25 miles from their communal roosts on the river. The birds return to the river area in late afternoon, probably for the safety in numbers that the giant flocks provide. Every day swallows leave the roost to move farther south in migration, but from August through mid-September, the flocks build in numbers, and at peak migration, there may be as many as 500,000 Tree Swallows roosting on the river, but no one knows the exact number of birds.

Tree Swallows
Tachycineta bicolor

Harbor Seal
Smaller, with a puppylike, rounded head profile

Gray Seal
Larger, with a thick, horselike snout

As with Bald Eagle cruises in the winter months, swallow cruises in late summer offer a much better view of the swallows than you might get from riverbank viewpoints. These larger passenger boats generally leave the dock in late afternoon from Haddam, Deep River, and Essex. The cruise boats typically hold positions off Nott, Goose, and Calves Islands just as the sun sets and the flocks gather. Swallow cruises are a great way to get unique views of other river birds such as Bald Eagles, Ospreys, Double-Crested Cormorants, and the multiple heron species that use the riverbanks for roosting and feeding. If the swallow cruises interest you, make your reservations early, as the boats usually fill up quickly by late August.

Mammals

Most riverine mammals are covered in previous chapters, but the Connecticut River estuary has some very distinctive mammals: seals. In the dead of winter, Harbor Seals are often spotted on the small beach areas on either side of the river mouth, particularly on the southern tip of Great Island and Griswold Point. Over the past twenty years, Gray Seals have become regular visitors to the Connecticut coastline in winter, and it's always worth inspecting groups of beached seals near the river mouth to see if the larger Gray Seals are mixed in with the Harbor Seals.

Diamondback Terrapins

Diamondback Terrapins are turtles native to brackish and salt marshes ranging from Cape Cod south to the Florida Keys and the Gulf Coast. Their common name derives from the diamond patterns of the shell carapace, which are highly variable but are always in a bold geometric pattern. The name "terrapin" is derived from the Algonquian word "torope," which the Native Americans used to describe the Diamondback.

Terrapins are shy and are fast, strong swimmers with large webbed feet and strong jaws for crushing their favored prey of small fish, clams, mussels, periwinkles, and mud snails. To see them, approach marsh creeks slowly and scan the water for swimming turtles as well as the water's edge along the mudbanks for basking turtles. In early summer, check roads near marshes for

HARBOR SEAL
Phoca vitulina

Harbor Seal pup

GRAY SEAL
Halichoerus grypus

The pelage colors and patterns of young Gray Seals can vary from almost pure white to yellow or gray

GRAY SEAL

HARBOR SEAL

Mark Bridge

Wim Claes

Estuary

Diamondback Terrapin
Malaclemys terrapin

female turtles seeking out nesting sites. Terrapins can survive in the wild from 25 to 40 years, making them one of North America's longest-lived animals. Diamondbacks are also unusual in that they can survive in a variety of water salinities, from freshwater (<5 ppt salt) to ocean water (32 ppt), but they prefer the brackish marshes (15–25 ppt). Special lacrimal glands near their eyes allow terrapins to drink salt water and then excrete the salt as tears.

Diamondbacks mate in late spring and lay egg clutches in June and July. The females prefer to lay their eggs in sandbanks but will also dig nests under vegetation in the high marsh. Females often wander long distances from the marsh to find suitable nesting areas, making them vulnerable to cars and domestic animal predation. Young turtles emerge from eggs in August and September and are a favorite food of herons, Bluefish, and Striped Bass. Diamondbacks overwinter by hibernating in deep marsh creeks under mud bottoms or high marsh vegetation, but the Diamondback's winter biology is not well understood.

Diamond-Backed Terrapin
Malaclemys terrapin

In the nineteenth and early twentieth centuries, the Diamondback Terrapin was nearly hunted to extinction for its meat, then used in a fashionable soup. As the popularity of turtle soup faded in the early twentieth century, Connecticut populations of Diamondbacks recovered somewhat. Today the main threat to terrapins is habitat loss. Biologists estimate that almost 75 percent of terrapin marsh habitat has been eliminated since colonial times. Accidental death owing to human activity is another problem: terrapins are often caught and drowned in crab pots and nets or hit by boat propellers or cars. In Connecticut, the Diamondback Terrapin is considered a Species of Special Concern, but terrapins are considered endangered in Rhode Island and threatened in Massachusetts.

Crabs and other brackish marsh life

Two large crab species are present in the Connecticut River estuary, the native Blue Crab and the invasive Green Crab. As the environment has warmed in recent decades the Blue Crab population of Long Island Sound and the Connecticut coastline has expanded. Blue Crabs may be inheriting the ecological niche of the American Lobster, a cold-water creature whose populations have plummeted since the early 1990s. Blue Crabs are well adapted to brackish estuary waters and may be found in numbers at least as far as the coves of Essex and the tidal rivers of Old Lyme. The Blue Crabs are highly mobile and occasionally wander well into the freshwater region of the lower Connecticut.

The Green Crab is an exotic species, one of the first major instances of a European species that made the jump across the Atlantic, probably by riding on the mossy bottoms of sailing ships or in wet ships' ballast stones dumped overboard in a Massachusetts port. Since 1817, the Green Crab has spread along the East Coast from Nova Scotia down to Cape May, New Jersey. Green Crabs are also voracious predators, particularly of mussels and Soft-Shell Clams, but because they are a primarily cold-water species, their local populations may fade as the Sound continues to warm.

Mud Fiddler Crabs are often abundant in salt marshes near the river mouth, but as you move north along the river the Mud Fiddlers are replaced by Red-Jointed Fiddler Crabs in the more brackish marshes.

Migratory insects

The estuary marshes of the Connecticut River are good places to observe migrating insects in fall. On a clear September or October day with a brisk northwest wind sweeping them down to the coastline, hundreds of

Lone Star Tick
Amblyomma americanum

Blacklegged Tick
(Deer Tick)
Ixodes scapularis

Carrier of Lyme disease

American Dog Tick
Dermacentor variabilis

Fresh, brackish, and salt marshes harbor several species of ticks that mostly parasitize wild mammals such as White-Footed Deer Mice, Meadow Voles, Raccoons, and Red Foxes. Always wear long pants when you explore away from trails in marshes and riverside woodlands and apply a DEET-based or Permethrin insect repellent on your clothes, socks, and shoes, as directed by the manufacturer.

Photos: Melinda Fawver, Sarah2, Dollar Photo Club

Estuary

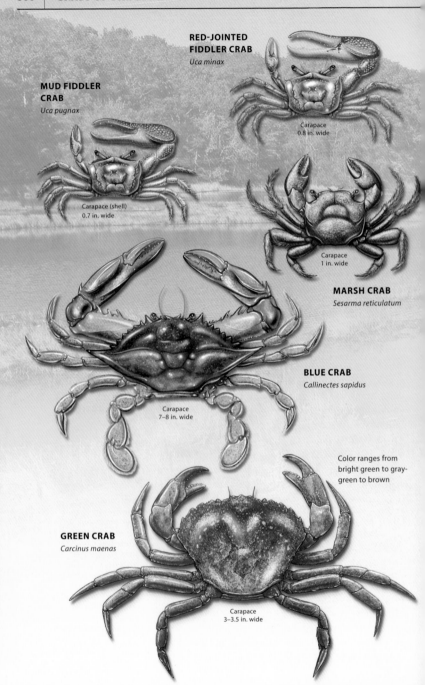

**RED-JOINTED
FIDDLER CRAB**
Uca minax

Carapace
0.8 in. wide

**MUD FIDDLER
CRAB**
Uca pugnax

Carapace (shell)
0.7 in. wide

Carapace
1 in. wide

MARSH CRAB
Sesarma reticulatum

BLUE CRAB
Callinectes sapidus

Carapace
7–8 in. wide

Color ranges from
bright green to gray-
green to brown

GREEN CRAB
Carcinus maenas

Carapace
3–3.5 in. wide

migrating Monarch Butterflies, Green Darner Dragonflies, and Black Saddlebags Dragonflies move along the river valley and the nearby shores of Long Island Sound, often using the marsh vegetation for rest and shelter. Unfortunately, the gorgeous flocks of migrating Monarchs may be a thing of the past. Over the past decade, scientists have seen a significant decline in the number of migrating Monarchs, which overwinter in just a few valleys in northern Mexico. Those Mexican valleys are now relatively well protected as conservation areas. Researchers are looking at the increased use of glyphosate herbicides by farmers since 2003 as a possible factor in their decline. Monarch Butterfly caterpillars feed on milkweeds. The significant decrease in milkweeds (particularly in the Midwest farming areas) is suspected in the 59 percent drop in overwintering Monarch populations in Mexico in 2012. So appreciate these black-and-orange beauties while we have them because they may be less common in the future.

Common Green Darner
Anax junius

Black Saddlebags
Tramea lacerata

Monarch Butterfly
Danaus plexippus

Tiger beetles
Tiger beetles are a fascinating group of tiny predatory insects, usually found in sandy areas and along dirt roads and exposed roadside sandbanks. Tiger beetles bask in bright sun to keep their metabolism high for

Monarch Butterfly
Danaus plexippus

Six-Spotted Tiger Beetle
Cicindela sexguttata

fast chases, and they are usually seen in sunny and not shady areas. The beetles are often highly colored, and the most common tiger in the estuary area is the brilliant green Six-Spotted Tiger Beetle. Tiger beetles are among the fastest running insects, and they often both run and make short flights when disturbed or chasing prey. Always keep an eye out for bright flashes of color and movement when hiking in sandy terrain in the spring and early summer. The Connecticut River is one of the last sites where the rare and endangered Puritan Tiger Beetle may be found in a few scattered sites around Middletown, Connecticut.

Puritan Tiger Beetle
Cicindela puritana

Seaside Dragonlet: The Connecticut River hosts dozens of species of dragonflies, but in the brackish marshes near the river mouth, Seaside Dragonlets (*Erythrodiplax berenice*) are the most common species. Seaside Dragonlets are unique in being the only regional dragonfly that can nest in brackish or salt water.

Seaside Dragonlet Female

Seaside Dragonlet Male

Old mill dams such as this one on Beaver Brook in Lyme, Connecticut, were a death sentence for anadromous fish runs, including those of Alewives, Blueback Herring, and Atlantic Salmon. Many older dams are being removed or breached to restore the fish populations of the Connecticut River watershed.

Estuary

The upper reaches of the Connecticut River estuary, viewed from Gillette Castle State Park in Lyme, Connecticut. The Chester–Hadlyme seasonal ferry is the second oldest ferry route in the state. Servi began here in 1769 as Warner's Ferry. The present ferryboat is the Selden III, 65 feet in length, first launched in 1949.

SALTWATER CORDGRASS *Spartina alterniflora*

SALTWATER CORDGRASS *Spartina alterniflora*

SALTMEADOW CORDGRASS *Spartina patens*

SALTMEADOW CORDGRASS, cowlicks

High marsh ditch with both Saltwater Cordgrass (in ditch) and Saltmeadow Cordgrass (surrounding)

SALTWATER CORDGRASS AND RIBBED MUS

MARSH ELDER *Iva frutescens*

GROUNDSEL TREE *Baccharis halimifolia*

SPIKE GRASS (in flower) *Distichlis spicata*

SWITCHGRASS *Panicum virgatum*

BLACKGRASS *Juncus gerardii*

BLACKGRASS, flower detail

Estuary

Common in salt marshes; unusual in brackish marshes
GLASSWORT *Salicornia sp.*

Common in salt marshes; unusual in brackish marsh
GLASSWORTS turn red in the fall frosts

Common in salt marshes; unusual in brackish marshes
ERECT SEA BLIGHT *Suaeda linearis*

SEA LETTUCE *Ulva lactuca*

Common in salt marshes; unusual in brackish marshes
GREEN FLEECE *Codium fragile*

Common in salt marshes; unusual in brackish mars
ROCKWEED *Fucus distichus*

mon in salt marshes; unusual in brackish marshes

A LAVENDER *Limonium carolinianum*

Common in salt marshes; unusual in brackish marshes

SEA LAVENDER, basal rosette

cially common in brackish marshes

ASIDE GOLDENROD *Solidago sempervirens*

MARSH ORACH *Atriplex patula*

RENNIAL SALTMARSH ASTER *S. tenuifolium*

COMMON REED *Phragmites australis*

Estuary

BLACK CHERRY *Prunus serotina*

COMMON JUNIPER *Juniperus communis*

WINGED SUMAC *Rhus copallina*

STAGHORN SUMAC *Rhus typhina*

NORTHERN BAYBERRY *Myrica pensylvanica*

BEACH PLUM *Prunus maritima*

POISON IVY *Toxicodendron radicans*

VIRGINIA CREEPER *Parthenocissus quinquefolia*

ASIATIC BITTERSWEET *Celastrus orbiculatus*

CATBRIAR *Smilax glauca*

EASTERN REDCEDAR *Juniperus virginiana*

SASSAFRAS *Sassafras albidum*

Estuary

PICKERELWEED *Pontederia cordata*

ARROW ARUM *Peltandra virginica*

ROSE MALLOW *Hibiscus moscheutos*

ROBUST BULRUSH *Scirpus robustus*

OLNEY THREE-SQUARE BULRUSH *Schoenoplectus americanus*

BIG CORDGRASS *Spartina cynosuroides*

[PU]RPLE LOOSESTRIFE *Lythrum salicaria*

NARROW-LEAVED CATTAIL *Typha angustifolia*

[AR]RROWHEAD *Sagittaria latifolia*

NORTHERN WILD RICE *Zizania palustris*

[NE]W ENGLAND ASTER *Symphyotrichum novae-angliae*

BUR-MARIGOLD *Bidens cernua*

Estuary

MALLARD *Anas platyrhynchos*

AMERICAN BLACK DUCK *Anas rubripes*

Dollar Photo Club

BUFFLEHEAD *Bucephala albeola*

Dollar Photo Club

GADWALL *Mareca strepera*

BRANT *Branta bernicla*

MUTE SWAN *Cygnus olor*

COMMON GOLDENEYE *Bucephala clangula*

HOODED MERGANSER *Lophodytes cucullatus*

RED-BREASTED MERGANSER *Mergus serrator*

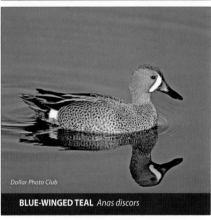

BLUE-WINGED TEAL *Anas discors*

GREATER SCAUP *Aythya marila*

LESSER SCAUP *Aythya affinis*

Estuary

RED-TAILED HAWK *Buteo jamaicensis*

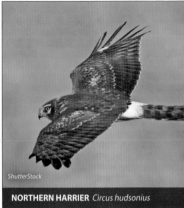

NORTHERN HARRIER *Circus hudsonius*

HERRING GULL *Larus argentatus*

GREAT BLACK-BACKED GULL *Larus marinus*

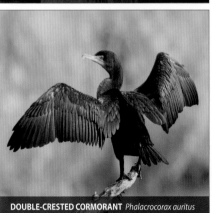

DOUBLE-CRESTED CORMORANT *Phalacrocorax auritus*

GLOSSY IBIS *Plegadis falcinellus*

GREAT EGRET *Ardea alba*

SNOWY EGRET *Egretta thula*

ar Photo Club

GREATER YELLOWLEGS *Tringa melanoleuca*

WILLET *Tringa semipalmata*

PIED-BILLED GREBE *Podilymbus podiceps*

COMMON GRACKLE *Quiscalus quiscula*

Estuary

NORTHERN MOCKINGBIRD *Mimus polyglottos*

RED-WINGED BLACKBIRD *Agelaius phoeniceus*

MARSH WREN *Cistothorus palustris*

CAROLINA WREN *Thryothorus ludovicianus*

COMMON YELLOWTHROAT *Geothlypis trichas*

SONG SPARROW *Melospiza melodia*

ELLOW-RUMPED WARBLER *Setophaga coronata*

SAVANNAH SPARROW *Passerculus sandwichensis*

erely threatened by population decline.

ALTMARSH SPARROW *Ammodramus caudacutus*

SNOW BUNTING *Plectrophenax nivalis*

ORNED LARK *Eremophila alpestris*

LAPLAND LONGSPUR *Calcarius lapponicus*

Estuary

Further Reading

Freshwater environments of New England

Alden, P., and B. Cassie. 1998. *National Audubon Society Field Guide to New England*. New York: Knopf.

Allan, J. D., and M.M. Castillo. 2007. *Stream Ecology: Structure and Function of Running Waters*. 2nd ed. New York: Springer.

Caduto, M. J. 1990. *Pond and Brook: A Guide to Nature in Freshwater Environments*. Hanover, NH: University Press of New England.

DeGraaf, R. M., and M. Yamasaki. 2001. *New England Wildlife: Habitat, Natural History, and Distribution*. Hanover, NH: University Press of New England.

Dodds, W., and M. Whiles. 2010. *Freshwater Ecology: Concepts and Environmental Applications of Limnology*. 2nd ed. New York: Elsevier.

Giller, P. S., and B. Malmqvist. 1998. *The Biology of Streams and Rivers*. Oxford: Oxford University Press.

Hammerson, G. A. 2004. *Connecticut Wildlife: Biodiversity, Natural History, and Conservation*. Lebanon, NH: University Press of New England.

Jorgensen, N. 1971. *A Guide to New England's Landscape*. Chester, CT: Pequot.

Jorgensen, N. 1978. *A Sierra Club Naturalist's Guide to Southern New England*. San Francisco: Sierra Club Books.

Kaufman, K., and K. Kaufman. 2012. *Kaufman Field Guide to Nature of New England*. Boston: Houghton Mifflin.

Mitsch, W., J. G. Gosselink, C. J. Anderson, and Li Zhang. 2009. *Wetland Ecosystems*. Hoboken, NJ: Wiley.

Mitsch, W., and J. G. Gosselink. 2015. *Wetlands*. Hoboken, NJ: Wiley.

Sinton, J., W. Sinton, and E. Farnsworth. 2007. *The Connecticut River Boating Guide: Source to Sea*. 3rd ed. Guilford, CT: Falcon/Globe Pequot.

Sperduto, D., and B. Kimball. 2011. *The Nature of New Hampshire: Natural Communities of the Granite State*. Hanover, NH: University Press of New England.

Thompson, E., E. Sorenson, and R. Zaino. 2019. *Wetland, Woodland, Wildland: A Guide to the Natural Communities of Vermont*. White River Junction, VT: Chelsea Green.

Connecticut River geology

Bell, M. 1985. *The Face of Connecticut: People, Geology, and the Land.* Bulletin 110. Hartford: State Geological and Natural History Survey of Connecticut.

Coleman, M. E. 2005. *The Geologic History of Connecticut's Bedrock.* Special Publication 2. Hartford: Connecticut Department of Environmental Protection.

Little, R. D. 2003. *Dinosaurs, Dunes, and Drifting Continents: The Geology of the Connecticut River Valley.* Northampton, MA: Tiger.

Lynch, P. 2017. *A Field Guide to Long Island Sound.* New Haven: Yale University Press.

McDonald, N. G. 2010. *Window into the Jurassic World: Dinosaur State Park, Rocky Hill, Connecticut.* Rocky Hill, CT: Friends of Dinosaur State Park.

Raymo, C., and M. E. Raymo. 2007. *Written in Stone: A Geological History of the Northeastern United States.* 3rd ed. Delmar, NY: Black Dome.

Skehan, J. W. 2001. *Roadside Geology of Massachusetts.* Missoula, MT: Mountain.

Skehan, J. W. 2008. *Roadside Geology of Connecticut and Rhode Island.* Missoula, MT: Mountain.

Stone, J. R., J. C. Ridge, R. S. Lewis, and M. L. DiGiacomo-Cohen. 2015. *Glacial Lake Hitchcock and the Sea.* Northeast Friend of the Pleistocene, 78th Annual Fieldtrip Guidebook, June 5–7, 2015. (https://www2.newpaltz.edu/fop/pdf/FOP2015Guide.pdf)

Van Diver, B. B. 1987. *Roadside Geology of Vermont and New Hampshire.* Missoula, MT: Mountain.

New England weather

Zielinski, G., and B. Keim. 2003. *New England Weather; New England Climate.* Hanover, NH: University Press of New England.

Environmental history

Cronon, W. 2003. *Changes in the Land: Indians, Colonists, and the Ecology of New England.* Rev. ed. New York: Hill and Wang.

Cumbler, J. T. 2001. *Reasonable Use: The People, the Environment, and the State, New England, 1790–1930.* New York: Oxford University Press.

Foster, D., and J. Aber. 2006. *Forests in Time: The Environmental Consequences of 1,000 Years of Change in New England.* New Haven: Yale University Press.

Judd, R. W. 2014. *Second Nature: An Environmental History of New England.* Amherst: University of Massachusetts Press.

Thorson, R. M. 2002. *Stone by Stone: The Magnificent History in New England's Stone Walls.* New York: Walker.

Ponds and lakes

Jacobs, R., and E. O'Donnell. 2012. *A Fisheries Guide to the Lakes and Ponds of Connecticut.* Hartford: Connecticut Department of Energy and Environmental Protection.

Reid, G. K., H. R. Zim, and G. S. Fichter. 1967. *Pond Life: A Guide to Common Plants and Animals of North American Ponds and Lakes.* A Golden Guide. New York: St. Martin's.

Streams and rivers

Travis, T., and S. Brown. 2011. *Pocket Guide to Eastern Streams.* Mechanicsburg, PA: Stackpole.

Utz, R. 2022. *Field Guide to Rivers and Streams: Discover Running Waters and Aquatic Life.* Essex, CT: Falcon/Globe Pequot.

Marshes and swamps

Eastman, J. 1992. *The Book of Forest and Thicket: Trees, Shrubs, and Wildflowers of Eastern North America.* Mechanicsburg, PA: Stackpole Books.

Magee, D. W. 1981. *Freshwater Wetlands: A Guide to Common Indicator Plants of the Northeast.* Amherst: University of Massachusetts Press.

Padgett, D. 2016. *Wetland Plants of New England: A Guide to Trees, Shrubs, and Lianas with Summer and Winter Keys.* Middleboro, MA: Spatterdock.

Travis, T., and S. Brown, 2014. *Pocket Guide to Eastern Wetlands.* Mechanicsburg, PA: Stackpole Books.

Vernal pools

Colburn, E. 2004. *Vernal Pools: Natural History and Conservation.* Newark, OH: McDonald and Woodward.

Bogs

Davis, R. 2016. *Bogs and Fens: A Guide to the Peatland Plants of the Northeastern United States and Adjacent Canada.* Hanover, NH: University Press of New England.

Birds

Dunn, J., and J. Alderfer. 2017. *National Geographic Field Guide to the Birds of North America.* 7th ed. Washington, DC: National Geographic.

Gallo, F. 2018. *Birding in Connecticut.* Middletown, CT: Wesleyan University Press.

Peterson, R. T. 2010. *Peterson Field Guide to Birds of Eastern and Central North America.* 6th ed. Boston: Houghton Mifflin.

Sibley, D. 2017. *The Sibley Field Guide to Birds of Eastern North America.* 2nd ed. New York: Knopf.

Fish

Jacobs, R., and E. O'Donnell. 2009. *A Pictorial Guide to Freshwater Fish of Connecticut.* Hartford: Connecticut Department of Energy and Environmental Protection.

Page, L., and B. Burr. 2011. *Peterson Field Guide to the Freshwater Fishes of North America North of Mexico.* New York: Houghton Mifflin.

Insects

Dunkle, S. W. 2000. *Dragonflies through Binoculars: A Field Guide to Dragonflies of North America.* New York: Oxford University Press.

Ellison, A., N. Gotelli, E. Farnsworth, and G. Alpert. 2012. *A Field Guide to the Ants of New England.* New Haven: Yale University Press.

Evans, A. V. 2008. *A Field Guide to Insects and Spiders of North America.* National Wildlife Federation. New York: Sterling.

Glassberg, J. 1999. *Butterflies through Binoculars: The East.* New York: Oxford University Press.

Glassberg, J. 2017. *A Swift Guide to Butterflies of North America.* 2nd ed. Princeton, NJ: Princeton University Press.

O'Donnell, J., L. Gall, and D. Wagner. 2007. *The Connecticut Butterfly Atlas.* Bulletin 118. Hartford, CT: State Geological and Natural History Survey.

Amphibians

Powell, R., R. Conant, and J. Collins. 1991. *Peterson Field Guide to Reptiles and Amphibians of Eastern and Central North America.* Boston: Houghton Mifflin.

Raithel, C. 2019. *Amphibians of Rhode Island, Their Status and Conservation.* West Kingston, RI: Rhode Island Division of Fish and Wildlife.

Mammals

Kays, R. W., and D. E. Wilson. 2009. *Mammals of North America.* 2nd ed. Princeton, NJ: Princeton University Press.

Wildflowers

Elliman, T., and New England Wild Flower Society. 2016. *Wildflowers of New England.* Portland, OR: Timber.

Newcomb, L., and G. Morrison. 1989. *Newcomb's Wildflower Guide.* Boston: Little, Brown.

Peterson, R.T., and M. McKenny. 1968. *A Field Guide to Wildflowers of Northeastern and North-central North America.* Boston: Houghton Mifflin.

Guides specific to the northern Connecticut River

Most of the information in this book on freshwater environments applies well throughout the length of the Connecticut River. However, readers interested in detailed information on northern New England environments will find these references very useful. I highly recommend them.

Brown, R. A., ed. 2009. *Where the Great River Rises: An Atlas of the Connecticut River Watershed in Vermont and New Hampshire.* Hanover, NH: Dartmouth College Press.

Davis, R. 2016. *Bogs and Fens: A Guide to the Peatland Plants of the Northeastern United States and Adjacent Canada.* Hanover, NH: University Press of New England.

Johnson, C. W. 1998. *The Nature of Vermont: Introduction and Guide to a New England Environment.* Hanover, NH: University Press of New England.

Sperduto, D., and B. Kimball. 2011. *The Nature of New Hampshire: Natural Communities of the Granite State.* Hanover, NH: University Press of New England.

Thompson, E., E. Sorenson, and R. Zaino. 2019. *Wetland, Woodland, Wildland: A Guide to the Natural Communities of Vermont.* White River Junction, VT: Chelsea Green.

Unfortunately, there are few state parks along the river in Vermont and New Hampshire. Even readers who do not canoe, kayak, or boat on the northern Connecticut River may find the following boating guides useful because they list public-access launch areas along the river.

Tougias, M. 2001. *River Days: Exploring the Connecticut River from Source to Sea.* Boston: Appalachian Mountain Club.

The Connecticut River Watershed Council, J. Sinton, E. Farnsworth, and W. Sinton. 2007. *The Connecticut River Boating Guide: Source to Sea.* 3rd ed. Guilford, CT: Globe Pequot.

ILLUSTRATION CREDITS

All photography, artwork, diagrams, and maps are by the author, unless
otherwise noted in this listing.

Additional photography credits

Images used with permission. All images are copyright 2024, by each source listed here. All rights reserved by the individual photographers.

46–47 Connecticut River at Chester, Matthew Male, 59 East Rock, Michael Marsland, 89 Winter Storm Nemo, NASA Earth Observatory, 103 Tropical Storm Irene, NASA, 119 Historic print, Connecticut River, NYPL Digital Collections, 120–21 *The Oxbow*, Thomas Cole, Metropolitan Museum of Art, 228–29 Common frog species, Twan Leenders, 230–31 Common salamander species, Twan Leenders, 232–33 Common turtle species, Twan Leenders, 246 West River, Robin Ladouceur, 257 Bald Eagles on ice, Matthew Male, 317 Red-Tailed Hawk, Janis Blanton, 338 American Bullfrog, Twan Leenders, 358 Deep Creek (top), Robin LaDouceur, 377 Saltmarsh Sparrow, Patrick Comins, 407 Saltmarsh Sparrow, Patrick Comins.

Images used under license from Adobe Stock

14–15 Guildhall, VT, Eli Wilson, 22–23 Cornish-Windsor Covered Bridge, Craig Zerbe, 34–35 Holyoke Dam, AerialMA, 50–51 Connecticut River mouth, Gregory, 58 Brownstones, Jon Chica, 62–63 *Coelophysis* Hunting, Catmando, 62–63 Argentine landscape, Miguel, 66 Deerfield River aerial, pics721, 75 Glacial till layering, duke2015, 77 Glacial till excavation, duke2015, 88 Panorama of White Mountains, Natalie Rotman Cote, 92 Black ice, Zach, 95 Smokestacks, martin33, 97 Stormwater drainage, boophuket, 98 Rain garden, Pavel Iarunichev, 100 Rain garden, auntspray, 101 Hartford aerial, Jacob, 101 Roof garden, Bonnie, 105 Boston in snow, f11photo, 109 Vermont countryside, Craig Zerbe, 115 Plimoth Museums houses, AndreasJ, 118 Plantain, Amalia Gruber, 119 Black rust on wheat, Tomasz, 122 Ears of corn, Larry Allen Peplin, 129 Aerial of Holyoke, MA, Joshua, 133 Polluted water, Brett, 133 Fish kill, Meen-Na, 135 Clear-cut forest, duke2015, 135 Forest path, jonbilious, 137 Fish kill, bearok, 140 Vermont landscape, SeanPavonePhoto, 142 Springfield, MA, John McGraw, 143 Hartford, CT, Mark Lotterhand, 144 Hartford, CT, SeanPavonePhoto, 145 Garbage on street drain, Natalie Schorr, 147 Rowers, aerial-drone, 151 Raindrops, Vera, 155 Winter stream, Valeriy Boyarskiy, 160 Eutrification in a small pond, fotosenukas, 175 American Mink, gallinago_media, 181 Binoculars, simmittorok, 181 Binoculars, Dmytro, 187 Black-Crowned Night-Heron, pferreira, 189 Night background, Solid photos, 192 Arrowhead, Sandra Burm, 192 Common Cattail, dule964, 192 Narrow-Leaved Cattail, noppharat, 193 American Bur-Reed, nickkurzenko, 194 Bloodroot, Margaret Burlingham, 194 Oxeye Daisy, bluehand, 194 Boneset, Erik, 194 Jack-in-the-Pulpit, Dave, 194 Trout Lily, Gerry, 195 Red Trillium, Hamiza Bakirci, 195 Painted Trillium, Jack, 196 Cardinal Flower, nickkurzenko, 197 Pickerelweed, tamu, 197 Yellow Water-Lily, danilag, 197 White Water Lily, Vitaliy, 198 Orange Hawkweed, skymoon13, 198 Ragged Robin, Imladris, 198 Fireweed, andreusK, 199 Swamp Rose, skymoon13, 199 New England Aster, Paul, 200 Coontail, 200 Watermilfoil, linjerry, 200 Spirogyra, Marius Burca, 200 Duckweed, Socoxbreed, 201 Ostrich Fern, scphoto48, 201 Royal Fern, knelson20, 201 Marsh Fern, Samuel, 201 Lady Fern, Ольга Жарликова, 203 Red-Osier Dogwood, Carmen Hauser, 204 Paper Birch, Zimmerman, 204 Yellow Birch, David Katz, 205 American Hornbeam, Jon Benedictus, 205 Black Ash, Diana Samson, 205 Pussy Willow, Blubird, 205 Sycamore, Batya, 205 Silver Maple, Aliaksandr Kisel, 205 Boxelder Maple, Anghi, 206 Water Strider, janmiko, 206 Whirligig Beetles, Olvita, 206 Backswimmer, float, 206 Water Boatman, GRFischer, 206 Giant Water Bug, evergenesis, 206 Diving Beetle, phototrip, 207 Fishing Spider, Michael, 207 Crayfish, AnikS, 207 Dragonfly larva, Vitalii Hulai, 207 Freshwater Mussel, AB Photography, 207 Mayflies, gordzam, 210 Ebony Jewelwing, J. Stone, 210 Familiar Bluet, Samuel, 210 Northern Spreadwing, phototrip, 210 Eastern Forktail, Ray Akey, 210 Eastern Red Damsel, fabiosa_93, 210 River Jewelwing, rbkelle, 216 Acadian Hairstreak, Beth Baisch, 216 Banded Hairstreak, Mark, 217 Coral Hairstreak, Brian Lasenby, 216 Gray Hairstreak, Annette Shaff, 216 Juniper Hairstreak, Paul Sparks, 216 Eastern Tailed-Blue, Randy Anderson, 217 Little Wood-Satyr, Paul Sparks, 217 Common Ringlet, Riverwalker, 217 American Copper, Andrea Izzotti, 234 Black-Crowned Night-Heron, rpferreira, 234 Bittern, FotoRequest, 235 Common Loon, Brian Lasenby, 235 DC Cormorant, elharo, 235 Red-Shouldered Hawk, William, 236 Great Blue Heron, Jeffrey, 236 Northern Harrier, Fritz, 237 Barred Owl,

Ron Dubreuil, 237 Killdeer, Brian E. Kushner, 237 Wilson's Snipe, amajk, 237 Woodcock, Steve Byland, 238 Mallard, havana1234, 238 Pintail, shaftinaction, 239 Sora, raptorcaptor, 239 Virginia Rail, Michael W Potter, 240 Northern Waterthrush, Alex Papp, 240 Swamp Sparrow, Chase D'Animulls, 241 Carolina Wren, Brian E. Kushner, 241 White-Throated Sparrow, tmtracey720, 242 American Mink, serhio777, 242 Muskrat swimming, Юрій Балагула, 242 Beaver swimming, Christian Musat, 242 Porcupine, hkuchera, 242 Black Bear, rima15, 243 River Otter swimming, patrick, 243 Raccoon swimming, AB Photography, 248 Pemigewasset River, J. Conover, 252 Groundwater spring, Temir, 254 Street drain, Volodymyr, 260 River and underwater, damedias, 267 Fly lure, gdvcom, 268 Trout in river, damedias, 272 Diving Beetle, jonnysek, 275 Black Bear, rima15, 275 Beaver, Christian Musat, 275 Underwater background, sergemi, 276 Stream, Daniel Vincek, 285 Background top - stream, Daniel Vincek, 285 Background bottom - underwater, damedias, 285 Fall leaves, Mara Fribus, 285 Screech Owl, pharry, 285 River Otter, ricktravel, 285 Mosquito, mrfiza, 285 Daphnia, micro_photo, 285 Daphnia, lukszczepanski, 287 Background - bottom, damedias, 287 Black-Crowned Night-Heron, rpferreira, 288–89 Illustration, bottom, underwater, aniphaes, 295 Beaver, Jordan Feeg, 306 Wood Duck, Ivan Kuzmin, 306 Pickerelweed, Sermek, 307 Muskrat, byrdyak, 307 Virginia Rail, Michael W. Potter, 309 Bittern, Paul, 312 Common Cattail, dule964, 312 Narrow-Leaved Cattail, noppharat, 320 Northern Waterthrush, cratervalley, 323 Beaver lodge, Jeff, 323 Muskrat lodge, Stan, 324 Beaver-chewed tree, Kaloa, 324 Brown Rat, Eric Isselée, 324 Muskrat, Iri-sha, 324 Raccoon, rabbit75, 325 River Otter, Cloudtail, 325 Beaver, jnjhuz, 328 Beaver dam, Ronnie Howard, 329 Woodcock, Daniel, 330 Eastern Comma, pimmimemom, 330 Wood Frog, ondreika, 330 Wood Frog egg mass, Mark Lotterhand, 330 American Toad, ondreika, 330 Spring Peeper, ondreika, 330 Gray Treefrog, Natalia Kuzima, 330 Spotted Salamander, ondreika, 330 Red-Spotted Newt, Melinda Fawver, 330 Common Garter Snake, Nynke, 330 Snapping Turtle, Mark Lotterhand, 331 Common Darter, Wirestock Creators, 331 Box Turtle, Brian E. Kushner, 331 Green Frog, sdbower, 331 Spotted Turtle, Hamilton, 331 Mayfly, Wirestock, 331 Amphipods, Aleksey Solodov, 331 Fairy Shrimp, phototrip-cz, 331 Fairy Shrimp, Rostislav, 331 Dragonfly larva, Vitali Hulai, 331 Daphnia, micro_photo, 331 Caddisfly larva, phototrip-cz, 334 Grass Pink, Kevin, 335 Round-Leaved Sundew, Matauw, 337 Pitcher Plant, martinrossi, 337 Grass Pink, scandamerican, 337 Labrador Tea, Amelia, 338 Bog Turtle, ondreika, 340 Balsam Fir, simona, 340 American Larch, steadb, 340 Red Spruce, Capucine Dieppedale, 340 Northern White Cedar, Михаил Балашов, 341 Labrador Tea, Amelia, 341 Sweet Gale, BestPhotoStudio, 342 Cranberry, pisotckii, 342 Bog Rosemary, lembrechtsjonas, 342 Royal Fern, Knelson20, 342 Spatulate-Leaved Sundew, brudertack69, 343 Starflower, Garry, 343 Pitcher Plant, martinrossi, 343 Grass Pink, scandamerican, 369 American Eel, Rostislav, 376 Piping Plover, Brian E. Kushner, 400 Bullrush, Tamor, 404 Great Black-Backed Gull, Christian Musat, 406 Carolina Wren, Brian E. Kushner.

Images used under license from Dollar Photo Club (now owned by Adobe Stock)
187 Black-Crowned Night-Heron – flight, Brian E. Kushner, 234 Belted Kingfisher, Dollar Photo Club, 235 Red-Tailed Hawk, Dollar Photo Club, 237 Greater Yellowlegs, Dollar Photo Club, 238 Wood Duck, Dollar Photo Club, 239 Hooded Merganser, Dollar Photo Club, 240 Yellow Warbler, Dollar Photo Club, 240 Yellowthroat, Robin Ladouceur, 240 Song Sparrow, Dollar Photo Club, 241 Marsh Wren, Dollar Photo Club, 241 Common Grackle, Dollar Photo Club, 241 American Goldfinch, Dollar Photo Club, 242 Eastern Cottontail, Dollar Photo Club, 275 Great Horned Owl, Dollar Photo Club, 275 Eastern Coyote, Dollar Photo Club, 275 Painted Turtle, Dollar Photo Club, 285 Raccoon, Dollar Photo Club, 285 Coyote, Dollar Photo Club, 287 Belted Kingfisher, Dollar Photo Club, 287 American Goldfinch, Dollar Photo Club, 287 Raccoon, Dollar Photo Club, 289 Osprey, Dollar Photo Club, 306 Screech Owl, Dollar Photo Club, 307 Red-Winged Blackbirds, Dollar Photo Club, 307 Kestrel, Dollar Photo Club, 337 Round-Leaved Sundew, Dollar Photo Club, 387 American Dog Tick, Dollar Photo Club, 403 Lesser Scaup, Dollar Photo Club, 404 Red-Tailed Hawk, Dollar Photo Club, 405 Greater Yellowlegs, Dollar Photo Club, 406 Marsh Wren, Dollar Photo Club, 406 Song Sparrow, Dollar Photo Club, 407 Yellow-Rumped Warbler, Dollar Photo Club, 407 Savannah Sparrow, Dollar Photo Club, 407 Horned Lark, Dollar Photo Club.

Images used under license from Shutterstock

16–17 Fairlee, VT, Bram Reusen, 141 Merritt Parkway (historic), Everett Collection, 207 Pond Leech, frank60, 221 Blacklegged Tick, Chris Ritchie Photo, 221 Dog Tick, Melinda Fawver, 221 Brown Dog Tick, Anton, 221 Lone Star Tick, ondreicka, 238 Green-Winged Teal, Shutterstock, 239 American Coot, Martha Marks, 240 Red-Winged Blackbird, BGSmith, 287 Common Yellowthroat, ShutterStock, 343 Dragon's Mouth Orchid, Lee Ellsworth, 385 Gray Seal, Mark Bridger, 385 Harbor Seal, Wim Claes, 387 Lone Star Tick, ShutterStock Melinda Fawver, 387 Black-Legged Tick, Sarah2, 404 Northern Harrier, ShutterStock, 406 Common Yellowthroat, ShutterStock.

Images used under Creative Commons or Public Domain from Wikimedia Commons

278 Mayfly larva, Bob Henricks, 278 Freshwater mussels, USFWS, 278 Collector micro, Lithium57, 285 Biofilm, Lamiot, 193 Woolgrass, Fredlyfish4, 67 I-91 and Higby Mountain, Mr. Matté, 130 Holyoke (historic), Paper City, Wikimedia Commons, 200 Elodea, Christian Fischer, 289 Hydrilla, Yercaud-elango, 289 Curlyleaf Pondweed, Christian Fischer, 289 Eurasian Watermilfoil, Donald Hobern, 289 Water Chestnut, Agnieszka Kwiecień, 330 Diving Beetle, Gilles San Martin, 336 Balsam Fir, Robert H. Mohlenbrock, 336 Bog Willow, Rob Routledge, 336 Round-Leaved Sundew, Agnieszka Kwiecień, 338 American Larch, AlbertHerring, 338 Balsam Fir, Superior National Forest, 339 Leatherleaf, Krzysztof Ziarnek, 341 Bog Willow, Rob Routledge, 341 Leatherleaf, Krzysztof Ziarnek, 342 Creeping Snowberry, Superior National Forest, 342 Round-Leaved Sundew, Agnieszka Kwiecień, 343 Swamp Loosestrife, Robert H. Mohlenbrock, 343 Rose Pogonia, wackybadger, 400 Olney Three-Square, Gordon Leppig and Andrea J. Pickart.

Index

It is interesting to contemplate an entangled bank,
clothed with many plants of many kinds, with birds
singing on the bushes, with various insects flitting about,
and with worms crawling through the damp earth, and
to reflect that these elaborately constructed forms, so
different from each other, and dependent on each other
in so complex a manner, have all been produced by laws
acting around us...

There is grandeur in this view of life, with its several
powers, having been originally breathed into a few forms
or into one; and that, whilst this planet has gone cycling
on according to the fixed law of gravity, from so simple a
beginning endless forms most beautiful and most
wonderful have been, and are being, evolved.

Charles Darwin
On the Origin of Species

Bird tracks

Tracks are shown at about 60% life size, as they might look in sand or firm mud.

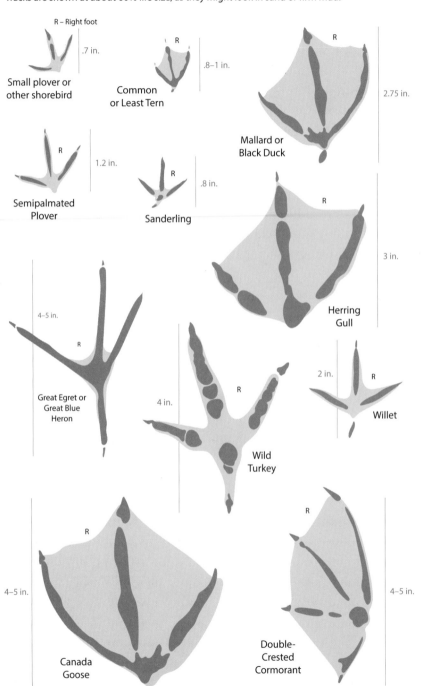

R – Right foot

Small plover or other shorebird
.7 in.

Common or Least Tern
.8–1 in.

Mallard or Black Duck
2.75 in.

Semipalmated Plover
1.2 in.

Sanderling
.8 in.

Herring Gull
3 in.

Great Egret or Great Blue Heron
4–5 in.

Wild Turkey
4 in.

Willet
2 in.

Canada Goose
4–5 in.

Double-Crested Cormorant
4–5 in.